PENGUIN BOOKS

ODDBALLS

Bruce Shlain is the co-author of *Acid Dreams: The CIA, LSD, and the 60's Rebellion*. He has written for *Rolling Stone, The New York Times Book Review,* and other publications, and also for television and film. He grew up a fan of the Detroit Tigers, and then, after graduating from the University of Michigan, moved to Boston and discovered the Red Sox. He currently lives in New York City, as a confirmed Met-aholic.

ODDBALLS

BRUCE SHLAIN

PENGUIN BOOKS

PENGUIN BOOKS
Published by the Penguin Group
Viking Penguin Inc., 40 West 23rd Street,
New York, New York 10010, U.S.A.
Penguin Books Ltd, 27 Wrights Lane,
London W8 5TZ, England
Penguin Books Australia Ltd, Ringwood,
Victoria, Australia
Penguin Books Canada Ltd, 2801 John Street,
Markham, Ontario, Canada L3R 1B4
Penguin Books (N.Z.) Ltd, 182–190 Wairau Road,
Auckland 10, New Zealand

Penguin Books Ltd, Registered Offices:
Harmondsworth, Middlesex, England

First published in Penguin Books 1989
Published simultaneously in Canada

10 9 8 7 6 5 4 3 2 1

Copyright © Bruce Shlain, 1989
All rights reserved

LIBRARY OF CONGRESS CATALOGING IN PUBLICATION DATA
Shlain, Bruce.
    Oddballs : baseball's greatest pranksters, flakes, hot dogs, and
hotheads / Bruce Shlain.
       p.   cm.
    ISBN 0 14 01.1128 X
    1. Baseball players—United States—Anecdotes.   I. Title.
GV873.S49   1989   88-30650
796.357′092′2—dc19

Printed in the United States of America
Set in Primer
Designed by Victoria Hartman

To my wife, Gayle,
for enduring various oddities
with rare generosity of spirit

"Sports do not build character. They reveal it."
—Heywood Hale Broun

Acknowledgments

I wish to thank all the current and former players, managers, coaches, and broadcasters who shared their thoughts with me—Jim Piersall, Al Hrabosky, Rick Dempsey, Roger McDowell, Ron Darling, Frank Thomas, Don Stanhouse, Jim Kern, Mudcat Grant, Frank Funk, Mickey Hatcher, Mike Scioscia, Pat Dobson, Boog Powell, Vern Hoscheit, Buck Martinez, Paul Blair, Jim Bouton, Ned Garver, Luis Tiant, Lee Mazzilli, Keith Hernandez, Tony Pena, Jeff Leonard, Joaquin Andujar, Pat Corrales, Bill Freehan, Al Kaline, Jack Morris, Ralph Houk, Ernie Harwell, Jim Northrup, Jim Campbell, Ochiai, Rob Murphy, Pete Rose, Dan Quisenberry, George Brett, Dave Rozema, Jim and Lee Walewander, Helen St. Aubin, Casey Candaele, Ted Williams, John Henry Williams, Dwight Evans, Stan Williams, Bill Lee, Dennis Boyd, Joe Morgan, Whitey Herzog, Vada Pinson, Tony Taylor, Roger Craig, and many others too numerous to mention.

Among the books that were most useful for my purposes were *The Truth Hurts* by Jimmy Piersall and Dick Whittingham; *El Tiante* by Luis Tiant and Joe Fitzgerald; *Remembrance of Swings Past* by Ron Luciano and David Fisher; *Baseball America* by Donald Honig; *Temporary Insanity* and *Over the Edge* by Jay

Johnstone and Rick Talley; *Moe Berg: Athlete, Scholar . . . Spy* by Louis Kaufman, Barbara Fitzgerald, and Tom Sewell; *A Catcher in the Wry* by Bob Uecker and Mickey Herskowitz; *No Big Deal* by Mark Fidrych and Tom Clark; *Dynasty* by Peter Golenbock; *Baseball's Wacky Players* by George Sullivan; *Where Have You Gone, Vince DiMaggio?* by Edward Kiersh; *Oh, Baby, I Love It!* by Tim McCarver with Ray Robinson; *Babe* and *Stengel: His Life and Times* by Robert Creamer; *Ty Cobb* by Charles Alexander; *Baseball . . . A Laughing Matter* by Warner Fusselle; *Greatest Stories Ever Told About Baseball* by Kevin Nelson; *The Pitcher* by John Thorn and John Holway; *Sweet Lou* by Lou Piniella and Maury Allen; *Ball Four* by Jim Bouton and edited by Leonard Shecter; *The Baseball Hall of Shame* series and *Baseball Confidential* by Bruce Nash and Allen Zullo; *Beyond the Sixth Game* by Peter Gammons; *The Wrong Stuff* by Bill Lee with Dick Lally; *The Best of Spitball* edited by Mike Shannon; and the complete works of Thomas Boswell, Bill James, and Roger Angell.

Thanks also to the media directors of several teams who allowed me to come and go freely—Dick Bresciani and Josh Spofford of the Red Sox, Greg Shea and Dan Ewald of the Tigers, Howard Starkman of the Blue Jays, Jay Horwitz of the Mets, Harvey Greene of the Yankees, Jim Ferguson of the Reds, Rob Matwick and Chuck Pool of the Astros, Kip Ingle of the Cardinals, Mike Williams of the Dodgers, and Dean Vogelaar of the Royals.

Special thanks to writer-producer Ouisie Shapiro and writer-broadcaster Warner Fusselle of Major League Baseball Productions.

I appreciate also the encouragement and diligence of my agent at ICM, Bob Tabian, and the invaluable assistance of my editor at Viking Penguin, Chuck Verrill.

Contents

Part Two
DIAMOND VOICES

Introduction:
From Out of Left Field

My involvement with baseball's oddballs began with my first trip to a ballpark at the age of nine. It was in Detroit's then Briggs Stadium in 1960 with my Cub Scout troop. My fellow Scouts were a nasty group of rabblerousers and malcontents. The motto "Be Prepared" meant being ready for somebody pulling your cap down over your eyes and lighting your neck hairs with a match. How some adventurous den mother ever thought she could control fifteen of us at the stadium was a mystery to me even then.

We were cautiously led through a concrete tunnel, smelling the pungence of crushed stogies, hot dogs, and spilled beer, a smell at once new and familiar, a smell that I believe even an alien visitor would associate with a ball game. The tunnel opened out onto a vast emerald field as well-tended as a putting green. It was something like seeing Oz.

We moved along an aisle down the left-field line, further and further until we finally found our seats behind the left-field screen at ground level. When the players in the infield moved around, a glowing nimbus surrounded their bright-white uniforms. Home plate looked to be a mile away. I had the idea that you weren't supposed to see anything at a ball game. But before the day was over, I saw plenty. For the visiting Indians left fielder in front of us that day was none other than Jimmy Piersall.

The den mother's daughter was sitting next to me. She was the prettiest girl in the whole neighborhood, with big white teeth and honey-colored skin, already at age eleven growing into the feminine right stuff that could casually torment whole male populations. I decided to impress her by telling her what I knew about Piersall, that he had been in a mental institution (in those days known as "the nuthouse") and that he had written a book about it called *Fear Strikes Out*.

It was a movie, too, I told her, with Anthony Perkins and Karl Malden, although she couldn't place Malden until I told her he was the guy with the big schnozz in *A Streetcar Named Desire*. I remember telling her that Piersall had never been able to please his father, and that he built up pressure on himself to excel until he was literally a basket case, once climbing the screen behind home plate in Fenway Park, howling at his father after hitting an inside-the-park home run, something I remembered from the movie. Her eyes brightened and color came into her cheeks— she was getting into the game. She passed this pertinent background information along to the others, and within seconds our group was buzzing.

Piersall in fact was horrified when he saw the film of his life and all the made-up things in it. The movie's most dramatic scene, when Piersall climbs the screen during a game at Fenway, never really happened, and neither was his crisis precipitated by problems with his father. "They made my father out to be a real bastard," Piersall complained in *The Truth Hurts*. "Well, he wasn't. I have never blamed my father for that breakdown. My father and I actually had a good relationship."

The baseball scenes in the movie also made him cringe, especially since Perkins, who would never be accused of being an athlete anyway, was a natural left-hander and had to throw righty for the film. "He danced around the outfield like a ballerina. . . . If you thought Perkins looked silly throwing the ball left-handed, you should have seen him flit it with his right hand."

Early in the game, I heard one of our group cast aside the Scout code and scream *"Meshugenah!"* (the Yiddish expression for "nut" or "fruitcake") at Piersall. Others took up the chant. We proceeded to behave as cruelly and badly as kids can, and then even worse when there was no response. Piersall, having heard it all before, ignored us, and let a couple of kids go hoarse trying to rile him. As a last resort, some took ice cubes out of their soft drinks and threw them at him. This went on for a couple of innings.

I had no way of knowing at the time that we were reenacting as kids an ugly scene that had occurred in Detroit in front of 50,000 fans one night in 1953. Piersall got into an argument with the umpire on a called strike three in extra innings and when he went out to the outfield, the fans began throwing wine bottles and paper cups with ice in them and shooting paper clips. Then out came a hammer, batteries, even some golf balls. The umpire stopped the game, and it took twenty minutes to clean the field.

In the newspaper the next day, the Tigers' general manager, Rick Ferrell, excused the incident by saying that Piersall had brought all of that stuff out on the field himself and dropped it. "Of all the general managers I've known," Piersall wrote in *The Truth Hurts,* "Ferrell has to be credited with the all-time most stupid statement I've ever heard—that I brought the hammer out, that I brought the batteries out."

So there we were, little suburban Cub Scouts in the cheap seats in left field, berating Piersall deep into the afternoon. And then, in the eighth inning, Piersall made an incredible leaping catch up against the fence to smother a Tiger rally. And then he made an even better one to save the game again in the ninth, rattling the left-field screen in front of us as he crashed into it just after gracefully cradling and protecting the ball.

Of course he was a terrific fielder. As Larry Doby once said of Jimmy, "He may be crazy, but not in the outfield." It was on his second catch that I caught a glimpse of his face. He looked totally impassive, grim even. I had hoped to catch him smiling, as if all was forgiven. But he just bounced off the fence and ran off the field, leaving the Scouts with their mouths gaping.

Watching Piersall that day changed the way I would follow baseball. What I saw was much more than a baseball game, it was a personal drama, and it burned something into my brain: that ballplayers were not just living embodiments of their baseball cards, not cardboard fantasy idols, but people, too, and some were real characters, complex individuals with unique personalities. Piersall certainly was.

"He was just such a high-strung, emotional kid," Ted Williams told me at Winter Haven, some thirty-five years after Piersall joined the Red Sox. "He went after every fly ball like it was life and death." Piersall in fact credits Williams with influencing the way he would approach the game. According to Piersall, Williams lived by the credo that it was far better to give an ulcer than to get one. "He told me never to hold it in, never to let it get at me," Piersall wrote. "I learned from him. That's why I've always popped my beak to get it out, so that it didn't stay inside of me."

Piersall was a player who always expressed himself, especially to umpires. Thrown out of a game for arguing, Piersall once continued heckling the umpire from the roof of the grandstand. Even nowadays, when he spoke with me at the Red Sox Old-Timers' Day at Fenway Park, having fully recovered from bypass heart surgery earlier in the year, he was as feisty as ever, and umpires still made him mad.

"You know what's fucking everything up?" he asked. "The umpires. I sit in the dugout today, and nobody says a word to the umpire. The catcher never complains about a strike, the pitcher never makes a face on the fucking mound, and the other day there was a close play, a half-swing, and everybody in the dugout says, 'Holy shit.' Nobody said a word to the umpire. But here comes the fucking umpire anyway, and the manager [Don Zimmer] comes out and he says, 'We ain't talkin' to you, for Chrissake, we just went "Aw shit." You want to stop us from spittin'?' It's just horseshit.

"One thing about the umpires when I played, they didn't hold grudges. Today they hold grudges. Nine-tenths of the umpires in the National League are fat and out of shape. It's a disgrace to the game. They're fat. One guy lost fifty pounds, and he's still fat. The umpires think the fans come out to see them. They got a fucking union, they can't be sat on, like that fuckin' Pallone. He looks into the dugout, looking for trouble. He threw out two fans paying fourteen a pop behind the screen.

"The umpires are villains, and fans come out to see them take shit. I understand that you shouldn't carry it on a long time, but the fans want a release, have some goddamned fun. Baseball is lucky today because they've got television. The game is fucking boring, it's so fucking long, and nobody's doing anything. I've seen Minnie Minoso knock an umpire down, really knock him down, and he got three days. But this new college cocksucker, this is what happened to baseball, they got a new memo now— no balks, don't take no shit from nobody, Heil Hitler, you know."

When Piersall went back to playing in 1953 after his breakdown the previous year, every game was a kind of test. There was not only the jeering of the fans to contend with; he got special attention from the umpires and other players as well. Whenever he lost his temper, the umpires would instantly become amateur psychiatrists, wondering if he had gone off his nut again, and say to each other, "Look in his eyes." Piersall would direct their attention toward the pitcher who threw at his head and advise them to look in *his* eyes, since he was the one throwing at him. As Jimmy was always fond of saying, "I've got them all on the run. They think I'm crazy because I act crazy. But I'm not crazy. I've got papers to prove it."

During a game at Yankee Stadium, Piersall hid behind the monuments in center field, and refused to come out and play. "Well, it was the second game of a doubleheader," Piersall told me, "and they used to walk in those pitchers, it would take a week to get in there, and some of 'em didn't even want to pitch. They had a big lead. So I sat on old Babe. It was so funny, the umpire [Ed Hurley] comes out and says, 'You can't sit on there.'

I said, 'Hey, they're in play! If I jump on there I can catch a ball, can't I? Then I can sit on it too, can't I?' He said, 'You're making a farce out of the fucking game.' I said, 'Watching you fuckers umpire is the farce of the fucking game.' "

Piersall had to take a lot from the players as well as the umpires. Some of it was malicious, but mostly it was in good humor, like Dick Williams sweetly singing "cuckoo, cuckoo" in the dugout. The fans were something else. There was the day two guys came charging toward him in front of 60,000 people at Yankee Stadium. One guy yelled, "You crazy bastard, Piersall, we're going to get you." Piersall decked the one that was shouting, then ran after the other and kicked him in the rear so hard that his toe was black-and-blue for a week.

Despite the various incidents—fights with other players, including a bout with Billy Martin, arguments with umpires, and tête-à-têtes with unruly fans—Piersall was for the most part a model of restraint. As teammate Mudcat Grant said about him, "He could handle everybody jeering at him as well as anybody that I knew. It's not as if he didn't pull some strange antics, because he did, but that was the way that he handled all the strange things that people were throwing at him, and if he didn't handle it that way, he probably would have become more mentally ill."

Frank Funk, now a coach on the Kansas City Royals, was also a teammate of Piersall's with the Cleveland Indians. "I'll tell you how Jimmy Piersall and myself first got to know each other. When I joined the team in the middle of the 1960 season, it was a Sunday afternoon, and I had to wait a day or two until I could get on the roster. They had me throw batting practice, and Piersall was in there, and I always had good control, and I threw a few that were not right in the middle of the plate, and he wasn't hittin' 'em that well, and he starts hollerin' at me. 'What's the matter with you, you damn rookie? You can't throw the ball over the plate? Get somebody else in there!'

"Well, he stepped back in, and I plunked him right in the ribs and down he goes, he's rolling around on the ground, and he goes in the clubhouse. When batting practice is over, I go into the clubhouse and sit down by my locker and I look up and here he comes. And I think, here we go, I'm about to lock assholes with one of the superstars of the game right now. And he gets right up to me, I jump up, and I'm ready to go at it, and he says, 'Sit down, sit down, hey, why'd you hit me with that goddamn ball?' And I said, 'Because I've got "Cleveland" written across here same as you, and you're no goddamn better than I am.' He says, 'That's great, that's fuckin' great, that's what we need on this goddamn club,' and from then on every appearance that he had, which was nearly every day, he always took me, and I got clothes and money and groceries."

Piersall was pretty much of a loner, but he adopted "Funkie" as his friend and confidant. Piersall especially liked when the public-address announcer informed the crowd that the fireballing Funk was coming into the game, because his name sounded like Piersall's favorite four letter-word. Funk even became his good-luck charm.

"I remember one time in New York," Funk recalled, "I was standing out in right center field, and Jimmy finished batting practice, and whenever he took his last swing he would run down to first base as hard as he could go, but this time he keeps on going right down the right-field line and comes running at me, and yells 'Here I come, Funkie, catch me!' and he jumps up and I catch him in my arms. And he goes three for four that night. . . . Now we have to do it every day. You just never knew what he was gonna do.

"We were in Detroit, and Jim Bunning was pitching, who used to always knock Piersall down, and he said to me 'Funkie, I haven't had any ink here, Bunning's always knocking me down. The first time he knocks me down today, I'm going after his ass. I hope somebody grabs me and grabs him before he knocks the hell out of me.' And sure enough, the first pitch, down he goes, and he jumps up and goes after Bunning, and he got his headlines in the paper, all right."

Piersall's behavior on the field sometimes made him a marked man. Ned Garver, a pitcher for the St. Louis Browns and later the Detroit Tigers in the '40s and '50s, recalled a time in Boston that Piersall's shenanigans got under the skin of Detroit manager Fred Hutchinson. Piersall got on first base and acted like an ape, scratching himself and making noises, and then he was on third and the batter hit the ball off the left-field wall, so Piersall got down on all fours and crawled home. Hutchinson warmed up his hardest thrower, Paul Foytack, for the express purpose of hitting Piersall.

When Piersall went to the National League for the first time in 1963, he played under Casey Stengel with the New York Mets. When teammate Duke Snider hit his 400th home run, Piersall kidded him about how small the article on it was. Piersall vowed that when he hit his 100th homer, he would get some major-league publicity, coast to coast. Snider was suitably impressed. "Get lost, bush," he told him.

Later that year Piersall got his 100th, and ran the bases backward, backpedaling at good speed (he had been practicing), and made the front page, not to mention all the sports pages. He kidded Duke that he was going to be on the Jack Paar show with Zsa Zsa Gabor, coast to coast. Stengel didn't appreciate it, and Piersall was released a few days later. He finished his career by playing for the Angels until 1967.

"You've got to remember," said Mudcat Grant, "baseball was *boring* most of the time in those days. You didn't have a lot of good teams, the Yankees won the pennant every year, baseball was really boring a lot of the time. So what he did, he just spruced up everything, that's all."

"There's no Vic Power today," says Piersall, referring to the style of one of the most flamboyant fielders. "You may have guys who can play well, but who do people really want to see besides Dawson and Mattingly? They used to say about me, 'Look at that crazy vegetable, you don't know what he's going to do next.' But they'd come to see me play."

Yet still, there will always be those who spring up out of nowhere like green grass growing through the cracks in old cement, who march to a different drummer, who will never fit into any regimented slot. They are the round pegs that don't fit into the square holes, the nonconformists, the iconoclasts, the oddballs.

Baseball has a name for these oddballs. They are generally called by a term what was first used to describe outfielder Jackie Brandt, who played for the St. Louis Browns in 1956—"flake." Brandt was the sort who once played twenty-seven holes of golf in 101-degree heat before a doubleheader. A teammate noticed that "things seem to flake off his mind and disappear."

Vada Pinson said that the late utility infielder Chico Ruiz was "the original flake," because Chico turned bench warming into an art. He brought a special cushion with him for doubleheaders, and for hot days always carried a portable fan.

Those of the oddball persuasion do not generally like the term "flake." Bill Lee, Oddball Chairman of the Board, said that the very word was "a right-handed, egotistic, consumeristic, exploit-ative, nonrecycling, carnivorous" word that no left-hander would have coined. And so for the purposes of this book we have adopted the term "oddballs," implying as little value judgment as possible. These players were just . . . different. By whatever name, odd-balls are oddballs. They make life interesting.

PART ONE

ODDBALL GUMBO:
Flakes, Pranksters, Hot Dogs, and Hotheads

THE MAD HUNGARIAN

Before he stalked in from the bullpen, the organist would play something appropriate, such as Liszt's "Hungarian Rhapsody No. 2." Before each pitch, he would walk behind the mound, his back to home plate, lower his head, and psyche himself up until he seemed about to explode. When he was finally ready, he would fire the ball into his glove, stomp to the pitching rubber, and glare in at the hitter. "I'm getting myself into a concentrated hate mood," he explained. "I want the hitter to wonder if maybe I *am* a little crazy."

If Al Hrabosky's modus operandi was really just an act, then De Niro has nothing on him. "The Mad Hungarian" not only acted like he was a little nuts, he kind of looked like it, too. He wore his hair quite long for most of his career, along with a fearsome Fu Manchu mustache that grew down into mutton chops. Today, in an unsettling contrast to his playing days, he is a clean-shaven, well-dressed television broadcaster for the Cardinals. The only thing really ostentatious about him is the huge diamond-studded World Series ring adorning his finger.

In baseball there is a long history of players who gave the fans a little extra for the price of admission to a ball game. Through

13

their flamboyance and natural showmanship, they became big draws because of their reputation as colorful performers. But if by "colorful" you mean a player who could pride himself on receiving a standing boo everywhere he went on the road, a player who regularly drove crowds to the edge of frenzy, then you have to go back to the '70s, when the hirsute Hungarian was being given the ball with a game on the line.

When Hrabosky was traded from St. Louis to the Kansas City Royals in 1977, he knew that on his first trip to Yankee Stadium he was going to receive "the greatest boo of my life." During batting practice, Hrabosky went out to right field to receive the malediction of the New York fans. Hrabosky has witnesses for this great moment in sports. "Ask Ken Kaiser," he told me at the Busch Complex in St. Petersburg, the Cardinals' training complex. (We know that's a reliable reference, because American League umpire Kaiser was once the second to humongous wrestler-actor Andre the Giant.) "The fans are yelling at me, 'You National League reject,' 'Get a haircut,' and all this shit, so I walk up to them and say 'Sit down and shut up.' And they did! So I said . . . 'Goddamn.' "

Hrabosky is most proud of his first American League win, because he beat the Yankees and that night Billy Martin and Thurman Munson had a serious altercation. "I took credit that Martin got so pissed off that I beat 'em, that when they left KC he got in a fight with Munson. Obviously he couldn't believe that I won the game."

The U.S. Army couldn't believe Hrabosky either—while serving his country, he was nearly court-martialed. "They were taking target practice, and one of the guys' targets fell down, and he ran out there to right his target. One of the gunnery sergeants behind me got so mad that he said, 'Shoot the dummy!,' so I shot him. And they tried to get me on court-martial charges for shooting him, and I said, 'Look, ever since I've been in this army, I've had to gear myself to the lowest intelligence, so I was just following orders.' 'Well,' they said, 'don't you realize that if you get a command and it's unreasonable that you're not supposed to follow it?' 'I know,' I said, 'but that's why I didn't shoot to kill, I just shot to stop him. I shot him in the leg.' "

Hrabosky admits that he was eager to get on with his career as a pitcher, and was trying to get out of the Army. He booby-trapped an infiltration course and wouldn't tell the top brass where his bombs were. "I said, 'Hey, are the Viet Cong going to tell me what they've booby-trapped? I thought this was supposed to be realistic.' " Three men got hurt pretty bad and the Army asked Hrabosky if he would be willing to accept a six-year stint in the Army Reserve rather than be on active duty. Hrabosky said they made him the offer "because they weren't sure which side I was going to fight for." He looks back on his weapons training with a certain fondness. "It's good training for coming to Shea Stadium."

When the Royals got off to a slow start in 1978, he brought a hand grenade into the locker room and told his teammates that if they didn't start playing better ball he was going to have to blow them up. He had defused it, but didn't tell anyone that, and the grenade lay there all season. The night the Royals clinched the pennant, he pulled the safety pin. Hrabosky kept his finger down on the pin for a while, then said his finger was getting tired, initiating calls to the fire department and bomb squad.

With all the talk about umpires displaying a newfound arrogance and threatening to take over the game, I asked Hrabosky if he ever had an experience of that nature with the men in blue. "Well, I had one with the late Bill Kunkel. The Royals were in Minnesota, we had a one-run lead, it was the top of the ninth inning, and I did not have very good stuff, I was struggling. I had Rod Carew at the plate, and I kind of went back there behind the mound with nobody on base, to make sure that I was mentally ready to throw the ball where I wanted to throw it.

"Kunkel came over, he was the crew chief and first-base umpire, and when I came back to the mound he was standing on it, and he says, 'Give me the ball.' He was kind of mocking me, rubbing the ball, and he's saying, 'How's Mike? How's Mike?' I knew who he was talking about, Mike was my college coach and one of his buddies. I'm sure Gene Mauch was gettin' on him about me taking too much time, the twenty-second rule, so he decided that he would come over and satisfy Mauch and make a joke with me, and he found out that I was deathly serious.

"I told him to get the hell out of there with some choice Hungarian words and then I think he got back and figured, you know, *he's cussin' at me*. So the batter fouls off a couple of pitches, then he comes out to me and says, 'We made a new rule, you can't go out behind the mound.' And I'm arguing, 'What the hell are you talking about, when did this happen?' He says, 'Two weeks ago.' 'Well, why hasn't this been brought to my attention if the rule is designed obviously for me? You're lying.' So Whitey [Herzog] comes out and says, 'What's happening?' And Kunkel says, 'You better warm somebody up because if he stands behind the mound, I'm going to throw him out.' Now Whitey is yelling and screaming at him. So it ends up, he got the best of me, where I wind up walking Carew, and threw a couple balls on the screen, I was just so mad—this is supposed to be an *impartial arbitrator*. So it gets to the point that Whitey comes out and says, 'I gotta take you out.'

"We end up getting a double play, the next guy hits a home run, so we're tied. We go to the twelfth inning, and [Fred] Patek checks his swing, he does go all the way around, but nobody asks for an appeal play. The pitcher's in the middle of his windup, and Kunkel starts whistling and screaming and yelling, running down the line, and calls time out. Everybody gets up and he says, 'He's out of there!' Nobody asked for an appeal play, so I'm yelling and screaming at him, sitting in the third-base dugout. And I get thrown out of the game, so I refuse to leave the dugout.

"And about two innings later, the second-base umpire tells Frank White, 'Al's been thrown out of the game, would you please tell him to leave?' So I'm sitting there, and I say, 'Tell him I'll leave, but I want that rule interpretation.' So after the game I asked the home-plate umpire, 'Would you stand here and listen to Kunkel's answer when I ask him about this new rule?' He says, 'No way.' And I say, 'Can I ask him the question then, man to man?' So I said, 'Bill, would you explain that new rule to me?' He puts his arm around me and says, 'Oh, Al, there's no rule change.'

"I wrote a letter to the league president, told 'em everything. The Royals were afraid I would be suspended. But when an umpire takes it upon himself to make up rules at a pivotal point in the game . . . It was not unusual for Kunkel. Once or twice a year he would go off the deep end and do something."

Hrabosky has fulfilled a boyhood dream by maintaining stables of pure-bred Polish Arabian horses, and his stables have given him that winning edge when it came to the occasional prank. One of his favorites was one he helped pull on Jerry Reuss. "I was retired when Stan the Man Unusual (Don Stanhouse) was playing in L.A., but we had a mutual friend that goes all the way back to college. The guy's an attorney out in L.A. and he pulled all these pranks against Jerry Reuss as 'The Phantom.' For a birthday, the Phantom once sent an elephant to his front lawn.

"I get a call, 'Hey, it's Jerry's birthday, he's in Atlanta, can you do something special for him?' He was starting-pitching, and on the board it said, 'Happy Birthday Jerry, from the Phantom,' and we had a cake delivered to the clubhouse, and he was gonna go stick his face in it. Well, I have a stable and I decorated it with my handpicked road apples. Fresh out of the stalls, manure. So he starts to bury his face in this cake, and there it was right on top, his name spelled out in shit, and decorated all around the side. I did it myself. How in the hell did the Phantom, he wondered, get this thing to Atlanta?"

Where did Hrabosky get his outlook on life? It could have been a genetic trait, or then again, if he picked it up somewhere, it might have been in some of the godforsaken spots where he played ball early in his professional career, such as Gausabe, Mexico. "This town was so small there were like two hotels, neither one had a restaurant, it cost you a dollar sixty a night to stay there. We had a couple guys who were blond, and all the kids wanted to touch them, because they'd never seen blond hair except in the movies.

"They called me 'El Cordobe,' or 'Bandito Loco' down there. I always had a gun on me, because we were hunting all the time, I'd shoot pheasants, and I wore like a Clint Eastwood cap and a serape. It was just bad news. I'd walk around the streets and go to one bar that closes at two, then I'd find the paddy wagon and go on patrol with the police until five in the morning. And I'd do this every night, there was nothing to do. One night we were drivin' around, and Bake McBride was down there, and we drove past his place, so I told the police to go in there and arrest him. So we get there and we knock on the door, it's 3 A.M., Bake didn't speak any Spanish, and they spoke little English, and they say, '*Policía!*' "

Other diversions were to go to the whorehouse at five in the morning because he was curious about the American player who had gone there the previous year and gotten killed. Or going up on the roof with Rick Sutcliffe and some others with some surgical tubing and rubber balloons. "We hit cars, we shot 'em into apartments that had doors open. We had a 300-yard capability."

Hrabosky also played for Licey in the Dominican Republic. One year the team owners were holding a Thanksgiving party for the team when the players' mounting dissatisfaction with the conditions reached a breaking point. Hrabosky was at that party. "They had a big dinner for us," he recalled, "but they didn't know that we liked food that was edible. They really tried hard but they butchered turkey."

Mickey Hatcher, Everyman's 1988 World Series Hero, got pretty well oiled at this gathering, and wound up with his pants off on top of the roof overlooking a pool filled with three feet of water. "Get yourself another outfielder," Hatcher bellowed. "This food is the worst. I'm going to kill myself." His teammates Mike Scioscia and Leon Durham immediately came to his aid, yelling,

"Jump, you chicken!" Hatcher did a modified belly-flop into the pool and splashed the club owners, the *presidente,* and their wives dressed in their finery. "Oh, good, I thought," said Hatcher, "they're going to send me home now. But they thought it was the greatest thing they've ever seen." Hrabosky just shook his head, recalling Hatcher's big splash. "They made him a hero down there."

DANGEROUS FUN

All it took for Rick Dempsey to take the plunge was a rain delay. It began harmlessly enough, but soon Dempsey's act became well known in the American League East cities.

"Well, it started in 1977 when Boston and Baltimore were both tied for second place, we were two games out, and the Yankees had won it," says Dempsey. "I was entertaining the fans for a while by throwing some baseballs out and there was one ball out on the tarp so I went out to get it, and the organist was playing, so I just started slidin' around out there. And then I led 'em through a song, and the people didn't want me to leave, and I didn't know what to do, so I did a pantomime of Babe Ruth's home run, calling his shot, mixed with an insert of an Alibi Ike movie with Joe E. Brown, with a funny windup, and then I continued to fool around and went around the bases and slid into home. The belly-flop across home was the finale."

Dempsey has mimicked several of baseball's more offbeat moments, including acting out the George Brett pine tar incident as an old silent movie, but his favorite rain-delay pantomime was the one he did in Milwaukee of the final regular season game in 1982 between Baltimore and Milwaukee when Robin Yount homered twice off Jim Palmer to win the pennant.

"When I went to Milwaukee I agreed that I would do the tarp act if somebody would give me Yount's jersey. So I put it on underneath mine, and when I pulled my jersey off, the fans in Milwaukee got a big kick out of it. Then Sammy Stewart came out on the mound wearing Jim Palmer's Jockey underwear, with tights underneath it. So we did a pantomime of the two homers."

It got so that every time it rained, fans would get pumped up at the prospect of seeing Dempsey get wet and make a fool of himself. So Dempsey began hiding. One time in Boston he hid in the commode for forty minutes until he was found and carried onto the field without his feet touching the ground. That was in 1984, the last time he did his celebrated act.

Showmanship is second nature to Dempsey. It doesn't just run in his family, it gallops—both his parents were vaudevillians. But besides being one of baseball's true entertainers, throughout his career he has played alongside some of the game's more colorful characters.

These "meetings with remarkable men" began very early on in his career. When he was playing Little League baseball at the age of thirteen, he was on a terrific team that had four players who later played in the majors. They traveled around to different tournaments with their inspirational and flamboyant manager, a big, tall man, who was always giving the players money to do things. When they rode through the Arizona desert on the way to one of their games, this guy would say, "There's money in those hills out there, there's money in that real estate," but nobody on the team paid him any mind.

When Dempsey's team finally lost a tournament in Pennsylvania after winning twelve in a row, their manager was arrested as they were leaving the ballpark. "Everybody was wondering what the heck is happening. Well, apparently, in every city where we had a tournament, he would have a guy that followed our ball club around, a short guy. They robbed a bank in every city we went to. They called themselves 'the Mutt and Jeff bank robbers.' They'd robbed a bank that afternoon. They'd always have pictures of us in the sports page, and a lady who was in the bank identified him as the bank robber.

"The police chased these guys for a long time before they caught 'em. They had the perfect alibi, coming into town with a Little League team. Finally, they made 'em 'fess up as to where they hid the money and they had buried $280,000 worth of stocks and bonds in the desert in Arizona. Now we understood why he was giving us money all the time."

When Dempsey tells stories about playing winter ball, he boggles the imagination. His team's shortstop got shot at one night going down the street, went over a wall, and then fell through the roof of somebody's house into the living room. But for cheap thrills there was nothing like driving around with Pete LaCock, son of game-show host Peter Marshall, who played with the Cubs and Royals from 1972 through 1980.

"We roomed together one time and he almost ran a policeman off a cliff in Aguadilla, Puerto Rico. Pete used to race, and he tried to pass as many cars as he could before he had to turn back into his lane. So he used to drive me nuts, saying, 'I'm going for the record, I'm going for the record,' and I'd be going 'No, Pete!' "

On one occasion LaCock was passing his eleventh car for a new record when a police car came around the corner and had to slam on the brakes to avoid a head-on collision. The cop did a 360-degree turn and came skidding to a stop right on the edge of a thousand-foot drop down into the water. Dempsey wasn't confident about their prospects of staying out of jail as the police car wailed its siren and lit out after them, but LaCock didn't have "the record" for nothing, and the cop never caught up with him. As with all of these brushes with near-disaster, Dempsey said, "It was fun to talk about later on."

Dempsey also got a kick out of watching teammate John Lowenstein deal with the many cakes delivered to the Oriole clubhouse. "In Baltimore we used to get a cake once a week from somebody for a birthday, and they put it out on the table for everyone to eat. John would come out, he had a special bat in his locker, just about twenty-four inches with a big head and a small handle, and John would walk over to the cake and stare at it until somebody came over to take a piece of it, and as soon as they got close—*boom*—he'd slam the cake and it would explode all over the clubhouse. Or he'd see somebody about to have some cake and he'd sit on it naked."

When Lowenstein, a native of Wolf Point, Montana, played for the Indians, he formed what he called the Apathy Fan Club. Usually about 70,000 of the 74,000 seats in Cleveland's Municipal Stadium were then empty, but Lowenstein claimed that every empty seat represented a member of the fan club. "I just like to keep myself entertained," Lowenstein explained. "Baseball is reality at its harshest. It's a stress existence. You have to introduce a fictional world to survive. But I'm not flaky."

If Lowenstein wasn't flaky, then neither is a pie crust. He wore sunglasses even for night games, earning the monicker "Captain Midnight." "John did a lot of crazy things," recalled Dempsey. "One time while playing against Seattle in Baltimore he ran into a concrete wall, and he held on to the ball, and then he didn't get up. It looked like he was passed out, and nobody could bring him to, so they came rushing out with the stretcher to take him to the hospital. And just before they went down the steps and into the dugout, he stood up from the stretcher and raised his hands up to the people in the grandstands and they all just cheered. They went crazy, he really had 'em."

Dempsey also was the catcher for pitcher Ross Grimsley in his last two years with the Orioles. Many veteran baseball observers were stunned by Grimsley's success throwing his assorted junk at major-league hitters. Dempsey offers a clue to how Grimsley became a twenty-game winner. "He had Vaseline or KY jelly over every part of his body, he had it on his socks, on his belt, on his hair, his arms, his glove. Anything that he bent over and touched, it was loaded."

If cheating didn't work, Grimsley figured that black magic might. During one bad stretch, he called in a gypsy woman to perform a voodoo ceremony. When he was going good, he went months wearing the same rank-smelling sweatshirt. Superstition prevented him from washing, combing his hair, or using deodorant when he was winning, causing his teammates to consider throwing games that he pitched.

It was more than superstition. For Grimsley, it was a life-style. He took great pride in being a walking pigpen, and had the nickname "Skuz." He would walk around town shirtless in torn jeans and sandals, and collected sleazy photos of disgusting-looking people, like bearded ladies and wolfmen.

"Ross just looked like a wild and crazy guy," Dempsey recalled. "One time in Boston he was being badgered really badly, and one kid threw something at him, so he threw the ball up and it went right through one of the squares in the fence and hit the kid right in the eye. And he got sued for it. I don't think he lost his case, but whether it happened by accident, you never really knew with Ross."

According to Dempsey, the player who was more of a prankster than anyone else on the Orioles was the six-foot-six-inch pitcher with the curly hair and the wild look in his eye, the incomparable Sammy Stewart, who would go through airports walking like a spastic, with his hands flipping this way and that. Dempsey would hold one of his arms until one of the sympathetic stewardesses came over to help with a stroller. Then Sammy would start crying uncontrollably and blubbering incomprehensibly, and the stewardess wouldn't know what to do with this 235-pound, helpless behemoth until it was time to board the plane. Then he would get up, say "Thank you very much," and kiss her on the cheek.

"Sammy had a personality that was just unbelievable," said Dempsey. "Everybody kind of knew Sammy was a party guy, and he liked to get out and kick up his heels a little bit, and he liked to make you believe that he was on drugs. He used to scare Tippy Martinez to death, because he used to grab Tippy and pretend that he was going to cut his throat or something, and Tippy would get scared, and just lose it.

"They were living together one spring the last week of the

season. Tippy was coming home from the dog track one night, so Sammy went into his bedroom, put a chair on top of his bed, took off all of his clothes, and sat down on the chair waiting for Tippy to come into the room.

"Tippy was yelling through the house, 'Anybody home?' There was no answer, but he heard the TV on, so he goes into the bedroom, flips on the light, and there was Sammy with his eyes wide open, just staring at Tippy from the bed. Tippy figured that Sammy had OD'd on a drug of some sort, and he wasn't safe. So instead of sleeping in the house that night, Tippy tiptoed out on the veranda and slept outside under this overhang, because he thought Sammy would come in the middle of the night and try to hurt him. It was hilarious because he was so afraid of Sammy all the time."

Apparently it was a running joke on the Orioles to try and induce some form of cardiac arrest, and Dempsey came close to doing just that one night at the Key Colony Hotel during spring training. Dempsey went to dinner with Tippy Martinez, Mike Boddicker, and Len Sakata, got their key, and sneaked back into their room, figuring he could scare them to death.

Dempsey hid in the closet as Tippy, Mike, and Len prepared to play their penny-ante poker game. Dempsey could see them through the door slats, although they couldn't see him. When they were in other rooms, Dempsey ran out of the closet and turned off all the electricity from the main power switch. He then got back in the closet and listened to Tippy talking to his wife over the phone in the pitch dark. "Tippy says, 'I'm scared. Don't hang up the phone because I don't want to be in here by myself.' So I'm just crackin' up because this guy is telling his wife that he doesn't want to be alone when there's three other men in the house."

They got the lights back on, and then settled down to their poker game, a bit uneasily. Then a brush thrown by Dempsey went flying past their table, and they heard a voice that sounded like it came from a man who was evidently big, probably black, probably ugly, and possibly criminally insane. "Okay, motherfuckers, move away from the table and leave that money down there!"

"Who the hell are you?" they yelled. "I'm gonna get all that money, and if you motherfuckers don't get out of that room, I'm gonna kill ya, I'm gonna kill ya!" Tippy ran into the kitchen and grabbed a butter knife. "You can't have our money, because I've got a knife!" he said. Dempsey retorted with "I've got a gun!" and Tippy replied, "Okay, you can have it!"

Dempsey held his teammates at bay for twenty minutes. Tippy tried to ease the change off the table into his pocket, and Dempsey could see him, so he yelled to leave the change right there, or he'd kill him. He ordered the three of them into the kitchen so he could take the money and run. Dempsey then stamped his feet on the floor as hard as he could and started running at them, screaming when he reached the kitchen, only to find Tippy ready to attack him with six butter knives in one hand and a can opener in the other. "He damn near stabbed me with 'em," recalled Dempsey, "and when he saw it was me, he just dropped everything and started pounding on me. And I think that was the funniest thing that happened in spring training with us."

Tippy, for his part, says Rick exaggerates a bit. He told me days before his release from the Minnesota Twins that Boddicker was in on it, for one thing, and besides, he only had "about three butter knives" in his hand when he attacked Dempsey.

When Dempsey was playing with the New York Yankees in the mid-'70s, he was witness to another episode in the dangerous-fun category involving Bill Sudakis and Lou Piniella. Sudakis came over to the Yankees from the Rangers as a reserve first baseman and catcher, and wasn't playing very much. Piniella was badgering him and Sudakis snapped. When he came out of the elevator of the Ponchartrain Hotel in Detroit and saw Lou, he ran after him and chased him into a janitor's closet. Right next to the closet was a fire hose and hatchet under glass. Sudakis was so mad that he broke the fire box, grabbed the hatchet, and told Piniella he was going to kill him.

"He took the hatchet and slammed it in the door, and it went right through the thin plywood. We all gasped. I'm sure Sudsy was just trying to be funny in his sort of way, but when the hatchet went through the door we figured, well, he may have killed Lou. But the door opened up and there was Lou with a couple of nails in his back up against the wall with the hatchet swingin' out from the door. If he had been leaning up against the door, it damn well would have killed him. We laughed about it after we saw that he didn't get hurt, but for a while there was some anxious anticipation."

Later, Dempsey had an epic fight with Sudakis at the close of the 1974 American League pennant race in Milwaukee. On the team bus, Sudakis was needling Dempsey about not playing, and as Lou Piniella tells it, "the needling grew more nasty as the beer flowed." Sudakis and Dempsey tried to go through the hotel's revolving door and the door jammed. "When it started," said Dempsey, "I hit Sudakis three times, and he went out, but he came to in a hurry." Dempsey was 170 pounds and Sudakis was around 230. Piniella said it was "like one of those bad movie fights in the Westerns."

By the time they were through, they had destroyed the lobby of the hotel and, by Dempsey's own count, taken out nearly half the team. "I hit my roommate and he fell across the table, I hit Walt Williams, he fell over the couch and broke it. Pat Dobson, I hit him. And Murcer broke his finger, I must have stepped on his hand." Dempsey described the bout as an ordeal, a live-or-die situation. "Finally Thurman came over and choked the shit out of me and I passed out for a second. Elston Howard picked me up, brought me into the bar, and I was so exhausted, I vomited. Two guys had to sit next to me because I couldn't raise my arms. Ellie fired a couple shots down me. Sudakis couldn't breathe for a while, and I was damn near dead myself." The Yankees then lost to Milwaukee in extra innings without Murcer, and the Orioles won the pennant. Dempsey looked back on it with a measure of irony. "I won it for Baltimore and didn't even know it."

HOTFOOTIN'

Another former Oriole who loved to scare the daylights out of his teammates was none other than the great Drabo, "The Snake Man" himself, Moe Drabowsky. A journeyman pitcher for much of his career, he had his moment of glory in the 1966 World Series when he set a record by striking out eleven Dodgers in six and two-thirds innings of relief.

Drabowsky was disappointed when he first was sent to the bullpen, but then realized that working in relief definitely had its points. "When I was a starting pitcher, I could pitch eight great innings, but give up a home run in the ninth inning to lose the game. And what did the fans remember? That I blew the game in the ninth inning. So as a starting pitcher I had to work more than two hours just to discover I was horse manure that day. But as a reliever, I could come into a game and give up a home run on my third pitch. So as a relief pitcher I only had to work about two minutes to find out I was horse manure."

The bullpen also afforded the impish Drabowsky (he once considered going to Hollywood as a Danny Kaye impersonator) enough time to pursue his various extracurricular activities. Drabowsky worked as a stockbroker during the off season, and often used the bullpen phone to check the latest market quotes—that is, when he wasn't calling a Chinese restaurant in Hong Kong to find out if they delivered.

Drabowsky was not above using the phone as a mind-control weapon during a ball game. When he was with the Orioles he impersonated Kansas City manager Alvin Dark and called the KC bullpen, ordering Lew Krausse to get up and start throwing while the A's pitcher, Jim Nash, was pitching a two-hit shutout. Nash, seeing how little confidence his manager had in him, threw his glove on the ground in disgust, and subsequently lost his concentration as well as the ball game.

Drabo did indeed enjoy doing the occasional impersonation. After he joined the Kansas City Athletics in 1969, he would call teammates and drawl in the distinctive voice of owner Charles Finley, engaging in fake contract negotiations. Among those who had their legs pulled in this manner was Rocky Colavito. Besides enjoying the ruse, Moe thought it might help him in his own negotiations. Another time he impersonated Finley and called a Baltimore talk show to tell a momentarily choked-up Brooks Robinson that he had just been traded to the A's.

Moe made a point of keeping up with his old mates on the Orioles, and in 1969 he set off a bullpen war that lasted the whole season. Under Moe's guidance, the Royals' bullpen synchronized their watches, blackened their faces, wore dark jackets, and bombed the O's bullpen with rocks and dirt balls during a night game at Memorial Stadium. Two days later the O's launched a counteroffensive, splitting eardrums with a loud firecracker that scared the Royals' relievers silly. Things escalated from there faster than a Chinese tong war.

"I guess I'm a frustrated soldier," Drabowsky admitted. "I would have loved being in combat. Baseball was the next best thing. I could defeat the enemy with a good pitch, and also play my war games." When the O's struck again by painting the Royals' bullpen pitching rubber black and orange, the Oriole colors, Drabowsky one-upped them by putting sneezing powder into the O's clubhouse air-conditioning system, and goldfish in the water cooler. Then the O's pulled out all the stops and painted the Royals' bullpen roof bright orange and wrote "Go Birds" on it.

The end of the regular season did not mean that Moe was through, as he took his parting shot at the first game of the 1969 World Series in Baltimore. He got a plane to circle Memorial Stadium and pull a banner with the message "Good Luck Birds. Beware of Moe." On the same day he sent Orioles utility infielder Chico Salmon a box containing a five-foot boa constrictor. Salmon got dressed for the game in the dugout.

Drabowsky did it all—throwing smoke bombs in the showers, letting air out of the tires, putting Limburger cheese in his teammates' cars. He got into an elevator once with Boog Powell and dropped some hydrogen sulfate on his shoulder. "It smelled like eighty barrels of rotten eggs," said Powell. "Everyone moved away from me as if I cut some vicious cheese. I was smelling that nasty shit all day. It didn't seem to bother Moe. Maybe he burned out the lining in his nose from sniffing that stuff."

The Chinese man who invented the firecracker could not have loved setting them off more than Drabowsky. Vern Hoscheit was the bullpen coach in Baltimore in 1968, so he can vouch for that. "He got some firecrackers," said Hoscheit, "and lined them up and put a slow-acting fuse between the packs. The fuse was way off somewhere—nobody could see it. And when he came to the bullpen he lit the fuse, it took maybe a half hour for the thing to blow. It was right under me, I'm sittin' there, and all of a sudden *bang bang bang*. I was jumping. And then I'm back to the game, I'm trying to steal their signs, and the next inning another pack goes off, and the next inning another one."

That was Drabowsky's trademark—surprise and overkill. In 1971, the Atlanta Braves' mascot Chief Nokahoma used to do a war dance outside his teepee in left field. Drabowsky set off a dozen cherry bombs next to the teepee, and when the smoke cleared, there was no sign of the chief. "I thought, 'By gosh, he's up there, he's with his ancestors in the Great Hunting Ground.' "

Drabowsky was called "The Snake Man" because he liked to use slithering reptiles to see how high he could get his more squeamish teammates to jump. Brooks Robinson was the mark when Moe was invited back to Baltimore in 1984 for a sports banquet. Drabowsky brought a four-foot Florida King snake with him and sneakily placed it in the basket of dinner rolls, putting a folded napkin on top. When Robinson asked for the rolls, he reached out and found instead a little black head looking right at him, flicking its tongue.

I read a story that he put a boa constrictor in Paul Blair's locker, causing Blair to run screaming onto the field. Blair told me what transpired on that day. "I was the first one in the clubhouse that day, so I was already in there, thank God. He came in and he had a four-foot snake wrapped around his neck. All year he was playing with rubber snakes, so he comes over, and I said, 'That's not real,' and then he started laughin' and it stuck its head up and I lit out of there. I was gone.

"He had five little snakes to put in guys' lockers. He put one in Aparicio's locker, and Luis got a bat, getting ready to fight everybody. And Camilo Carreon came in, he was getting ready to sign for the fans, and Moe just threw the snake right on him. I thought he was going to have a heart attack. Then Bauer came in and made him take all the snakes out of the locker room. I didn't let him put snakes in my locker, I got there first. I don't like snakes at all, I can't even watch 'em on TV. I knew Moe, and we used to play cards every night on the road. So I was always the first one in the room so I could search the room and check Moe out. I didn't want no snakes in the card game."

While Drabowsky liked employing firecrackers and snakes, he probably got more mileage out of the old standby, the hotfoot. But Drabo brought some new wrinkles to one of baseball's greatest traditions after learning the fundamentals from Davey Johnson. One match wasn't enough for Moe, so he went to an entire matchbook.

Paul Blair said, "He gave more hotfoots than anything. In our locker room we had the rubber kind of mat. He would put the matches in your shoe while you were talking and leave a trail of lighter fluid and go all the way into the trainer's room and light it and catch you. And you'd see the flame go all the way across the room. Moe Drabowsky was absolutely crazy."

"Certainly my greatest hotfoot," Drabowsky said, "was administered to Baseball Commissioner Bowie Kuhn in our locker room after we'd won the World Series. I placed an entire book of matches under his foot and laid a lighter fluid trail from the matches to the trainer's room. I hid in the trainer's room and lit it. Have you ever wondered how high a baseball commissioner can jump?"

Whether it was his good fortune or his special curse is hard to figure, but bullpen coach Vern Hoscheit served time not only with Moe Drabowsky but also with Roger McDowell of the Mets, enduring all manner of mischief. McDowell and his mates lovingly called Hoscheit "Dad," and obviously liked the guy, otherwise they would not have tortured him so much. Hoscheit is not a tall man, and McDowell would put the bag of balls on a shelf higher than Vern could reach. Frequently Vern would pick up the bullpen phone and it would be "loaded" with Vaseline or shaving cream, and he was hotfooted so many times he considered wearing asbestos socks.

Sometimes Hoscheit would retaliate by putting some dirt in McDowell's coffee, but it was a token gesture. Hoscheit actually ran a relatively strict bullpen, forbidding cheeseburgers, pizza, fried chicken, *and* girlfriends in his lair, allowing only coffee and Coke. But in the early part of the game he would let Orosco and McDowell work off their boredom by playing golf using a bat for a club.

I spoke with McDowell soon after the Mets opened their new spring training facility in Port St. Lucie, Florida. He had just arrived in camp a few days earlier, casually sporting a cast on his arm, a prank that hardly fazed his manager, Davey Johnson, who's grown quite accustomed to his reliever.

After his workout, Roger was eating a bowl of egg salad from the training table spread, which is a bit out of character for him, since he could easily exist on a steady diet of fried foods. Port St. Lucie, being a relatively new resort development, has few restaurants, but as soon as McDowell found a McDonald's, he knew he was set. "My typical order at McDonald's is two Quarter Pounders with cheese, a Big Mac, a fish sandwich, two cheeseburgers, a large order of french fries, a large iced tea, a vanilla milkshake, and a piece of cherry pie. Only one order of fries because I need room for the cherry pie."

When the bell rings late in the game, Roger McDowell is ready to go, and has been for several years now. He's the right-handed reliever that Johnson has successfully relied upon in tandem with

Jesse Orosco for three years and now with Randy Myers. Since 1985 he has gotten big-league hitters out with one of the nastier sinker pitches around, having his biggest year in the Mets' championship season of 1986, when he won fourteen games and saved twenty-two. And, not so incidentally for a reliever who often comes into the game in bunting situations, he is acknowledged as one of the best fielding pitchers in the National League.

It's just that when he isn't pitching, he spends a lot of time plotting ways to set his teammates' shoes on fire, and has earned the reputation as one of the league-leading hotfoot specialists. Curiously, McDowell had always heard about the hotfoot, but he never knew how to do it before he reached the majors. Howard Johnson came to the Mets from the Detroit Tigers in 1986, and schooled McDowell on the method he learned from Lance Parrish. "Howard had a lot of time playing behind Ray Knight," said McDowell, "and we had a lot of time to work on it."

McDowell's preferred foot warmer is created like this: Take the staple from a pack of matches, wrap the cardboard around a lit cigarette, which serves as the fuse, and then attach it with bubble gum to the shoe. All of the Met starters serve as McDowell's setup men, especially Ojeda and Aguilera, who must help to somehow distract the victim. Most of the Mets have been lit up at one time or another, but the prime target has undoubtedly been first-base coach Bill Robinson.

On one memorable occasion, Robinson got that warm sensation after he went out to the coaching box, and his foot caught fire in front of 25,000 people. After his foot cooled off, Robinson did his own slow burn, but, all things considered, took it in good humor. "There were 20,000 fans at Shea Stadium all looking at me and laughing," Robinson said. "Now that's embarrassing. I wanted to kill him."

Robinson is now ever-watchful of McDowell. "Every two minutes you have to check the back of your shoes because they might be on fire thanks to Roger." Before the '88 regular season began, Robinson told McDowell he would never get him again, and they bet a dinner on it. McDowell and his various setup men had their work cut out trying to distract Robinson enough to allow Mc-Dowell to crawl underneath the length of the dugout bench to the front where the coaches sit. There's no question it would be difficult, but McDowell seemed up for it. "It's a challenge to get him," he said.

It was in Cincinnati that McDowell sent his man Bill out to the first-base coaching box with his foot ready to go up in flames. The Mets saw it about to happen, and so did the Reds. McDowell was especially proud of his timing; there was already one out in the inning when Robinson's foot caught fire. Roger even has the videotape of it for his personal library.

When McDowell first made the major-league roster in 1985, he had to be reassured that it wasn't an April Fool's joke, because when Bobby Valentine coached in the Mets organization he used to tell young players that they were being sent down to the minors as a joke. Like most rookies, McDowell was very quiet when he first came up. He admits that a player has to have a certain amount of success before he can feel comfortable doing the things he does. And McDowell has had success, with the pinnacle coming in what some observers call the greatest game ever played, Game Six of the Astros-Mets '86 playoff. In that historic contest, McDowell pitched five innings of one-hit relief.

McDowell may have the perfect makeup for a relief pitcher. Some fans would like to see him act ticked off after he gives up a key hit or a home run, but it is just not his nature. He thought he made a good pitch to Terry Pendleton when he gave up a pennant-turning home run in the '87 season, but that's the breaks. (When I visited the Cardinals' camp, someone had stuck McDowell's baseball card above Pendleton's locker.)

"Some of them are harder to forget than the others," Roger admitted. "But you have to leave 'em on the field. I use them for learning. Then I throw the bad memories away. You should see the letters I get. 'How come you don't care?' People write that all the time, because I guess I don't look upset enough out there.

People tell me I shouldn't act like I do after I give up a home run. I want to tell them, I act that way so I can get on with things and not give up another homer." (In the '88 regular season, McDowell gave up only one homer.)

McDowell's approach is a nice complement to that of his new bullpen partner, Randy Myers, who comes into the game breathing fire. Disgusted with his control one night, Myers snatched Gary Carter's return toss with his bare hand. Myers gives a new meaning to the phrase "pumped up." He is so enamored of weight lifting that he even works out on the weight machines after he pitches. While Randall K. Myers is a blithe spirit, he is also the most inscrutable of Mets. As McDowell put it, "Probably the only guys who can understand him are the Green Berets."

When I saw McDowell during the season he was sitting by himself in the dugout at Shea, squirting the Mets who were warming up in front of him with a high-powered water pistol. On the Mets of '85 and '86, McDowell considered himself only one of a whole bevy of crazies. He views the '88 collection of Mets as a younger and more serious bunch. In '85 there was Larry Bowa on the bench doing his Harry Caray impression in the ninth inning while sitting next to Davey Johnson. There was Kevin Mitchell in '86 flashing his gold teeth, gold chains, and nonstop street rap. Few things in baseball are as much fun as winning, and it was the Mets' dominating '86 season that helped create the anything-goes atmosphere on the ball club.

One of McDowell's favorite moments from that season happened in Atlanta. "There were some guys down on the end of the bullpen bench looking at a porno magazine centerfold, and a fly ball comes over. Terry Harper runs in, leans over the fence, and catches the ball, and the pitcher's legs go up, and the centerfold is exposed on TV. I think it was too fast for most people to see what it was, but when we saw the highlights, we could see it very plainly."

Now McDowell is pretty much on his own as the team prankster. "If something happens now," he says, "I'm the person everybody looks at." McDowell has never felt that he can get away with virtually anything. He knows his limit, when to lighten things up and when not to, which is something everyone appreciates, including Davey Johnson. And McDowell in turn appreciates the leeway that Johnson gives him without trying to curtail his prankish nature. McDowell was most interested to find that his manager was the one who taught Moe Drabowsky the rudiments of hotfooting when he was with the Orioles.

"Davey doesn't try and mold anybody into the kind of player he was, or anybody else was, he lets the individual go his own way. I think he knows that we know we have a job to do, and if something gets out of hand, he'll let us know." McDowell's approach to playing baseball seems to set just fine with most of his teammates. He is the Mets' good-natured Huck Finn, specializing in the pursuit of good, clean, inoffensive fun. "Roger's a beauty," says Keith Hernandez.

McDowell also has a large, ever-growing mask collection. He has tried to find a mask to match every player on the Mets, and frequently visits joke shops on the road. His mask for Hoscheit, for instance, was a wrinkled 150-year-old-man mask that he wore as he presented the lineup card to the home-plate umpire. Now that Vern has retired, McDowell may have to put that mask in retirement. He is still looking for a mask that captures his old roomie in the minor leagues, Lenny Dykstra. "I think they broke the mold when they made Lenny," he said, shaking his head. In a store in Los Angeles, he spotted a three-foot-high Tasmanian Devil mask, for which he paid $99.99. It's a mask that he brings into the dugout whenever the Mets have a chance to sweep a series.

When the Mets played the second-place Pirates in Pittsburgh in June of 1988, a radio campaign described the Mets as "one more thing to hate about New York" and exhorted the fans to come out to Three Rivers Stadium and "bring some hate." The result was a fiasco, with fans throwing beer and cups on the Mets' relievers, along with pennies and nickels. McDowell retaliated by visiting a novelty store and armed himself with a pig nose, buck teeth, and, in case anyone requested an autograph, a stump arm.

Ron Darling recalled the night when he and his wife went out with the McDowells. "A grandmother came over after dinner, and I think she had a few drinks. She asked Roger to sign a ball for her, saying that her four-year-old grandson Mark would just die if he didn't get McDowell's autograph." With no hesitation, McDowell jauntily signed for the kid. "He wrote, 'Dear Mark, Hope you make five, Roger McDowell.' "

While McDowell is a naturally funny guy, he is probably at his best as a visual cosmic. When the controversy raged during the '87 season about pitchers cheating by ball-scuffing, McDowell showed up at the ballpark wearing a sanding belt, complete with drills, sandpaper, and a bit of cork donated by Howard Johnson. Likewise, when an outbreak of chicken pox threatened to infect valuable Mets, McDowell showed up in the locker room wearing a surgical mask.

McDowell created his most famous sight gag on the spur of the moment in Los Angeles in 1987. It was about ten minutes before batting practice, and they were having a battle of the marching bands. One band came in wearing Davy Crockett uniforms, so McDowell wanted to change uniforms with the tuba player, but the bandleader was not very happy about the switch, and squelched the idea. McDowell went back to the dugout, and then, he says, "It just hit me."

He decided to dress himself upside down. "I had to put my sanitaries over my hands, I had to tape 'em. I put my shirt on upside down, putting my legs through my sleeves, and took off my socks. Then I took one of my masks and taped it to several towels and taped a hat to that and used it for a head, and I roped the sanitaries to the mask and then tied that around my waist." Then he walked out and they put him on Dodgervision.

STUNTMEN

McDowell's stunts are really not bizarre compared to some of the behavior that has been exhibited in the big leagues. Where is a Bill Faul, the '60s pitcher who had himself put under hypnosis to help his control, and who once ate a live toad? Where is a Brad Leslie, one-time Yankee prospect, who bit the head off a chicken before Ozzy Osbourne made heavy-metal history with the same routine? Now we get Bert Blyleven picking his nose on camera and showing the resulting find to the home audience. It's just not the same.

The old-timers could really pull some stunts. In 1914, the Dodgers were down in Florida for spring training, and the players went up in airplane rides, enjoying the novelty of this newfangled diversion. Their rotund manager, Wilbert Robinson, a former catcher, boasted that he could catch a ball dropped from a plane, so his players took him up on it. So a plane flew over the ballpark, with "Uncle Robby" looking up for the ball. Somebody (Casey Stengel took credit for it in later years) dropped a grapefruit instead of a baseball, and when it came down it splattered Robinson with wet pulp, knocking him flat on the ground. Robinson lay there, thinking he was mortally wounded, and everybody had a good laugh.

That was just par for the course, as it was in the '20s when catcher Gabby Hartnett caught a ball dropped from the top of the Washington Monument. Players didn't back down from a challenge in those days. One of the most incredible stunts pulled on a ballfield was done repeatedly by former Phillie and Met Frank Thomas, a power hitter who played in the '50s and '60s. Thomas had a little trick he developed—he caught fastballs barehanded. The first guy he did it to was pitcher Bill Pierro in Waco, Texas, in 1949.

"I did it on a dare," recalled Thomas. "I went out in the outfield and he's poppin' off about how hard he can throw, so I said, 'I'll catch your best fastball barehanded.' And he says, 'Like heck you will.' So I said, 'Go down to the bullpen and warm up.' He says, 'You won't catch it if I don't warm up.' I said, 'Well, that's what you're going to say after I catch it.' So he went out sixty feet six inches and he threw it and I caught it, and he says, 'I'm not really warm.' So I said, 'I knew you'd say that, so go down to the pen and warm up and when you're warm you come down here and I'll catch it again.' So I caught five in a row. That shut him up pretty good. It hit him in the ego, and that's what I did it for more than anything else."

I kept looking at Thomas's huge hands while he was telling me this. When he was growing up he toughened his hands by playing fast-pitch softball without a glove. "I'd catch anybody," he said. "I caught Mays. In New York Richie Ashburn comes over and asks Mays, 'How'd you like to make a quick hundred?' Willie says 'Yeah, man, what do I gotta do?' 'I'll bet you Thomas can catch your fastball barehanded.'

"So then I said to him, 'Willie, I want you to be warm when you throw it.' I thought he was ready so I dropped the glove and caught it. But he wasn't ready yet. Then he turned to Ashburn and said, 'Let's make it a ten-dollar bet.' He threw me a couple and I caught 'em. He never paid me. When I see Willie, I always ask him how a guy can make $125,000 a year and he can't pay a ten-dollar bet.

"The toughest one I had to catch was from Don Zimmer. Zimmer had a great arm, he marked off sixty feet six inches, went back twenty feet, took a running start and threw me a spitter. I had to catch it like this, coming up underneath. I caught it and he just threw his glove up in the air."

When asked if he wasn't at all worried about injuring his hands, Thomas answered, "Looking back, you have to wonder how crazy could you have been, because you could have gotten hurt, but I never did. I just caught 'em in the palm of my hands. If you know what you're doing, you can do anything."

Can you imagine a major player today trying to psyche out Roger Clemens or Dwight Gooden by catching their best fastball barehanded before a game? It would never happen, and if it did the ball club would have the player's agent on the phone the same day.

Players have to protect their own as well as the team's investment in them, so they just won't attempt the kind of stunts that players used to do almost casually. That's not to say they don't do fairly amazing things now and then. In 1988, on NBC's "Game of the Week," Pirates second baseman Jose Lind took a running start and jumped clear over the bald head of a standing Joe Garagiola. It seems that Joe was taking the risk with that little stunt.

How does that compare with a player the Pirates developed named John Candelaria? When "The Candy Man" was just beginning in pro ball, he became so bored in spring training that he announced that, for the right price, he would jump off the two-story roof of the Pirate City Motel at midnight. His teammates anted up $4.50, and that was enough for Candelaria. He jumped off the roof, and walked off laughing, never telling anyone that he had broken the big toe on his left foot.

Joe Charboneau, the Cleveland Indians' former Rookie of the Year in 1980 and self-professed "punk-rock ballplayer," would try anything. On a dare he once ate five filter-tip cigarettes. In a bar one night with a teammate in the minor leagues, Charboneau got involved in a little contest. Joe's teammate opened a bottle of beer with his forearm, so Joe did that, and then one-upped him by opening the next bottle with his eye socket. It hurt like anything and left a scar under his right eyebrow, but Joe wasn't finished. He blew everyone away and ended the contest by boasting that he could drink beer through his nose, which he had never done, and proceeded to drain a cold one nasally. Surprisingly, no brewery asked Charboneau to endorse its product, even after he hit it big, however briefly.

Today, stunts during games are strictly verboten. If some enterprising player tries to pull something creative while a game is in progress, then it could be his last shenanigan. That was certainly the case with Dave Bresnahan, a minor-league catcher for the Williamsport Bills in Pennsylvania whose great-uncle was Hall of Fame catcher Roger Bresnahan. Bresnahan peeled a potato before the game and put it in a reserve mitt. Then in the fifth inning he called time, saying something was wrong with his mitt, and changed gloves. The new glove had the potato in it. There was a runner on third base and Bresnahan threw the potato into left field. The runner tried to come home and Bresnahan tagged him out with the real ball.

The management of the Bills was not thrilled by his trick play. They fined him fifty dollars and the Cleveland Indians' director of player development released him. But baseball fans across the country loved it, and the Williamsport fans just about deified him. Bresnahan wound up doing over a hundred interviews. So eventually he was flown back to the scene of the crime where, naturally, the Bills retired his number. (Bresnahan sold T-shirts reading "This Spud's for You" and donated the money to the American Cancer Society.)

⚾

THE THREE STOOGES AND THE CUCKOO'S NEST

It's a sign of the times that a stunt like Bresnahan's is so unusual today that the player is drummed out of the game and becomes a cause célèbre. It's hard to imagine what present-day baseball's corporate leaders would do with baseball's original flake and oddball, Rube Wadell.

When they describe a pitcher as having a million-dollar arm and a ten-cent brain, that was Rube. His fastball and curve were good enough to get him into the Hall of Fame after pitching for Connie Mack's A's in the 1900s, but many wondered what he might have accomplished if he hadn't been just an overgrown kid. Between innings during a game he could occasionally be found playing marbles with local urchins. The Rube was a farm-boy who loved parties, parades, fishing, pretty girls, red neckties, and fire engines. He once left a game in progress to chase a fire truck.

Attendance was definitely not one of his strong points. He might pitch a game, then disappear for three or four days. When he did show up at the park, it was often at the last minute and with great dramatic effect. Minutes before he was scheduled to pitch, someone would spot him storming through the stands. Amid the commotion he would jump onto the field, tearing off his shirt as he walked toward the clubhouse to change his clothes. When he reappeared later to take his warmup pitches, the crowd would go nuts.

Waddell's roommate Ossee Schrenkengost had one complaint about living with Rube on the road, and that was his penchant for eating animal crackers in bed (at that time two players often shared the same bed for economic reasons when the club was on the road). Ossee demanded that the club write into Rube's contract a clause forbidding the consumption of crackers in bed.

One night, when he and Shreck were in their cups, Rube announced that he could fly and leaped out the window to prove it. When he came to in the hospital the next day, he asked his roomie why he didn't stop him. "Heck," said Shreck, "I bet you could do it." Maybe Shreck was thinking about the time in Florida when Rube watched a professional alligator wrestler and asked if he could give it a go. Waddell then pressed his snap-jawed opponent in no time flat.

He beat Cy Young in a twenty-inning game and left the mound turning cartwheels. He later sold the ball used in that game for drinks, many drinks. About twenty bartenders around the league displayed the historic ball above their bars. Soon after he began pitching for Philadelphia he could be seen in the saloons, where he would often step behind the bar and begin serving and drinking at the same time. He could just as frequently be found in a local jail, for he was married and divorced several times and invariably spent his alimony payments on booze. He gave up a homer once and was so drunk that as he turned dizzily in a circle to watch the hitter round the bases, he fell flat on his butt.

In 1905, he had won twenty-six games when he got into a fight over a straw hat, fell and hurt his shoulder, and began his decline. One of the game's most loved players, he died in 1914 at the age of thirty-seven, an alcoholic with tuberculosis. Many said at the time that we would not see his like again, and they were right.

The contemporary flake is characterized not by his total naiveté, but by his extreme self-consciousness. When Jay Johnstone, who terrorized eight different teams, joined the Los Angeles Dodgers, manager Tommy Lasorda told him quite frankly that the clubhouse was too quiet and that he wanted Johnstone to loosen people up. He was the Dodgers' Designated Flake.

Johnstone revived the Green Hornet, a gag that had been started by the Dodgers' Jim Lefebvre and Wes Parker years before. Johnstone would spray a big "GH" on players' shoes, bats, or even the walls of their hotel rooms. He had his accomplices, so frequently he had a perfect alibi. But that was only the beginning.

In spring training at Vero Beach, with the help of catcher Steve Yeager, he tied a sailor's knot around a palm tree and tied the other end to the door of manager Tommy Lasorda's room, making it impossible for him to get out. They disconnected his phone before that, and so he was trapped. He screamed until a hotel employee let him out, but by then—tragically for Lasorda—it was too late for breakfast if he wanted to catch the team bus.

One of Johnstone's favorites on a hot day was putting a melting brownie into Steve Garvey's glove and wiping some of the chocolate on the pants of pitcher Jerry Reuss. When Garvey came in from first base and saw the chocolate on Reuss, he pummelled the surprised pitcher for messing with his glove, while Johnstone conveniently made himself scarce. Johnstone and Reuss once dressed as groundskeepers during a ballgame and dragged the infield. Johnstone changed back into his uniform just in time to hit a pinch-hit, game-winning home run.

Reuss, with his deadpan delivery and bold imagination, can be a dangerous prankster. When the Dodgers were in Chicago to play the Cubs, the Yankees happened to be in the same city to play the White Sox, and that was all the coincidence Reuss needed to floor Yankee manager Lou Piniella. Reuss reported to the Yankees and told Piniella that he was ready to do whatever he wanted, start or relieve. Piniella thought that George Steinbrenner had made another deal without consulting him, and was thoroughly flabbergasted.

For one very unusual year in Los Angeles, Reuss and Johnstone were united with relief ace Don "Stan the Man Unusual" Stanhouse, who joined the Dodgers as a free agent. They were known on the Dodgers as "The Three Stooges." "Jay made me laugh as much as anybody," Stanhouse said. He pegged Reuss as "the kind of guy who would stand back, but you never knew when he was going to go off. You never knew what was going through his mind." Stanhouse doesn't play favorites, however. "They should have been committed, both of 'em."

He recalled the day that he and Johnstone taped Reuss's hands and feet together, and then proceeded to tape him up entirely, like a mummy, and left him until game time. But Stanhouse's absolute favorite was the time that Tommy Lasorda came into his office only to find that all of his treasured autographed pictures of himself with Hollywood celebrities like Frank Sinatra and Don Rickles had been replaced by pictures of Johnstone, Reuss, and Stanhouse. "He yelled the loudest he's ever yelled, and it was the fastest he'd moved since he went after a heavy plate of spaghetti," recalled Stanhouse. When Lasorda finally cornered the culprits, they responded by asking, "How many games did those other guys win for you?"

Stanhouse remembers Johnstone as the kind of guy who would stay up all night dreaming up new ways to prank. He takes credit for doing a lot of the nuts-and-bolts detail work for Jay, but Stan-house had his own concerns. A girl bought him a big stuffed monkey, and as soon as Stanhouse brought his new pet into the clubhouse, the Dodgers went on a winning streak. Henceforth, when Stanhouse celebrated a win with a beer, the monkey had one, too. On team flights he had the monkey strapped in right next to him.

Stan the Man was basically left to his own devices by that time in his career, having been one of the best relievers of his time. He had the arm for it, having been a high school All-American quarterback who could have played college football. Charlie Fin-ley signed him as a third baseman, "but ground balls kept hitting me in the face," so they put him on the mound and three years later he was in the big leagues.

It was Dick Williams, the manager who made Rollie Fingers into a relief pitcher, who told Stanhouse over cocktails that he was going to be getting the ball on a daily basis. Stanhouse took to the role because he always hated sitting around between games as a starting pitcher. He wound up with ten wins and ten saves and summed up his first season in the bullpen as a smashing success—"I pitched in fifty ball games, I had a lot of fun, I occupied my summer, I went out there to do a job, and I enjoyed the shit out of it."

He had that attitude that can't be taught. Even with 50,000 people screaming in a ballpark and runners on base in an im-portant game, he would feel in control. "I don't think I ever got real tight once," said Stanhouse. "You have to go out, 'What do we have here, Ollie? Let me see what I can do with this mess.' You go in, you're supposed to paint this car red, you paint the fucking car red. When's it supposed to be painted? You get it done.'" It's the simplest perspective that is finally the most unusual.

Earl Weaver called him "Full Pack" because that's how many cigarettes he would have to smoke in the runway while Stanhouse finished ball games. This was a result of Stanhouse's philosophy of walking the guys that could hurt you, and getting the other guys out. He simply would not give in to the hitters. In one memorable fifty-minute ninth inning against the California Angels in the playoffs, Stanhouse kept allowing dinky hits, seeing-eye ground balls, a flare that hit the chalk line, a couple of walks. "There was nothing to get excited about, I felt I was in complete control of the situation."

Stanhouse finally retired Brian Downing for the last out in a 9–8 marathon, and walked into the dugout. "Earl must have smoked a carton. I came in, he was wringing wet, I never saw him so worked up. And he just looked at me, gritting his teeth, 'Why did you do this to me?' I said, 'You think I was doing it on purpose? It was hot out there.' "

Stanhouse says that the Earl of Baltimore spoke to him three times in 1978 and twice in 1979. He just kept giving him the ball. "For two years I must have warmed up 800 times. Anything went wrong, 'Get Stan up.' I think he did it to punish me." For those two years The Unusual One led the league in ERA [earned-run average] with more than twenty saves. One year he didn't give up a home run, and went to the World Series and the All-Star Game. He did it all, and he did it his way, meaning that often during the team meeting, he'd be reading a newspaper.

He got the nickname "Stan the Man Unusual" from Mike Flanagan. "During my tenure in Baltimore, the first two years I was single," explained Stanhouse, "and I managed to get there on time, but sometimes I looked a little strange." It must have looked strange to see him hanging upside down in the bullpen, but that's what he would do when he was having a little back trouble. A camera just happened to be panning the bullpen, creating the impression that this was business as usual for him—or unusual, as the case may be.

Stanhouse insists that you have to have characters on a ball club. The group he really wishes he could have played with was the '71 Orioles group, with Boog Powell, Pat Dobson, and many others. "If everything was strictly business, and you live together every day more than you live with your wife for nine months, you're gonna have tension, and you're not gonna perform."

Stanhouse met his share of great characters in his career, had Billy Martin, Lasorda, Weaver, and Dick Williams as managers, but one thing that stood out were the words of wisdom from the great enigma, former batting champion Alex Johnson. "We used to have a kid by the name of Joe LoVitto in Texas here when I was twenty-one years old. The conversations between Joe, our catcher Rich Billings, and Alex Johnson were something I'll never forget. The Mike Tyson of baseball. Johnson told Billings, 'You know, you hits because you has to. I hits because I want to.' That cracked me up. I lockered next to him. He said, 'Stanley, I'm going to hit one right here, right here, and right here.' And he brought the bat in to me after the game, didn't say a word, held it out, and there they were, three spots, sweet as ever. He hit when he wanted to.''

Stanhouse had known Tiger pitcher Mark Fidrych since he came up. "We met each other in a bar and had a great conversation between me and him and his glass. It was off the wall. I was worried about him." He caught up with Fidrych again when he was down in Rochester on rehab with Ross Grimsley in 1982 and Fidrych was then pitching for Pawtucket in Triple A and they wanted to see if the Bird "had any brain cells left." They found an obituary for a man and got his number and left a message for Bird—"Dear Mark, really had a good time last night. Don't forget the tickets. Jack Smith." "We're sitting outside the clubhouse, he's scratching his head, going 'Well . . . shit,' he goes over to the phone and calls and asks for Jack Smith. 'No, you can't talk to him, he's dead.' Bird says, 'What do you mean he's dead? I'm supposed to leave him some tickets for today's game!' Then he slowly turns and sees Grimsley and I walk by the door and you could hear him yelling, 'You son of a . . . !' "

Relief pitchers have the edge when it comes to thinking and doing the unusual because they have all that time out in the bullpen to think of strange things to do. When Jim Kern was in the bullpen in Cleveland, the relievers used to kill moths and put them in spiderwebs, then watched the spider go after the moth and eat it. "We figured if we got a spider big enough," said Kern, "he could answer the phone and warm up five people at the same time."

You remember Jim Kern, don't you? He was the fireballing right-hander for the Indians and Rangers who referred to games in the minor leagues when he didn't hit anybody as "no-hitters." He told the writers once that he was working on a new pitch. "It's called a strike," he deadpanned. Kern always held that "playing baseball is much easier if everyone thinks you're an off-the-wall babbling idiot.

"I got in trouble at the New York Writers banquet when I got the Rolaids Award in 1979. I got up and said, 'I want to thank everybody that made this possible. Brad Corbett, for trading for me, Gabe Paul for trading me away, and our starting pitchers who could never get into the ninth inning.' That was it, then I just spun on my heel and booked it. Don't give 'em a chance to jump on you."

Kern was known during his playing days as "The Amazing Emu," the emu being a tall, skinny Australian bird. "I got that name from Pat Dobson and Fritz Peterson. I was walking through the clubhouse in 1976. I was six foot six at the time and probably weighed about 180 pounds, and I would squawk occasionally— *Ruawwk!* They were doing a crossword puzzle and the clue was 'The world's biggest non-flying bird' and I walked by squawking, and it's been 'Emu' ever since."

Pat Dobson, former Tiger, Oriole, Indian, and Yankee, and now the pitching coach for the Padres, has given a lot of players nicknames. In the Detroit bullpen, he called John Hiller "Ratso" and Fred Lasher "The Giant Hamster." It was Dobson who gave Dick Tidrow the name "Mr. Dirt." Dobson and Kern became close friends during their four years in Cleveland, and Kern explained a baseball life-style of semi-lunacy by admitting that he patterned his own sense of humor after Dobson's.

"I spent many a night with Snake," Kern recalls. "The first night I came into the big leagues in '74, I came up in September, and we went to Milwaukee, so Booger and Dobber took me out drinking that night to a place called Oliver's. Dobber loved this place because everybody in there had either an overbite or an underbite. He called it 'The Bite.'

"They wanted me to see the show at this place. They had a huge fish tank. And when everybody got drunker than hell at this bar at about one or two in the morning, they'd start feeding the two-pound piranhas. There were goldfish on one side of the tank, and when they'd put the fish food on top of the water, when a goldfish came up to grab it, the piranha would get him, and you'd see nothing but scales flying, and that was the entertainment for the night. I remember about three in the morning Booger having me slung over his shoulder walking back to the hotel."

Dobson recalled his initiation of Kern into the big leagues. "Kernie's a great guy," he said. "I used to have to embarrass him. He was a cheap bastard when he started out because he'd just sit around and never buy a round. He pulled it a couple of times. He'd wait until it was his turn to buy and then the sumbitch would leave. I broke him of that habit by telling the waitress as soon as we got into the bar, 'The first one's on him.' When he first came up he probably wasn't making any money, but hell, none of us were."

"There were nights," Kern recalled, "where I sat in the room and listened to Boog Powell and Dobber tell stories and one time in Anaheim I laughed so hard that the next morning I woke up and my cheeks hurt, my cheeks just ached. The Booger and the Dobber were very tight. Dobson called Powell 'Count Schmagma' because he smoked so many cigarettes. Booger tells a story about batting in the World Series and Booger took a nasty hack at a slow curve and it wasn't even in the same area code, and Dobber yells from the dugout 'Hey, Booger, after that swing you better check your pants for a steelhead!' and Booger said he was laugh-

ing so hard it took him thirty seconds of kneeling down and looking at the ground before he could get back in the batter's box.

"I hung around with the Dobber in Cleveland," said Kern. "We
were best friends for about four or five years, and a bigger piece
of work you've never seen. Snake had one of the best one-liners
you've ever heard in your life. We were on an airplane and we
were sitting there playing backgammon at about three in the
morning, inebriated, and the stew comes by. I'm by the window
and the middle seat is open, and Dobber is on the aisle. And the
stew came over and stuck her head in his lap, and said, 'My, you
smell good, what do you have on?' And Dobber, just that quick,
without a second's hesitation, said, 'A hard-on, but I didn't know
you could smell it.'

"Bill Melton fell out of the seat in front of us into the aisle
laughing. He didn't hesitate for a tenth of a second. As she was
leaving, she was just going, 'Uh, uh, uh . . .' I asked Dobber,
'How'd you come up with that so quick?' He said, 'I heard that
line ten years ago and I've just been waitin' for a place to use it.'
You didn't trade one-liners with Dobber because you were going
to lose. I hung around with these guys, and that became my
hobby, playing with waitresses or stews. I called it 'fucking with
the public.' "

Dobson had lain in the grass like a snake for ten years waiting
to use that line, and so I asked if that was how he got his nickname
of "Snake." No, he said, he'd been called that since high school
for throwing so many curve balls. He throws pretty good curves
to anyone asking him a stupid question as well. One time after
practice a *USA Today* interviewer was videotaping Dobson and
finished by asking him one of their trademark priceless queries,
in this instance, "If you could be any animal, what would you
like to be?" Dobson said, "A whale." Why? "Because then I'd
have a seven-foot tongue and a hole in the top of my head to
breathe through."

"So he started laughing and the guy holding the camera was
laughing," said Dobson. "I've seen the part on ESPN where we're

laughing, but they've never put the line on TV anywhere, so I'm sure to wind up in one of those X-rated shorts that they put in a video."

Dobson feels that the good-time players are often misunderstood. "With the way the public views professional players of any sport, it seems like automatically if you do some crazy things or want to have a good time, they feel you're not really concentrating on your job, but I honestly believe that a lot of times humor and screwing around is a way to vent frustration and forget about the games and not worry about it.

"The game is played between the lines. And as long as you don't screw around when you're on the field . . . I always felt that being a relief pitcher you always had to have a kind of 'I don't give a shit' attitude. I played with Sparky Lyle and had Rollie Fingers as a pitcher, and those guys didn't care about *anything*."

These types of players always seem to gravitate toward each other, and basically remain close for as long as they're teammates. "You never make lasting friends, unfortunately," said Kern, "because you have no control over your life. You walk into the clubhouse and they say 'You've been traded,' and all you can say is 'Oh, who to?' You have a lot of loose friends and no real tight friends. Boog Powell and Dobber were probably two of the best friends I ever had in my life and I talk to them maybe twice a year. I bet Dobber and I have played 100,000 games of backgammon in our three or four years, just sitting there playing backgammon and tellin' lies. It's not an extended family, it's just the family for the day, it's definitely the here and now and not a long-term thing."

Kern moved from Cleveland over to the Texas Rangers, and there he played with Richie Zisk, Rusty Staub, Oscar Gamble, Mickey Rivers, and many more. "We could have fielded the all-time good-time team," he said. Numerous curiosities on that team made an impression on Kern, such as the way Ferguson Jenkins would shag flies. "His thing in the outfield was to never catch a fly ball. If a fly ball was hit right to him he would step to the side and then pick it up. If it hit the ground in front of him, he would catch it. But he had a superstition that he would never catch the ball in the air."

On the Rangers, Kern was joined in the bullpen by Sparky Lyle, and together they formed one of the classic character lefty-righty tandems in relief history. The Rangers' bullpen of the early '80s became known as "The Cuckoo's Nest," a too-friendly place where a rookie reliever grabbing his glove and starting for the mound ran the risk of dislocating his shoulder, because his mitt would invariably be nailed to the bench.

"We were warming up in the bullpen in '80," Kern recalls, "and I was throwing in Texas Stadium with my back to the hitter and Sparky was standing behind me backing up and Sparky's hands were kind of like feet, so you worried a little bit. The batter hit a drive and I turned around to look and at the same time Dave Roberts threw the ball back to me and hit me right in the mouth, broke my jaw, knocked out three teeth, and opened my lip up about an inch and a half, and I fell off the back of the mound. They said my knees never bent. So I was lying on my back next to Sparky, with a broken jaw, knocked-out teeth, and bleeding like hell, and what does Sparky do? He looks over his shoulder and says, 'Kernie, quit fuckin' around. Corrales is watchin'!' "

Then there was the last day of the '79 season, when Lyle undressed for the fans. "The fans had been egging him on," said Kern, "saying, 'It's the last day of the season, gimme your jersey, gimme your hat.' Sparky got tired of this trash after about a half hour. So after infield practice they're yelling for his hat, so he throws 'em his hat. Somebody yells, 'Can I have your shirt?,' so he throws 'em his shirt, and a good-looking girl yelled, 'Sparky, can I have your pants?,' so he took his pants off and threw 'em up to her. Then he threw off his stirrups and his sanitaries and his T-shirt and walked in wearing a jockstrap. Oh, it was beautiful."

Sparky Lyle was one of baseball's all-time relief pitchers, but he was just as well known in major-league clubhouses for his cake-sitting streak. Lyle obviously wanted to make a "good impression" for his teammates, so every time a cake was delivered to the clubhouse, Sparky would drop his pants and sit right down on it.

It all started one day in Boston on Ken Harrelson's birthday, when Harrelson received a lemon meringue pie and hit Lyle in the face with it. Lyle vowed revenge, and found it the next day when someone sent Harrelson a huge birthday cake with green icing in the shape of Fenway Park. Harrelson just loved the cake. Lyle undressed, got the Hawk's attention, and then plopped down on top of the cake, and a dubious tradition was born.

Late in his career he was a little leery about doing it, worried that somebody was going to load one of the cakes with a needle or a razor blade, but he sat in the custom-made cake that his Ranger teammates got him for his birthday.

"The first year with Texas in 1979 Sparky had a birthday in Boston," recalled Kern, "and Doc Medich and I went out and bought him a cake that we had made that looked like two buns and it had icing stenciled across the top that said 'Sit Here.' When he sat in the cake, we had six Boston cream pies, Zisk and Darwin and Staub and me and Medich had 'em, and we pelted him with the pies. It was the most beautiful mess you've ever seen. He said it was a birthday he'd never forget."

ON YOUR CASE AND IN YOUR FACE

It's not hard to explain how Jim Kern got his angle on the game. He spent four years in A Ball and two years in Double A and a year in Triple A. "By going to the minor leagues for four or five years, you learn what it is to be a turd," he said. "The low minors in the late '60s were like death. I wouldn't want to see what D Ball was like in the '50s. *Bull Durham* was great. People say, 'The minor leagues aren't like that, it portrays a bad picture.' I'll tell you what, the minor leagues in the '70s were *just* like that. You played in damn chicken wire cages."

A long stint in the minor leagues is something like the armed services. It's rough, it's tough, and years of that life-style can put warps in the mind and burrs on the soul. Going through this kind of experience can make you lose your hair or lose your mind—it builds character and characters. That's the road that Jim Kern traveled.

"When you got to the big leagues," said Kern, "you really appreciated it because you rode buses forever and played with the five-dollar-a-day meal money. Now the average life expectancy in the minor leagues is about two years. It's almost the same thing as when a football star comes out of college right into the pros."

Kern's career ended when he blew out his elbow at the age of thirty-four. He was in the last year of his contract and had always been a power pitcher and he wasn't given the chance to be a transition pitcher who learns how to finesse hitters. "I was viewed as a one-trick pony," he says. "As they rightly should, they were looking to the future. At thirty-five, I had three to five years left in me, a twenty-year-old kid has fifteen. So you're just gonna put your eggs in that basket. The only problem with getting old is realizing that you're a commodity. Once a commodity is used up, you're trashed."

Kern says the biggest change in the big leagues compared to when he played is that it used to be hard to come up to the majors because you had to be better than the older players. Teams kept their young kids in the minors to get experience and filled their pitching staffs with veterans. But with the success of organizations like Minnesota, Toronto, and Oakland in developing their young players in the majors, the system has changed. It's an extra bonus for the owners, who don't have to go to arbitration with a young player for three years.

This change has had an effect on the type of people who populate the big leagues. They're younger, and haven't spent as much time in the minor leagues, and the older guys with the kinky senses of humor are out of the game unless they're very productive.

Bob Uecker also commented on the change in today's major-league ballplayer, feeling that they do take themselves more seriously. "Today's players are more secure in their planning. Most of them have already picked out other careers. They have investments. They want to be seen and treated as responsible people. When the players board a plane, you see so many three-piece suits it looks like they have evacuated the offices of E. F. Hutton. You get the impression that management now picks a roster with the idea of getting the best possible team photograph."

Jim Bouton was also struck by the marked change in the type of ballplayer today. "The minor leagues have been replaced gradually by the colleges, so more and more players are coming out of college. And so what happens is that you have a more homogeneous type of player. They all have college experience, you don't get an eighteen-year-old kid out of high school who is only partially formed as a person and is more liable to be a real character, a kid off the farm in Iowa, or a kid off the streets of New York.

"Another factor is the computerized scouting system and the central scouting system. All the players look alike, they're all six feet two and they're all big and strong guys, guys who made it on talent. They're there because they've got all the talent, they've got all the tools. So you get guys that look like they're all from the same planet, they look like clones of each other. You can't call a guy 'Stuffy' or 'Shorty' when he's six-two, one eighty. Also, ballplayers today are corporations as much as they're people. Someone pointed out that you wouldn't call your chief executive officer 'Walt No-Neck Williams.'

"In my day," said Bouton, "guys made it because they were winners at whatever league they were playing in, they were smart and scrappy, guys like Pete Rose and Whitey Ford, these guys would never get signed today. Yogi Berra would never be signed today. Can you imagine Yogi Berra walking across the campus at the University of Arizona? If not, forget it. That's why guys like that aren't in the game anymore. If you look funny, there's a box on the computer scouting card today that says 'strange-looking,' and if that box is checked, forget about it."

Don Stanhouse felt the same way about computerized scouting. "It's the closest thing to the Third Reich that you can get," he said. "We want everyone to be German, six-eight, blond, blue eyes, throw a hundred miles per hour and take orders."

A lot of former players assess the attitudes of today's major leaguers and conclude, as Boog Powell did, that "they just aren't having any fun." Of course, some people think that making a couple of hundred thousand dollars is a lot of fun. But just what do we mean by fun? Take rookie hazing, then and now. In the '60s, when a rookie came up to the big leagues, they'd send him out to the bullpen with catcher Duke Sims. Sims had the enviable talent of being able to regurgitate on command, so when they sent a rookie pitcher out there, Sims would throw up for him all game. Could anything be more fun than that?

Jim Kern was hazed by the best, Gaylord Perry. "I remember the first time I came up, and I had pitched the night before, and I was lying on the training table getting some work about forty-five minutes before the game, and Gaylord Perry just grabbed the side of the table, picked it up, rolled me off onto the floor and said, 'My turn, rook.' And I was laying there like 'Oh, this is the big leagues, okay.' "

Each generation that you go back in baseball, the hazing of first-year big leaguers was more cruel. Of course, some players get hazed worse than others. Phil Rizzuto's career as a prankster mark began when he was a rookie. Phil was deathly afraid of mice and insects, flying things, and sometimes even his own shadow. But most of the jokes pulled on him related to his fear of anything that crawled, as they would put worms, soggy chaws of tobacco, or even dead mice inside of his glove when he put it down. Until one of the Yankees removed the thing in his glove, he wouldn't put it on again.

After a while, players could walk up to him with their hands closed and chase him all over the ballpark. In the clubhouse, the players would hang a dead bird or rubber spider from a string above his locker. They would lower the string until it came down to eye level and scared him out of his wits.

One time Specs Shea and Charlie Keller locked Rizzuto in a trunk and then they couldn't find the key. Rizzuto was hollering to let him out, but a clubhouse meeting was about to start, and so they told him to keep quiet. When clubhouse man Pete Sheehy got the key and let the Scooter out, he was on the way to asphyxiation.

Rizzuto was what was known as a professional victim. On one airplane flight, they convinced Phil that the engines were on fire. Yet, when they played these endless and sometimes cruel tricks on him, he liked it, because to him it meant the guys still liked him. Measuring by that yardstick, he was a much-beloved player, but in my opinion they may have gone too far when they painted his genitals purple before his honeymoon.

When George Steinbrenner bought the Yankees in 1973, he aimed to put an end to such shenanigans. A practical joker slipped half a hot dog into the glove of light-hitting shortstop Gene "Stick" Michael, who had Rizzuto's fear of squirmy things. Steinbrenner went into a rage, had a security guard confiscate the wiener, and then demanded that manager Ralph Houk find the culprit who perpetrated the foul, un-Yankee-like deed. The statute of limitations has run out on this prank, and to this day the caper remains unsolved.

Tim McCarver was treated like a typical rook when he came up to the big leagues; that is, he was treated like a dumbbell. "In 1959, my first year, I was with the Rochester Red Wings, and Dick Rand, an old catcher, sent me into the clubhouse to get the key to the batter's box. I innocently asked him where it was, and he told me it was 'next to the glove stretcher.' "

McCarver survived these small humiliations to become a veteran player who would in turn put the screws to young rookies, perpetuating the never-ending cycle of pranksters and victims. When Keith Hernandez first joined the Cardinals, somebody put analgesic balm in his jock strap, and as soon as he went out on the field for practice and started sweating, the burning was incredible. "It was a dirty trick," Hernandez told me, and it, too, remains an unsolved crime, though Tim McCarver remains to this day on Keith's list of likely suspects.

Today in the big leagues there are some oft-repeated pranks intended for rookies. One trick has been played so frequently that most rookies hear about it and become immune. This classic prank is known as the Three-Man Lift. It works when someone says he can lift three people at once. When the mark says he doesn't believe it, they tell him to lie on the floor and two others interlock his arms and legs with theirs. When the rookie can't move his arms or legs, everyone in the clubhouse comes over and pours shaving cream, soda, dirt, ketchup, mustard, and various other effluvia over the guy.

Casey Candaele told me about his experience with the ultimate shock tactic directed at unsuspecting rookies, the Mongoose. There's no real mongoose involved, just a big bushy tail. "Most of the guys know the Three-Man Lift but the one in Cincinnati where the guy has the mongoose, that's a good one, that's scary. You're lookin' in there, the thing jumps at you, yeah, they got me, they got most every rookie. You come in and one of the veterans will come up to the clubhouse guy and say 'Hey, you still got that mongoose you had around here?' 'Yeah, he got three mice last night, pretty big ones, too.' The rookies are listening, wide-eyed. 'You let it out at night?' 'Yeah, it does a really good job. He's pretty mean, though, you just have to stay away from him, he crawls back into his box when we come in the door.' 'Let's get him, let's look at him.'

"So in the back room he walks and brings out this cage, with a little tail sticking out. 'Oh, he must be asleep,' and he starts hitting it and the tail starts shaking, and the vet says, 'Don't get him mad, he might do something.' 'Oh, I want to wake him up so you guys can see him.' Then he hits this little thing and this tail comes flyin' at you. Oh, man, it's amazing. I just ran, started screaming. It is funny, it's a good joke, it's probably the best one that's set up for puttin' sheer terror in you. That's part of the game."

Things aren't as bad for rookies as they once were, when they were caddies for the regulars, fetching beers, and waiting their turn to board the bus, with all the privileges of a fraternity pledge. When Glenn Wilson joined the Tigers, Lance Parrish, the former bodyguard for Tina Turner, did go up to him and say, "Give me your meal money, or I'll beat you up." But in general, today's game is more genteel than it used to be, and this can be seen in some of the little things that the game is losing.

Many players lament the virtual end of the era of bench jockeying. Baseball was a rough game in its early days seventy years ago, when the crowds in the northern cities were made up of burly German and Irish immigrants, mobsters, and racetrack touts who used language that even a moral degenerate could not invent. The ballparks of the early 1900s were not places for women and children, when mobs would sweep out of the stands to beat up umpires, and the umpires fought back. The vociferous fans took their lead from the rough-hewn players of the day, for whom giving the well-sharpened dirty needle was a vital part of the game.

Profanity of some form, it seems, will always be a part of baseball. Many players don't use profanity in their daily life except when they get near a locker room, and then everything is instantly bleep this or bleep that. It's the rare player who can go through a career without at least one nearly unprintable blowup. Tim McCarver made a point in his book *Oh, Baby, I Love It!* of what a great moment in sports it was when Stan Musial pointed his finger at the ever-obnoxious Durocher in the opposing dugout, and the ultra-decent, normally staid Stan the Man responded to a whole day's worth of Durocher's off-color screaming. Musial pointed at Durocher and said, "You're up and strutting now, but just you wait. We'll get you, you *prick*!"

It is interesting to consider just where the players in the old days drew the line. In the World Series against the New York Giants, Babe Ruth was being jockeyed unmercifully by a small infielder named Johnny Rawlings. After the game, Ruth barged into the Giants' clubhouse, looking to throttle the little guy. "You little bastard," Ruth said, "if you ever call me that again I'll choke you to death."

Rawlings egged Ruth on for not being able to take it. When the rest of the Giants started getting into it, Ruth let on as to what had made him so mad. "He called me a nigger," Ruth explained. "Don't get me wrong, fellows," he said seriously. "I don't mind being called a prick or a cocksucker or things like that. I expect that. But lay off the personal stuff." And he turned and walked out. Apparently the impervious Sultan of Swat was not so thick-skinned when it came to insinuations about same.

Ty Cobb was sensitive about the same kind of slur, which, before the color line was broken, was hurled at white players. Cobb's vicious style of play frequently inspired some down-and-dirty bench jockeying, but most opposing players learned to go easy on a guy who sharpened his spikes daily and would gladly fight you under the stands. But one day in New York in 1912, there was a loud fan who called Cobb a "half-nigger," which pressed Cobb's crazy button.

Cobb, who has been described by some as a high-functioning psychotic, jumped into the stands and beat the guy senseless. The fan, Claude Luecker, had lost one hand and part of another. Cobb hit Luecker in the face, spiked him, and started kicking him. Someone in the crowd shouted that his victim had no hands. Cobb answered, "I don't care if he has no feet!"

But that was Ty Cobb, the genius in spikes, the Georgia Peach. When Cobb came up to the majors there were few Southerners playing pro ball in the northern cities, and Cobb, an unreconstructed bigot, rubbed many the wrong way. In one of several such incidents, he slapped a black groundskeeper and one of the Tigers, Charley Schmidt, intervened.

Schmidt was a burly ex–coal miner from Arkansas who had once fought a short exhibition match against Jack Johnson. One of the strongest men in baseball, Schmidt sometimes amused himself by pounding nails into wood with his fist. Schmidt called

Cobb a coward and the two grappled and were separated. Shortly thereafter an article appeared in a newspaper quoting Cobb as saying he could whip Schmidt or anybody else on the Detroit club. So Cobb and Schmidt fought and Schmidt broke Cobb's nose and shut both his eyes. Undaunted, two weeks later Cobb jumped Schmidt again, with the same results.

In his later years, Cobb was a bitter man. Despite having made a fortune by investing in Coca-Cola stock before 1920, when he got fan mail requesting his autograph he would burn the letters and use the stamps enclosed for his own correspondence.

Cobb didn't make many friends in the game of baseball. He was elected to the Hall of Fame ahead of Babe Ruth, but only three people from the baseball establishment attended his funeral in 1961. As one wag sadly put it, "The only difference now is that he's a bad guy who's dead."

When Pete Rose was approaching the all-time hit mark, he was asked by a reporter if he thought Cobb might be looking down on him from above when he broke the record. Rose, a long-time student of Cobb's life, paused. "From what I know of Cobb," he said, "he might not be up there."

Whatever Cobb's shortcomings, as a player it was well known that it was a bad idea to get him mad. Many in the game today subscribe to the theory of letting sleeping dogs lie instead of picking out a player and impugning his masculinity, family ancestry, or how he looks in his uniform. Stirring up the opposition in this manner is now pretty much frowned upon.

OVERINDULGENCES

One of the most piercing barbs recently directed at a ballplayer came from late-night talk-show host David Letterman. One night Letterman was watching the Atlanta Super Station when Terry Forster came into the game, and he couldn't believe that a profes-

sional athlete could have such a physique. So he used his mono-
logue to point out that Forster was not just large, but "the fattest
man in professional sports . . . a fat tub of goo . . . a silo."

Forster, to say the least, wasn't pleased. At first he wanted to
sue, then relented. Eventually he appeared on Letterman's show
and took it all in good humor, saying he didn't know how he got
so heavy. "It just snacked up on me," he joked. "A waist is a
terrible thing to mind."

Letterman later said that "fat tub of goo" was an unfortunate
choice of words. In his defense, he was just trying to express his
incredulity that a man shaped like a Florence Flask could be
wearing a major-league uniform. (Letterman hasn't completely
reformed, however. When he interviewed David Cone in 1988,
he asked him this "thought question": Would he rather have a
career-threatening injury or have Whitey Herzog's haircut? Cone
replied, after deliberating, that he would "probably rather blow
out my knee.")

Singling out Terry Forster was not really fair. There have been
some pretty hefty ballplayers in the big leagues. At the end of
his career, Charley Spikes, the Bogalusa Bomber, could have been
rolled down a bowling alley. But with Charley's attention span,
it might be exaggerating to say that Spikes ate his way out of the
big leagues. One time he was standing reverently, head bowed,
for the National Anthem and was still meditating on "The Star-
Spangled Banner" when a first-pitch fly ball fell right at his feet
without his even moving.

Among the prodigious eaters in big league history, Ruth stands
as tall as he does among the batting leaders. The Babe was legendary for his hot-dog-and-beer binges. If there was a long inning
in the field, players swore that they could hear his stomach rum-
bling. As Yankee pitcher Waite Hoyt said about the Bambino, "If
you cut that big slob in half, most of the concessions at Yankee
Stadium would come pouring out."

For some players, making weight is a neverending struggle,
as it was for Boog Powell. Jim Kern relates this nugget on the

Booger's valiant attempt to get into shape in spring training with Cleveland in 1976. "Frank Robinson threatened to fine Booger $1,000 a pound for every pound he was above 265. Booger had not eaten for five days or had a drink of beer. The first morning he weighed in at 264. He works out and then weighs in at 262. We went out that night and I came in about eight o'clock, and he'd already been through two twenty-two-ounce steaks and just piles of beans and bread. He was celebrating, and he ate another steak with me and drank beer and such till midnight. The next day he stepped on that scale and it just went *tilt*. He weighed 274 and Frank wanted to hang him. He had put on twelve pounds of fluid in one day!"

In 1968, Hank Bauer once gave a 260-pound Powell one week to get to 240, or he would fine him ten dollars a pound for every pound he was over. At the end of one week, a starved and dehydrated ballplayer weighed in at 240½ pounds. "You know," said Powell, "that son of a bitch fined me five bucks. What a chickenshit thing to do."

Anyone who saw Frank Howard eat has to say he was the biggest eater they ever saw. Let's say Howard was playing cards with three other guys. Frank would call down and order four hamburgers, four fries, and four milkshakes, then look at the other three guys and say 'You guys want anything?' But Howard is one of those who has won the battle of the bulge. At a recent old-timers' game he looked exceedingly trim.

A classic food legend in the big leagues is the story about the Tigers' pinch hitter Gates Brown, who was called on to hit as he was in the clubhouse having two hot dogs. As soon as he took a bite out of his first dog, he heard his manager right behind him. The Gator stuffed the dogs in his jersey, and hit a double. When he slid head first into second, he squashed the dogs and stood up with mustard and ketchup and smashed hot dogs all over him. "The fielders took one look at me, turned their backs, and damn near busted a gut laughing at me. My teammates in the dugout went crazy. That had to be my most embarrassing moment in baseball." Brown's hit helped win the game but Brown was still "pissed off because I messed up my hot dogs and I couldn't eat them."

Even more embarrassing was what happened to the Astros' Charley Kerfeld during the 1987 season when he was caught snacking on ribs in the bullpen in front of the metropolitan New York television audience. First he was caught on TV passing money through a gate in the bullpen to one of the grounds crew in exchange for a couple of plates of ribs. The telecast would cut back every once in a while to Charley's head bobbing up and down as he munched. He was fined an undisclosed amount by the Astros' management.

Kerfeld was always a big man. Although one of his baseball cards listed his weight as 175, he hadn't tipped the scales at that number since the seventh grade. When the Padres got their first look at Kerfeld, Graig Nettles stared, and then stared some more before he had to ask, "How did they get Denny McLain out of jail?"

Charley had a fine season in 1986, going 11–2. Who could forget his first national television interview with Marv Albert, wearing his Jetsons T-shirt underneath his uniform, and Dave Smith hitting him with a pie in the face? He pitched in the National League Championship Series against the Mets and claimed not to be intimidated by all the hoopla. "I've only been intimidated by one thing in my life," he said, "and it's not human. It's a scale."

A journeyman pitcher who is currently prospering in the big leagues with the White Sox is Dave "Snacks" LaPoint, who freely admits that he'll never look good in a uniform. His weight has ballooned up and down throughout his career. He said he knew he lost twenty-five pounds one time when he went into the stretch position and didn't have anything to rest his hands on. While pitching in the 1982 World Series, he was covering first base and dropped a toss from Keith Hernandez, who quipped after the game, "If it was a cheeseburger, he wouldn't have dropped it."

In the late innings, there are always players on the field who are thinking about the postgame spread in the clubhouse. Teammates say stopper Lee Smith works especially fast when he's in an extra-inning game, because he knows there are other players already in the clubhouse attacking the spread before he's got a chance. Dick Allen once turned down an appearance on "Kiner's Korner" because he was also worried that there would be no food left in the locker room.

Dodger Manager Tommy Lasorda wears a T-shirt that reads "Please Don't Feed the Manager." "When we win, I'm so happy, I eat a lot," he explained. "When we lose, I'm so depressed, I eat a lot. And when we're rained out, I'm so disappointed, I eat a lot."

The same vicious cycle has held the game's greatest drinkers in thrall. That was the case with the hard-throwing reliever Ryne Duren, who starred for the Yankees in the '50s. Ryne was subject to abnormal highs and lows, soaring and drinking when he won, depressed and drinking when he lost or wasn't pitching well. Either way, he drank heavily, and he was not alone. "I think on every team I played on," he said, "75 to 80 percent of the guys drank, and about 50 percent drank heavier than most."

Duren joined the Yankees in 1958 and for two years he was one of the most respected and feared pitchers in the game. He wore very thick glasses, having had rheumatic fever when he was twenty. The illness affected the muscular balance of his eyes, so he wore thick corrective lenses. He used his Coke-bottle glasses as an intimidating weapon. He would feel for the pitching rubber with his toe as if he couldn't see it, and invariably his first warmup pitch would sail over the catcher's head and hit high on the screen. As Stengel said, "I would not advise hitting against Duren because if he ever hit you in the head you might be in the past tense."

Pitcher Ned Garver confirmed that there was a contract out on Duren in the American League. "The word went around," he said, "that if you were pitching and Ryne Duren happens to come up to bat, your job was to hit him. Very few people ever got a shot at him, because as a closer he seldom pitched long enough to come to bat. Duren didn't see all that great, I think he'd be pretty easy to hit."

Duren's biggest problems, however, were not with American League pitchers, but with alcohol. When Duren drank he became overly friendly, often with someone's wife or girl friend, and would get into fights. When his career went down the tubes he found himself alone one New Year's night in 1965 in San Antonio, Texas. Duren drank a dozen beers and drove his car onto the railroad tracks, waiting for a train. The police beat the train and he was hospitalized, then got into a rehabilitation program. Today, a survivor, he works as a counselor to alcoholics.

How fearful would batters have been if they were aware that Duren, by his own admission, "never knew what it was like to pitch a sober inning." It probably doesn't make hitters very comfortable to learn that some of the hardest throwers in the history of the game had serious problems with alcohol. Sam McDowell was one of those pitchers who threw it all away by losing a battle with the bottle during his career. Recently, at the age of forty-five, he took the mound in a minor league park and threw a fastball that still registered in the nineties on the radar gun.

Steve Dalkowski, an Orioles prospect in the early '60s, may have had the greatest fastball of all time, but he had no idea where it was going. How else do you walk twenty guys in one game? For all his promise, Dalkowski never became a major-league pitcher, and his drinking problem accelerated. Ron Shelton, writer and director of the film *Bull Durham,* played for five years in the minors, and recalled seeing Dalkowski, after his career was over, looking for handouts in the locker rooms of the International League.

Of course, when we talk about a drinking problem in baseball, it's naturally assumed that we are talking about beer and distilled spirits, but for Denny McLain, his swig of choice was always Pepsi. Early in his career with the Tigers, pitcher Phil "The Vul-

ture" Regan discovered that McLain carried a suitcase of Pepsi
with him on the road. While some players worked off their tension
by smoking or having a beer, chewing tobacco or chewing on the
heel of their hands, as Jackie Brandt used to do, for McLain it
was Pepsi. He would drink two Pepsis before a game, five after
a game, one before dinner, three watching TV . . . you get the
idea. It was not uncommon for him to drink more than twenty
Pepsis in a single day.

It could be embarrassing, as when Denny would call room
service and order seven Pepsis, and the waiter would come up
with seven glasses and find only one person in the room. "I'll tell
you," he said, "they don't have to be cold for me to enjoy 'em. I
even like 'em warm." He had one rule about Pepsi, that he never
drank one at mealtime, when he had a glass of milk. But he
would go to bed with a Pepsi on the nightstand, drink three-
quarters of it, then finish it off before he got out of bed the next
morning.

McLain's soft-drink addiction turned out to be the least of his
problems. Soon after his playing career ended, his weight ballooned to 300 pounds, he consorted with criminal elements, and
in 1985 was convicted on charges of racketeering, conspiracy,
extortion, and cocaine possession. He was freed after serving two
and a half years of a twenty-three-year sentence because of ju-
dicial error in his trial. At the retrial in the fall of 1988, he was
still found guilty on two of the counts, and at this writing awaits
sentencing.

One of the frequently recounted *alcohol*-drinking stories in
baseball is that of Gene Conley's famous bender when he was
pitching for the Red Sox. The year was 1961. Conley was a 6–
8 pitcher whose personality, it is said, resembled his favorite
pitch, the screwball. At that time he was playing pro basketball
for the Boston Celtics in the off season, and the strain of playing
two sports was wearing him down. He was getting bombed, both
on and off the mound.

When the team bus was caught in a traffic jam in Manhattan,

Conley convinced infielder Pumpsie Green, the first black to play for the Red Sox, to leave the bus with him. They started boozing, and for a couple of days they attempted to hit every bar in New York. At one point, Conley tried to convince Green that they should visit the Wailing Wall in Israel. "If we can visit the Holy Land and find God," Conley told Green, "you'll hit .350 and I'll win twenty games." Green thought better of it and rejoined the team, paying a fine. But Conley continued on to the airport with no luggage or passport. "I was so tanked up I didn't have to fly," he said. When reporters asked him why he wanted to go to Israel, Conley replied, "I guess I must have thought they had weaker hitters over there."

Conley was traded the next year. The story is usually recounted as a funny, bird-brained quest to find God. It has become, oddly enough, the signature story of his professional sports career, passed on to future generations, which Conley realizes now that ten-year-olds ask him about it. When I spoke with Conley, he offered another angle on the episode. After playing two sports, "doubling up," as he put it, for ten years in the majors and seven years in pro basketball, Conley had only $11,000 in the bank, and his chronically sore arm was giving him a lot of trouble. A little desperate with a family to support, he had nothing to lose by freaking out in a major way, and so he went with the flow.

"Looking back, it was serious," he said, "but people made a joke out of it." Conley was not especially close with Pumpsie Green—he just happened to have been the one who got off the bus with him. Conley was missing for three days, unaware that Red Sox owner Tom Yawkey was very concerned about his welfare. When he came back to the team, he was so embarrassed about the incident that he considered throwing in the towel, but Yawkey would have none of it. "No," said Yawkey, "you're startin' in three days against Baltimore, big boy."

The warm-hearted owner told Conley that there were indeed times when he'd like to be bending the old elbow with him for a few days. "We'd probably have ourselves a good time," said

Yawkey, "but it's just one of those things you can't do when you're in the limelight." Conley took a good bit of razzing from opposing teams the rest of the year, and received more of the same when he resumed playing professional basketball in the fall. "Auerbach thought I was crackin' up, Red thought I'd flipped," said Conley, "but I played three or four more years of NBA basketball after that."

Billy Martin's most recent bar fight was, no real surprise here, drinking-related. A few months into the '88 season, Martin went into a topless nightclub called Lace near Arlington Stadium. Martin had been ejected from the ball game that night, and according to witnesses, returned to the club's hotel and began drinking heavily with Mickey Mantle and Yankee first-base coach Mike Ferraro. "Drinking heavily" in this case means ordering the next round as the current round is being served. Mantle went home to nearby Dallas, but Martin and Ferraro left the hotel and continued drinking at Lace.

Martin later said he went into the men's room and a couple guys jumped him. But other reports held that Martin got involved in name calling with two men, threw a punch at one, and then was forcibly thrown out an exit, hitting his head on a concrete wall and leaving a smear of blood. Martin might have sneaked back undetected into the team's hotel, but as luck would have it, a fire drill had everyone in the lobby and parking lot in their pajamas to witness the return of the bloodied Yankee manager.

He had a nasty gash near his ear and stopped counting after forty stitches. When he reappeared at the ballpark he resembled Frankenstein. Some of the players were somewhat distracted by the injury, finding it disheartening to look down the bench and see blood leaking out of their manager's ear.

It wasn't the first time that Martin had gotten into a fight off the field. He had slapped Rangers secretary Burt Hawkins, punched journalist Roy Hagar for refusing to give back his interview notes, and then there was the famous bout with a Minnesota marshmallow salesman.

In a TV commercial for Miller Lite beer, Martin joked "I didn't punch that dogie." But as these incidents continue into his sixties, they grow increasingly pathetic. There was something about his latest reign as Yankee manager that smacked of Captain Queeg in *The Caine Mutiny,* something nihilistic about the way he self-destructed.

In two months of managing the Yankees, Martin aged like the picture of Dorian Gray: his teeth clenched behind pinched lips, his jaw jutting defiantly, his eyes darting suspiciously as if looking for those trying to do him in. His latest firing was one of the few times that his baseball sense was seriously questioned. Martin had a vendetta against the New York sportswriters who criticized his moves, and seemed determined to show them that he knew more about the game, that he could not only win but do it his way—pitching forty-two-year-old Tommy John on short rest, making Cecilio Guante his stopper rather than Dave Righetti, inserting pitcher Rick Rhoden as his designated hitter, batting league-leading hitter Dave Winfield sixth (this reportedly on strict orders from Steinbrenner)—moves that literally had no rhyme or reason.

When he kicked dirt on an umpire, an edict was laid down by Richie Phillips of the umpires' union that Martin's "tap-room behavior" would not be allowed, and prohibited him from leaving his dugout during the game. Phillips only succeeded in making Martin into a victim of discrimination. No one really has to victimize Martin when he's so good at doing it himself.

He was fired a month after the Lace incident when the Yankees relinquished first place by losing three close games in Detroit, one in ten innings. After the second loss, Martin overturned the food table in the clubhouse, sensing the end was near. At this writing, George Steinbrenner has hired and fired Billy five times. Martin was fired for the first time after becoming so enraged by the owner's constant calls and suggestions that he ripped the clubhouse phone out of the wall. Over the years, they have nearly come to blows, and yet their stormy relationship remains intact.

It would require about four nineteenth-century Russian novelists to explore the *folie à deux* in which these two men have been embroiled.

Adding up the number of drunken brawls Martin has been involved in would require a calculator. Early in his career as a player, he learned that a shot in the mouth was worth two to left field, as he became a great draw for the Yankees. One of his infamous on-field bouts got started when pitcher Jim Brewer brushed him back in 1960. Martin took the next pitch and then let the bat slip out of his hands toward the pitcher's mound. Brewer picked up the bat and held it out to give to Martin, who was approaching the mound. Martin said he was just coming out to get his bat, but when he got to the mound, he threw a right that shattered Brewer's cheekbone just below the eyeball socket, requiring two months of hospitalization and two operations.

Once he began managing, Martin learned to occasionally take out his anger on inanimate objects as well, most notably the urinal he decimated with a bat one night in Cleveland. And then there was the time he went ten rounds with his office over a contract dispute when he was managing at Oakland. And there was the time he threw a watch given to him by Texas Rangers owner Brad Corbett against a wall. Breaking that timepiece got him fired the next week, but a lot of different things have gotten him fired.

He started his career as a manager at Minnesota, where he won by a knockout over one of his pitchers, Dave Boswell, outside a bar. As Martin described it, he hit Boswell with "about five or six punches in the stomach, and a couple to the head, and when Boswell came off the wall, I hit him again. He was out before he hit the ground."

Another time Martin had to be restrained from going at it with Thurman Munson at Chicago's O'Hare Airport, not to mention the time he fought in the dugout with his star, Reggie Jackson, after pulling him from the field in mid-inning during a nationally televised game. One of his all-time doozies was the protracted brawl with unhappy free-agent acquisition Ed Whitson in 1985. It began in the hotel bar in Baltimore, with later rounds held in the parking lot and hotel corridors. Whitson was so juiced that he just kept coming, even after Martin had broken his own arm. As Whitson charged him once again, eyes blazing with hatred, Martin got off the line that could serve as his epitaph: "What's wrong with you, can't you hold your liquor?"

Martin grew up fighting. It was his primary form of recreation in West Berkeley, California. His father left home before he was born, and his family was poor. Martin shared a bedroom with his grandmother until he was fifteen. His mother never forgave her husband, swearing that after he died she'd go to his funeral to piss on his grave. His mother, the indomitable Jenny Downey, gave Billy his lifelong credo: Never take any shit. She wore a button that said, "I'm Italian. If you don't like it, kiss my ass."

That's the attitude that got Martin to the majors as a young, fiery-tempered second baseman with the Yankees. The chinks in his armor were the actual and psychosomatic ailments that he suffered, including hypertension, anxiety, insomnia, and acute melancholia. But Casey Stengel liked him and played him regularly. He called Martin "my big-nosed kid," which may have goaded Martin to get a nose job as soon as he could afford it.

Stengel liked having a "spark plug" like Martin around, and stuck by him despite the numerous fights he was involved in. Martin remained a central figure on championship Yankee teams, setting records in the World Series and always outhitting his Dodger counterpart Jackie Robinson in the big ones.

Martin frequently partied with his pals Ford and Mantle, drinking and horsing around. They'd have a few drinks and have dinner and then have a few more drinks, and after a couple of years, said Mantle, "we skipped the dinner part." One time Martin and Mantle were playing chicken with golf carts and Mantle fell out and hurt his knee. Yankee management wasn't thrilled by these shenanigans, but the final straw was the catastrophe at the Copacabana, on the occasion of Martin's twenty-ninth birthday.

Martin went to the Copa with teammates Ford, Mantle, Berra, and Bauer, to watch Sammy Davis, Jr., when a bowling team at the next table yelled racial slurs at Davis and made it impossible for others to enjoy the show. A headline-making fight broke out and Martin was made the scapegoat, although in this case the altercation truly wasn't his fault. But, as the Yankee company line went, it was Martin who was leading the blue-chip stars, Ford and Mantle, astray.

Stengel tried to stand up for him, but Martin was traded to Kansas City. To Martin, whose whole sense of self-worth was tied to being a Yankee, it was a bitter betrayal and he didn't speak to Stengel for years. But he later patched things up with Casey, and the plaque on Martin's stadium monument reads, across the top, "Casey's Boy."

The drinking that has always gone on in the game has been whitewashed time and again, while many of the teams remain financially tied in to lucrative sponsorships with beer companies and distributors. The film made of the life of the great pitcher and all-time lush Grover Cleveland Alexander, with Ronald Reagan in the lead role, was typical of how dishonestly the great drinkers in the game have been depicted. In the film, Alexander drinks because of recurring dizzy spells. Wasn't it probably the other way around?

Until very recently, the ballplayers themselves have generally made light of the serious drinking that often goes with a career in baseball. Bob Uecker said it was easy to play when you're sober, "but it's a challenge to go out there when you're all likkered up." In the contemporary game, baseball's cocaine scandals have put all variety of substance abuse, including alcohol, in a new light. Few in the game are going to brag or joke today about their drinking exploits, not when the Pirates are suing Dave Parker to get back the millions they paid him when he was allegedly starting his day with cognac and cocaine.

Still, there have always been players who are candid about their drinking habits. As journeyman pitcher Dickie Noles said,

"I could put away three cases of beer a night. Now I can't handle that much. I have fifteen beers now and I'm totally gone." Drinking has always persisted in the game because the bottom line is doing the job, and many players have been able to perform at a very high level while drinking at night as hard as they played in the day. After the Cleveland Indians finished sixth in 1988, their DH, Ron Kittle, spoke out. "We led the league in card games and crossword puzzles. What happened to the guys who drank all night, threw up the next day, and went out and won ballgames?" As Bill Freehan told me, "If I knew that by going to church and never drinking, it was going to make me a Hall of Famer, I'd be doing it." But a heavy drinker like Paul Waner made it to the Hall with hundreds of hits to spare. He explained how he was able to hit the ball so well after drinking sprees—"I see three baseballs, but I only swing at the middle one."

Stocky outfielder Hack Wilson hit fifty-six home runs in 1930, still the National League record, despite being a high-ball hitter off the field as well as on. "I never played drunk," he said. "Hung over, yes, but never drunk." He was out of baseball by 1935, and when he died in 1948, a $350 grant from the National League was all that saved him from a pauper's unmarked grave.

There is even a story, a rare tale indeed, about someone who tried to discourage drinking in baseball. After a workout, Giant slugger Johnny Mize came into the clubhouse, flung off his sweatshirt, and hit the showers. Trainer Frank Bowman soaked his shirt with alcohol and then asked Mize how he was when he came out, toweling off. Mize said he was fine. Frank said, "You better stay away from the hard stuff, John. That's what really takes it out of a player." Mize swore that he hadn't broken curfew, he only had two beers the night before. "Don't kid me, John," Bowman said, dropping a lit match on John's sweatshirt, which immediately burst into flame. "Look, John, you're sweating out pure alcohol." Mize, completely taken in, pleaded with Bowman. "Please, Doc," he said, "don't say anything about this to anyone."

There were not enough Frank Bowmans, finally, to discourage

mounting substance abuse by well-paid young professionals with a lot of time on their hands. In an attempt to curtail drug use, urine testing was instituted, but even this was not enough to save several promising careers. When A's pitcher Mike Norris, a twenty-game winner, flunked his drug test in 1985, which showed traces of alcohol and codeine, he explained the test results by saying that he had shrimp cooked in wine for lunch.

Dwight Gooden had a drug-testing clause in his contract, but apparently he wasn't deterred by it. Paul Blair saw Gooden's situation as a sign of the times. "He was mature as far as baseball was concerned, but out here in the street he was just like another kid. It's unfortunate for Gooden he had his 24–4 year his second year in the big leagues, because if you do it early, they expect you to do it every day. You don't duplicate those kinds of years. Pressure is a motherfucker and some people can't handle it, some people don't respond to it.

"How to stop the drugs? You know why you never hit an umpire? Because if you hit an umpire, you're gone. If you have that rule, why don't we have the same rule for drugs? If the superstar goes out and kills somebody, he's gone. If you tell every major-league ballplayer, 'If you get caught with drugs, you're out,' I guarantee you they won't get caught. They won't be out there in the public eye. They'll never do it, and that's all it would take.

"Now that would do one of two things. You'll either stop it, or you'll never see it, and you still serve the same purpose, because in actuality, when you go out on that field, if you're straight and hit .320, you're fine, and if you're high and hit .320, you're fine.

"When I came to the game, all the guys I played with drank like fish, but come game time, they were ready to play. They'd stay up all night, drink all day, go to the ballpark, and they'd play, it was all they cared about. Nowadays I think too many people want to know what these guys do on and off the field. But when I go out on the ball field, and nobody knows what I'm doin', and I'm doin' my job, who cares? If I can get high in my room and I got five or six fucking women in my room that night and ain't bothering nobody but me and my girls, it shouldn't bother nobody.

"If I don't do my job, I get released. If I go out and abuse my body and abuse my time, all I'm doing is shortening my career. But that's my choice. Everybody's got choices to make, and you make yours and I make mine. Everybody's human, and everybody's gonna make mistakes. So you pay for yours, and I pay for mine."

Blair acknowledges that ballplayers are role models today, even if they shouldn't be. "Basically that's why society has gone down the way it has, because both parents have to go to work, and TV has taken the part of the parent so the child likes the game of baseball and relates to a ballplayer. When I was growing up, the mothers were home. Nowadays one normal man can't raise a family, so now the kids are raising themselves. Whether a ballplayer wants that responsibility or not, he has it. Whether you walk that straight line or not, the public should think you are."

FAMOUS RAKES: THE OTHER NATIONAL PASTIME

There is another way for a player to overindulge himself out of the game of baseball besides overeating and overdrinking and using controlled substances, and that is to screw your way out of the game. Some players may have hindered their careers because of their sexual profligacy, but this is not an easy thing to do. If it was, many observers hold that it would have been very difficult to fill out major-league rosters year after year.

The night life has always been a part of baseball. As Casey Stengel saw it, "It ain't sex that's troublesome. It's staying up all night looking for it. You gotta learn that if you don't get it by midnight, chances are you ain't gonna get it, and if you do, it ain't worth it."

Ron LeFlore, former prisoner and All-Star, maintained that baseball is an instinctual game, and the more relaxed you were, the better you could perform. He said it was in fact preferable to engage in sex before a ball game for these reasons. "How close before game time?" asked an intrepid reporter. "As close as possible," Ron replied.

One of baseball's more celebrated rakes was Bo Belinsky, bon vivant, pool hustler, dog fancier, ladies' man, and occasional left-handed pitcher. Whatever he did, it seems that Belinsky always got his share of ink. As Bo himself put it, "I have never considered myself a great talent. I think I have gotten more publicity for doing less than any player who ever lived."

Baseball for Belinsky was initially just a ticket out of Trenton, New Jersey. He was a wild kid who ran with an older crowd in the streets. "I didn't have a lot of choices growing up in Trenton. You rob gas stations or you book numbers. But I think if I never played baseball, I would have been a professional pool player."

His first minor-league contract was in Class D for $185 per month, but the money didn't matter. Baseball got him to the nightclubs and beaches he loved. He kicked around the minors losing as many games as he won, and didn't really distinguish himself until he played winter ball in Venezuela in 1961. He found out *bobo* was the Spanish word for dunce, clown, or fool, and he clowned it up and became the biggest draw in Venezuelan winter league history. He also drew some attention by having a great year, and the timing was right.

Expansion in 1962 brought Belinsky to the big leagues, as the Angels drafted him out of the Baltimore farm system. As soon as he hit Los Angeles, he had two questions. First, "Where are the pool halls?"; and second, "Where are the movie stars?" The Los Angeles writers couldn't wait to turn him into hot copy, this slight, sinewy, thin-lipped twenty-five-year-old with a crooked smile who grew up with a cue stick in his hand. Bo surely didn't disappoint. He had never pitched a game in the major leagues, and yet, upon his arrival in spring training, he held a poolside press conference. He was nine days late for spring training, explaining his tardiness by saying he was delayed by a pool tournament. He then announced that he was holding out for more than the $6,000 he was offered.

Eventually he accepted the Angels' contract, and the rest is oddball history. Belinsky won his first six games of the year. On May 5 of the '62 season, the Cinco de Mayo celebrated by the Hispanic community in Baja California with fireworks and heavy partying, Belinsky took baseball by storm when he pitched a no-hitter against Baltimore. (The last rookie to pitch a no-hitter was twenty-seven years previous, when another *bobo,* Alva "Bobo" Holloman, pitched one. Holloman never won another game in the major leagues.)

Belinsky did have good stuff. He had a live fastball, a good changeup, and despite a so-so curve, at times had a devastating screwball. He strode from the mound cockily that night after the final out of the no-hitter, and said to manager Bill Rigney, "How do you like that for a rookie?" He was especially pleased that it happened against Baltimore, the team that had let him go. "It couldn't have happened to a nicer team," he said.

A headline in the L.A. papers screamed FANTASY! NO-HITTER FOR BOBO! Belinsky was an instant media sensation. "It didn't impress me that much," he said. "But it seemed to impress everybody else, so I went along. It was luck, that's all." Columnist Walter Winchell helped with introductions to Hollywood starlets such as Tina Louise, Ann-Margret, Connie Stevens, and Mamie Van Doren, with whom he became involved in a highly publicized romance.

His major-league salary was still paltry, and the most he had ever made in his six years of kicking around the minor leagues was $550 a month, but he moved into the fast lane nonetheless. When Bo Belinsky partied, it was Dom Pérignon he liked to have flowing. He'd drink it with his "female associates" and friends, and pour so much of the bubbly in his suites that you could wring a quart out of the rug. "Nothing makes you feel so loose as good champagne running down your arm."

He wore the monogram "BB" on his sportsclothes, undershorts, and his gold watch, fittingly suggesting both Brigitte Bardot and the base on balls, as well as his own name. He wore custom-made suits, and there was talk of a movie role in the winter, as Belinsky was wooed by all the major talent agencies. Meanwhile, he was still scuffling, trading the ball he threw for the no-hitter for ten payments on his Cadillac, or about $1,000.

Belinsky led a double life as a Casanova with a curveball. "I like his body," a minor league scout once said of Belinsky, and many young women apparently came to agree. Belinsky would hang out on the beaches of Malibu and soak his face with a mixture of iodine and baby oil to effect the George Hamilton look. Even his mother seemed to wink approval: "He's out in Malibu Beach now," she told a reporter. "That ain't Coney Island, you know."

Bo's off-field antics had helped the Angels double their attendance. "Let's face it," he said without false modesty, "I put that team on the map." Bo was a victim of the sophomore jinx, and when his record fell to 2–9, he was farmed out to Hawaii, where he spent the summer ogling bikinis on Waikiki. "When the Angels called me back," he confessed, "I was depressed."

Bo was never anything but honest about his priorities, admitting that he never felt deeply about anything except having a good time—"I never was truly dedicated to the game." Bo adopted a simple philosophy of life: "Happiness is a first-class pad, good wheels, an understanding manager, and a little action."

After he slugged a sixty-four-year-old sportswriter, he was traded to the Phillies, where his love affair with the fans came to an end. "Fans there would boo a funeral," Bo said. In Philadelphia, he finally proposed to Mamie Van Doren, who sent his ring back. "He bought it on credit and needs the money," she sniped. Bo did not look back, however, continuing his escapades unabashed. He married former Playmate of the Year Jo Collins, and adopted a stray part–cocker spaniel named Alfie.

"I have no regrets, not one," Bo said. "I was there. I saw it and did it all. I heard music nobody else ever heard." Prodigious though Belinsky's feats may have been in the boudoir, they were naturally exaggerated. "If I did everything they said I did," he admitted, "I'd be in a jar at the Harvard Medical School." Belinsky has mended his ways. At present, he works as a drug rehabilitation counselor and lives in Hawaii.

Joe Pepitone is remembered for many things. Being a ladies' man was one of them. He said, looking back, that one of his downfalls, among the several, was the discovery shortly after he joined the Yankees that "I could hit .996 on the street. It cost me thirty points on my batting average." When he became a matinee idol with the Yankees, he started a new Yankee tradition by having the clubhouse attendants bring girls to him under the stands.

Pepitone got his start in Brooklyn with a semi-pro team from Brooklyn fittingly called Nathan's Hot Dogs. The Yankees realized that he might not fit into the Yankee mold when he showed up for his first big-league spring training in his Thunderbird trailing a fourteen-and-a-half-foot motorboat.

Pepitone spent so much time combing his hair that when he went north he found in his cubicle a mirror at the back, and mirrors on both sides, with a telephone and a shoeshine box. This was the first of many attempts by his teammates, who called him "Pepinose," to puncture his vanity. His mirrormania actually derived from his concern that he was losing his hair in the front. But Pepitone conquered his baldness with creative styling, and has the distinction of becoming the first player to bring a hair dryer into the locker room.

The real sexual controversy in baseball today revolves around the Wade Boggs case. Margo Adams, who lived with Boggs for four years on the road, asked him for $100,000 or so to make up for wages she lost while in his company, claiming that Boggs had promised to do so. When he didn't agree to fork over the cash, Adams went public with their affair. She upped the ante on Phil Donahue's program when she said that Boggs had a way of dealing with players who might testify against him in court. She said

Boggs had something going called the "Delta Force," which involved getting teammates in compromising situations and then breaking into their rooms and taking pictures. Adams also claimed to have the negatives. Her story came on the heels of an unexplained fight between Boggs and a few Red Sox players, including Dwight Evans.

It has already been well documented that Boggs has been overindulging himself for years when it comes to eating chicken. He eats chicken every day, using a twelve-day rotating recipe schedule. Will the notoriety over his private life lead to the publication of Margo Adams's secret chicken recipes? When all is said and done, this case may wind up having the effect on ballplayers that the movie *Fatal Attraction* has apparently had on the general public.

⚾

HOT DOGS

To some players, overdoing it comes naturally, no matter what they're involved in. Some overdo it on the field. They are the game's showmen, players with style to spare, who do everything with a little flourish. This gesturing, strutting, and clowning has long been a staple of the game, and yet some players are not given their due because of their propensity to play to the crowd.

Ned Garver, a pitcher with the St. Louis Browns and Detroit Tigers in the '40s and '50s, feels that the great Satchel Paige was definitely slighted because of his showmanship, along with the fact that he was well past his prime before the color line was broken. "People don't appreciate his pitching prowess. I don't think that people comprehend that Satchel Paige was probably the greatest pitcher that ever took a breath."

Garver was a teammate of Satchel's on the Browns, and got to know him better on barnstorming tours. "I got to know Satchel primarily after he joined us in 1951, and then we became very,

very good friends. He told me he went on barnstorming tours with a guarantee against a percentage of the gate. He didn't go for a share. He told me any time you want to get together a barnstorming tour, he gave me his unlisted number and said, 'You call me, I'll go, I'll get the team, and I'll go for just a share.'

"But I did a few things for him along the line. I did what I thought was right, and in the process he appreciated it. On the tours they wouldn't even feed his people, including his wife in one of the towns in Indiana. We were one time in Corpus Christi, before we got to San Antonio, going north to spring training in 1952. Satchel got off the train and he couldn't ride with us in our bus. We drove off with him standing there.

"We went to the ballpark that night and Satchel didn't show up. We got on the train that night and went to Houston, and he's there. The manager fined him $500. Satchel said, 'You're gonna fine me $500 without asking me why I wasn't there?' The manager said, 'That's not my job. Your job is to be there. The next time it happens you'll be fined twice that.'

"Then we went to San Antonio. I played two years in San Antonio, and my wife and I rented from some friends there. She drove from California to San Antonio, Texas, so my car was there. So I've got a car, and Satchel can't stay where we are. And he can't ride in any cabs or buses, because they won't pick him up, and he's supposed to be there and ready to go. So every morning I would go and pick him up, go to the ballpark, then I'd take him to where he stayed.

"After about the fourth day, he introduced me to his friends there. And I went in, the door was only about so wide, low ceilings, I wouldn't have gone in there with an armed guard. I'm not telling you it was a bad place, but it was a place that looked bad. But if he wanted to introduce me to his friends, that was fine, I went in. And I felt so embarrassed that he had to stay there. But I managed to pick him up and get him to the games on time so the manager had no excuse to fire him. That's how we became friends.

"When we would be in our compartment traveling, we'd talk, and he didn't think it was right that Jackie Robinson was the first, he thought he should have been the first. I'm not going to criticize [Branch] Rickey's decision because he picked the guy who was most qualified to handle all the flack, and he was probably right, but as far as having earned the right to be the first black to break through . . .

"He pitched every night. We're playing the Major League All-Stars against the Satchel Paige All-Stars, and we'd have maybe five or six pitchers. I'd have a day off, but Paige pitched every night, go five or six innings, a major portion of every game. It was unbelievable. I'm not talking about batting practice, I'm talking about every day, show 'em that you're Satchel Paige.

"I saw him in York, Pennsylvania, one time against the Browns farm club, a '51 exhibition game. He walked the bases loaded and acted as if he was truly unable to throw a strike. He just looked like he was in all kinds of trouble. And that crowd, of course they had a packed house, thought their hometown team of York was giving Satchel Paige a fit. And they were making all kinds of noise. So they got the bases loaded, nobody out. He threw ten pitches, one guy fouled one off, every one was a strike, he struck all three of them out. What a show. He could clown, he could showboat, but if the situation called for pitching and not letting the guy even bunt, he could do that, too.

"He brought out a scrapbook one time and showed it to me. It showed where he started in Mobile, and an article had a date on it. Let's say he was sixteen years old at the time. Even if you say he was sixteen, and maybe he was eighteen, he figured to be closer to fifty than forty-two years old when he finally pitched in the major leagues. He pitched winter and summer for twenty-seven years in a row, just pitch, pitch, pitch. He'd get done with the barnstorming and play on the islands, play winter ball. How many innings that man pitched, how many games he was in, there's no way of ever knowing, but it was phenomenal. He was the greatest and most incredible player that I saw in all my time playing baseball. Satchel Paige was a fun person, fun to be around. He was a marvel."

Baseball has a derogatory name for players who treat the diamond as their private stage: hot dogs. It's one thing to swish the bat in a big swing, connect, and drive the ball into the far reaches of the upper deck. But it's quite another to drop your bat, stand there, and admire your handiwork. Reggie Jackson always loved to watch his homers disappear into the ether, gazing at them as if seeing a good friend for the last time. Maybe it was because he loved hitting so much, having made the famous declaration that he would "rather hit than have sex."

Whether it was his love of hitting or his enormous ego that inspired him (Reggie made popular the sportspeak habit of referring to oneself in the third person), Reggie made the home run into theater, with himself as the star. Whenever he knew a ball was gone, he would go into his well-honed act. His home run trot was a piece of work, just oozing arrogance. After all, he did have a lot of practice, with 563 career dingers.

When some players hit a home run, teammates will start a stopwatch to see if he can break the record for the slowest home run trot. Dave Parker has been clocked at a tortoise-like pace of thirty-one seconds, easily qualifying him as a hot dog of jumbo status. As Willie Stargell said, when told that Parker had called Stargell his idol, "That's pretty good, considering that Dave's previous idol was himself."

Parker's histrionics, however, are relatively tame compared to what Willie Montanez did on one of his homers. People talk about a player being such a big hot dog that there isn't enough mustard to cover him. That's Montanez, who could have done a how-to video on hot-doggism.

During his fourteen-year career, most of it spent in the National League, Montanez was known as one of the most stylish players in the game, an artist, really, who recalled the graceful flamboyance of American League first baseman Vic Power. Montanez had a way of catching the ball as if he were at a picnic competing in an egg toss. On a good day, he could throw a paper wrapper off the field and bring the crowd to its feet. Everything he did looked choreographed by Balanchine. One day Montanez, if it's possible, outdid even himself. He hit a ball that nicked the scoreboard, a 450-foot shot. He stood stock still at home plate until the ball came down, then turned to the bat boy and yelled, "*Mira! I don't need this anymore!*" and flipped his bat thirty feet in the air, then set out on a super-slow home run trot.

You don't have to be a home run hitter trotting slowly around the bases to be a hot dog. All you have to do is come up to bat. If taking a lot of time makes you a hot dog, then Mike Hargrove was one hell of a frank. Hargrove became known as "The Human Rain Delay" for his fidgety routine of adjusting his batting glove, his helmet, his shirt, whatever. It always took him ten minutes to hit, insuring him as much time on television as the starting pitchers. As Mickey Hatcher said after a trade was finalized, "I'm glad we got Pat Putnam instead of Mike Hargrove. We'll play three- instead of four-hour games."

Then there is the Bat-Twirling Competition. Montanez was also an outrageous bat twirler. Whether he was swinging or taking a pitch, he would spin that baby like a baton. Mickey Rivers also used to put on a show, his expertise being in shifting the bat from one hand to the other after he swung. But the all-time twirling bat master was probably Tito Fuentes. Tito was one of those guys who wore rings on every finger. At the plate he would have that bat snaking around his body after every pitch, behind his head, between his legs, places a bat was never meant to be. Fuentes didn't like it when pitchers irked by his mannerisms brushed him back. "They shouldn't throw at me," he said. "I've got five or six kids."

It's a little more risky to be a hot dog in the field while making a play. The one-handed catch used to be a hot dog move before the advent of the big gloves that make the relaxed one-handed play almost a sure thing. Willie Mays's basket catch was an astonishing way of catching a fly ball in the '50s, and he has not really been imitated very much. Rickey Henderson took it to the next level when he came up with his "snatch" catch, where he plucks the ball out of the air with a head-high sideswipe. Incredibly, Henderson first used the snatch when he was catching the last out of A's teammate Mike Norris's no-hitter. On the spur of the moment, Rickey felt that something extra-special was called for, although I'm sure Norris thought catching the ball would have been enough.

Most pitchers get used to the game's biggest hot dogs, but once in a while they get pretty ticked off, as happened in the case of Jeffrey Leonard in the '87 National League Championship Series. For years, the Giants' Leonard was generally considered a surly player, perhaps because his typical expression is a baleful stare atop a moon-faced frown—that's how he got the name "Penitentiary Face." (Leonard didn't like the name, so it became "Correctional Institute Face.")

On the back of his warmup jacket, his more commonly used nickname is spelled out in orange letters—"Hac-Man." Leonard got that moniker when he was in Triple A ball at Phoenix in the Giants' chain, and he was so ticked off in general that he made it known that he would swing at the first pitch for the entire season, which he did. He is also the only current major-league player wearing the number double-zero, which he claimed in one of his efforts to start anew from his numerous injuries.

But in the 1987 NLCS between the Giants and the Cardinals, Jeffrey Leonard emerged as a most theatrical performer. His homers (one in each of the first four games, a playoff record), his slow, distinctive home run trots, and his inflammatory remarks about the Cardinals made him the focus of the fans, the players, and the national media. With all this storm swirling around him, Leonard not only came through, but when the dust cleared he was named the Series' Most Valuable Player. (Before the season, his agent Tom Reich negotiated a clause in Leonard's contract calling for a $50,000 bonus if he received the award.)

Leonard homered in the first game of the playoffs, dropping

his left arm in a pantomime he calls "one flap down." The Cards won the first game, but after the contest Leonard continued swinging, beginning the war of words by saying pitcher Greg Mathews had a fastball that was "mediocre at best." His remarks earned him a full afternoon's worth of raspberries in St. Louis for Game Two, in which he also homered. He turned up the flame in San Francisco in Game Three when he homered again and this time, in front of the home fans, took fifty seconds to circle the bases with, naturally, "one flap down."

I asked Leonard when he first came up with this most original way of running out a homer. "The first time was a few years ago. I pinch-hit a homer off Scott Sanderson in Candlestick. Boom, I hit the ball, I'm running to first base, and when I touched the coach's hand, my arm just fell. Everybody was asking, 'Is your arm all right?' I just did it. That was the very first time. I didn't do it again until next spring training, when I hit a home run, and instead of putting it all the way down, I kept it in here. Somebody asked me, 'What is that?' and I said, 'That's my Sling Trot,' like if you have a sling on.

"In the playoffs I told one writer what one particular home run trot meant, and he said I put a flap down on pitches that were nothin', but that was bullshit, that was one particular pitch, but I hit a lot of home runs off good pitches. That was just emotion, having fun, creativity, whatever you want to call it."

Of course, if you're going to play with the idea of agitating or irritating or frustrating the other team, you have to expect some retaliation. The Cards took exception to his extracurricular showmanship after the Game Three home run trot in front of the Giant fans. The next time he came up, Bob Forsch drilled him on the right forearm. Leonard wasn't fazed by it. "My trots dictated that something like that might happen," he said.

Leonard remained a marked man during the Series. In Game Four he tried to score from first base on a double by Will Clark, and tried to run over Tony Pena. Pena slammed a vicious tag on Leonard's neck, which he admitted was a lot more painful than the pitch that hit him. "But that's baseball," Leonard said.

If he could get the Cards mad and thinking about him, then he thought he was messing up their concentration. He didn't fear that he was firing up the Cards. "You're telling me they weren't ready to play hard in the playoffs if I didn't get them mad? They're professional ballplayers. They're thinking about what they have to do. They can't worry about me."

But they obviously were worrying about him. Leonard likes to play the inner game of distracting his opponents, but he most definitely doesn't appreciate it when someone tries to break his own concentration. Catchers, for instance, love to make small talk with hitters, chattering away about their families and the weather, anything under the sun to distract them. Leonard considers Tony Pena to be the absolute worst in this regard. When Leonard feels a catcher is too loquacious, he brings a special bat to the plate. He calls it his "nasty bat." In place of his signature on the barrel of the bat are carved the words "Fuck you." He takes his stance and slowly waves the barrel in front of the catcher's face. And if the umpire happens to notice it, that's okay, too.

When he returned to St. Louis for Game Six, there were an awful lot of fans carrying signs denigrating the Hac-Man. Leonard wasn't really disturbed. "How many ballplayers can come up and have 40,000 signs directed at you? Man, I was flattered. Absolutely fucking flattered. Full house, sixty grand, and I got 40,000 people with signs about me. It was like *whoa*, know what I mean? I had fun.

"I look back on it now differently than when I went through it. I look on it now as an achievement. I could have easily gone the other way mentally, getting uptight or whatever. I look back at it as a part of my life, which was a challenge, and I dealt with it."

When I spoke with Leonard only days after the suspension of Pedro Guerrero for throwing a bat at Mets pitcher David Cone, we discussed the never-ending controversy of the knockdown pitch. "I look for it," he said. "I look for the ball in. If I hit a home run and put a flap down or use a real slow trot, then when you hit, you look for it. That's the way the old guys played it, and that's the way I think. I'm not as old as the guys who came through the Drysdale era, but that's the way I was taught."

When Leonard was first called up from A Ball he hit a triple off pitcher Wayne Simpson, and the next time up, the first two balls were right near his head. Two years later, he was in Triple A and Simpson was his roommate. Leonard asked him about it, and Simpson explained that that's going to happen when a rookie hits a triple. "I learned it right there," said Leonard.

"It really doesn't tick me off, a close pitch just to let you know they don't want you leaning over there to hit the ball out of the park. But nowadays it seems that pitchers, after a home run, want to get ahead of the next batter, and the pitch comes right down the cock, strike one. That's now. But it happened so much that it became a part of the game. Now you get back to back to back home runs, if you're the fourth hitter, you've got a problem.

"I think hitters still expect to get knocked down. But a decent knockdown pitch starts below the shoulder. Throw at me anywhere from here down, and I don't care. If I get hit, I say, 'Oh, I'm hit,' but if you start throwing that knockdown pitch up near the head, that's a different ball game, so that's the only part of it I don't like."

As far as what hitters can do to retaliate, Leonard fondly recalled the tutelage of Willie Horton when they played together in Mazatlán. "We called him the Malldigger. He was a funny character. He said, 'What am I gonna do, fight on the field? I don't need to fight anymore on the field.' He said, 'You meet the fuckin' team at the hotel, you know where he's stayin' at. If I get hit tonight, I don't worry about it, I get in my car, drive to their hotel, and when the bus pulls up to the hotel, and they're comin' down off the bus, that's a *shock* for that sonofabitch to find you standing there in street clothes!'"

Booing Jeffrey Leonard is not the way to get to him, not after growing up going to Connie Mack Stadium and hearing the treatment given to Dick Allen. "I love Dick Allen. I saw him booed tremendously. If a guy can remember things like that, and go out here and get booed, you can just go 'Ha ha ha, you ain't doin' shit to me.' They can't even touch me if I go through Chicago."

Leonard sloughs off being labeled as a hot dog. What he does, he says, was nothing ten years ago. "My teammates, they love it, they look for me to do something crazy. I hit a home run in winter ball one year and slid home headfirst. I did the bump with the great Lyman Bostock at home plate. I'm not even thinking about being a hot dog, everywhere I go they say, 'Put a flap down,' they call me 'Hac-Man,' nobody calls me Jeffrey, nobody calls me Leonard. Hot dog? It doesn't bother me at all, man. Anybody who knows how baseball is played, who knows baseball, they know I'm not a hot dog. I play the game basically the way it's supposed to be played. What about Michael Jordan and all these guys doing all this crazy-ass shit when you know damn well they could just lay it off the glass? It's the same thing, and they say I'm a hot dog.

"What do you think people come out here to see? They come out to see stolen bases, hits, a high-scoring game. There's not a lot of people that come out there to see a pitching duel. There's nothing wrong with that. I love to see that, too—as long as I'm not in the motherfucker, I love to see it. But people come out to see the great catches, the great throws, the great slides, the collisions, the near-collisions, they want to see all that. And everywhere I go, people say when I hit a home run they want to see the flap down."

They won't be seeing the flap down in National League cities, at least for a while. A week after I spoke to Leonard, he was traded to the Milwaukee Brewers for infielder Ernest Riles. It was the last year of Hac's contract, and the Giants were very high on outfielder Mike Aldrete, and so Hac was shipped. He left a legacy in San Francisco as not only a mighty mouth, but a competitor, a student of the game, and a leader. He also left a can of spray deodorant with "OO" marked on it to teammate Kevin Mitchell, who explained that he was "in his will."

When informed of the trade, Leonard said, "At least I hope to play every day in Milwaukee, wherever that's at." He took it all in stride, almost philosophically. "It's not good or bad, it's just . . . Milwaukee."

Leonard's first ten days in Brewtown were business as usual. He got five standing ovations in his first ten games in Milwaukee. When he hit his first home run, he put a flap down on his trot like everyone wanted, and his next time up, the pitcher hit him with a fastball.

Joaquin Andujar has been called a hot dog, among other things, but at the Astros training camp in Kissimmee, he told me that he doesn't care what people call him. "Pete Rose used to play hard, and they call him hot dog, and he's a Hall of Famer. All the good players they call hot dogs because they play hard."

Andujar was happy to be back in the National League after being banished to Oakland for a year. He had put himself in a bad position vis-à-vis the Cardinals with his outburst in the seventh game of the '85 World Series. The Cardinals had lost Game Six on a blown call by umpire Don Denkinger. The seventh game, which the Cards felt they shouldn't have even been playing, was a blowout in favor of the Royals, and Herzog called on Andujar, the human time bomb, to relieve. Denkinger was behind the plate, and when Joaquin disagreed with a couple of calls, his yelling got him thrown out of the game. Then there was a hysterical scene where Andujar had to be carried off the field screaming curse words.

Unfortunately, there was more. On this night of ignominy, Joaquin was interviewed in the clubhouse as to what he said to Denkinger. Joaquin calmly repeated his invective, expletive for expletive, unaware that his remarks were being piped into Royals Stadium over the public-address system, where the fans, who had hung around to celebrate their championship, stood and cheered every blue word.

Andujar had broken the cardinal rule of flakedom: Never freak out during the seventh game of the World Series. He had a pretty good idea that he would be traded. "Wherever they trade me," he declared, "I win twenty games. If they send me to the moon, I win twenty there." It didn't quite work out that way. He was on the disabled list five times with the A's, and couldn't get accustomed to the American League. "It's a softball league," he joked. "Ozzie Smith would hit twenty home runs here."

Andujar comes from a small community in the Dominican Republic, San Pedro de Macoris, which has spawned so many major leaguers, including George Bell. When Bell was beaned, he said he was still thinking about it after he recovered and asked Andujar to throw to him to help him work it out. Joaquin hit him high on the cheekbone with the first pitch. Bell didn't even hit the dirt. "Thanks," he reportedly said. "I needed that." There was no need to continue the batting practice. Bell's problem was solved after taking that fastball in the face. After all, what are friends for?

When I asked him about the George Bell incident, he didn't want to talk about it; he was willing to talk, but only about Joaquin Andujar. I could understand Andujar being suspicious of my questions, especially considering the way he is generally treated in the daily papers and in books of this nature—as a volatile, almost extraterrestrial flake.

He is a great believer in luck, always feeling that unseen forces control the game of baseball. When he won after a long slump, he would say things like, "God is back in the National League. Matter of fact, He is staying at my house. I'll have to have a barbecue for Him."

Andujar grew up marveling over the pitching of Juan Marichal, but was playing center field when a scout suggested that he could make the big leagues as a pitcher because of his great arm. It was the former Indians, Twins, and Yankees second baseman Pedro Gonzalez who really taught him the fine points of being a pitcher, and that's what he has always been, instead of just a thrower. Keith Hernandez said Andujar was one of the smartest pitchers he ever faced, a great competitor who was always in control when he was on the mound.

Hernandez used to hang out with Andujar when they were in St. Louis, drawn to him because "he was loose." Tony Pena is a friend of Andujar's, and considers him a very smart man indeed who wants hitters to think he's crazy to gain an advantage.

Whitey Herzog told me he got along fine with Joaquin when he was with St. Louis, because all he wanted to do there was pitch. Herzog always found it tough to take him out of a game. "I would go out there to take him out and he'd say, 'I can get this cocksucker, I got him out before,' and I'd say, 'Yeah, but it was *this inning.'* "

The '88 season began and Andujar immediately went on the Astros' disabled list with a torn rib cage muscle. As soon as he came back he was fined by the National League office—$200 for hitting Andre Dawson of the Cubs, $200 for throwing close to his friend Tony Pena, and $100 for charging Pena after the close pitch. Our talk in spring training turned out to be prophetic. "Everybody knows I'm going to pitch inside," he told me, "so they should be ready. If the other team don't knock nobody down, I don't knock nobody down, but if they knock my teammate down, hell yeah, somebody going to go down. That's the way you Americans teach me to play, and it's too late to change."

After he was fined in May of '88, the Astros sent him down to Florida to work back into shape, and there he made a few of his notorious declarations. He's always made his living pitching inside, he said, and now he was afraid to do so. He claimed that "someone big" was trying to run him out of baseball. "There is some guy, some big guy in United States baseball, he doesn't want me in baseball. He wants me out of the game. I don't want to pitch no more. I am afraid for my life to pitch because if somebody is trying to get me out of baseball and they see that they can't, what would they try then?"

When asked to elaborate on the Joaquin Conspiracy, he said, "There are 300,000 sportswriters, and they are all against me— every one. They must be leading a campaign. They always write bad things about me. The other day, I got my one thousandth strikeout. Did anybody write about it? No. You never see me on the highlight film. I tell you, there's something going on." Andujar then said, perhaps wisely, that he would stop talking to reporters. One would think that after so many years in the big leagues, Andujar would be prepared for anything. After all, it was his never-wavering philosophy that baseball could be summed up in one word: "youneverknow."

EXCEPTIONS TO THE RULE

Some players really defy categorization, being so difficult to understand that they will forever remain enigmas. They're rebels, usually without a specific cause other than protecting their own individuality. Perhaps that was at the root of why Richie Allen kept insisting that people call him "Dick." Many players still call him "Richie" and he wears a bracelet with "Richie" on it. Back home in Wampum, Pennsylvania, they called him "Sleepy" because of his drooping eyes. When he came up to the Phillies, they already had Richie Ashburn, so he was listed as Richard Allen and it was shortened to Richie. Allen just didn't want an organization giving him a new name.

One thing baseball people are in agreement about is that Dick Allen had, without question, the talent of a Mays or an Aaron. He was recognized as a true superstar, the first player to make over $200,000, but by the time he was through, he had the dubious distinction of being the most misunderstood, criticized, and unhappy superstar ever to play the game. He was not only the first black man, but the first ballplayer of any color to assert his independence in the manner of a Muhammad Ali in boxing, a Kareem Abdul-Jabbar in basketball, or a Jim Brown in football.

His tape-measure homers were legendary. There were guys who hit the ball as hard as Allen, like McCovey, Stargell, or Frank Howard, but all of them were either four to six inches taller or fifty pounds heavier. Players and coaches still remember drives that he hit almost twenty years ago.

They still talk about the line-drive homer hit on such a low trajectory that the shortstop leaped for it. Larry Hisle recalled another epic blast, "a line drive into the second deck in Busch Stadium that surely would have killed somebody if it had hit them. It bounced off the glass of the Stadium Club and everyone stopped eating in there for a long time." Ralph Houk recalled a Dick Allen homer hit in Tiger Stadium that broke the old wood facing of the second deck, releasing a flock of pigeons.

When Dick Allen was in high school, he led his team to eighty-two straight wins. The Phillies signed him for $70,000, at that time the largest bonus ever paid to a black athlete. After a few years in the minors, the Philadelphia organization made a critical mistake with him, sending Allen down to Little Rock, Arkansas, where he would be the first black ballplayer ever to play there.

The year was 1963, and Allen was exposed to the harsh realities of segregation. When he got off the plane, he saw a man carrying a sign, "Let's Not Negro-ize our baseball." The Phillies had promised him that he would only be down there for thirty days, but they left him there the whole season. To Allen, it was a serious betrayal.

When he was brought up to the majors, the Phillies changed his position from second to third base, where his league-leading number of errors opened him to ridicule. Allen was nonetheless spectacular—the Rookie of the Year, hitting .318 with twenty-nine homers. But it was also the season of the Big Choke, where the Phillies, with a six-and-a-half-game lead, lost their last ten games of the season, and blew the pennant on the final day. Allen unfairly took a major share of the blame.

The booing, the rebellious streak in Allen, his increasingly strained relationship with management—all contributed toward making him an outcast. Pat Corrales came up to the big leagues the year after Allen did, and became his only friend on the team. "We were close friends," he said. "He took me to a nightclub one night, we had a night off, we took our wives, and it was dark when we walked in. I started laughing because there were like four people in this nightclub. I said, 'Boy, she's really famous.' He said, 'She will be.' It was Aretha Franklin, in a nightclub in Philly. Two years later she was a star, but in '64, nobody in the northeast knew her yet."

Allen had amazing strength that enabled him to wield a forty-ounce bat. The lower half of his body was that of a wide receiver, the top half was that of a defensive end. Corrales said, "Dick Allen was probably the best athlete I ever saw. He had the greatest physique that I ever saw, and he never touched a weight. This guy looked like Charles Atlas, ooh, he was awesome. His waist was like twenty-eight or thirty and he had the biggest arms I've ever seen on a man."

"I used to pick him up and make sure he'd come to the park," said Corrales. "If I didn't pick him up he would come to the game fifteen minutes before game time. He didn't have any other friends on the team, he was a loner, so when I was traded he was very upset about it. After I left, he got into a lot of trouble. I never asked him about it. But I was the only guy he could talk to, and I left in '65.

"Gene fined him a lot of money. It never fazed him. 'You can take my money, I don't care.' He'd get it at one thousand a whack. But Gene was right, you have to set rules for everybody. He was a friend of mine, we used to have a beer together, but I never tried to figure him out. He loved horses. We'd go riding on his day off, and this was his bag. Everybody thought he was strange, but I didn't think he was strange. Dick was Dick."

"I just wanted to be left alone," Allen said. "I did my thing on the field, but I wanted my privacy. Reporters would never leave me be, and management, they wanted to call every shot, from the way I walked and talked to my clothes or my mustache. Everything had to be Joe College or the corporate image. You ever wonder why baseball loves big, dumb farmboys? Well, big, dumb farmboys don't say very much. I was a grown man, not a kid. I have my own thoughts, and when something happens that I don't think is right, I have to express myself. I guess I have to rebel."

An unfortunate incident in the '65 season made the jeers grow even louder and more hostile. It was a fight he got into with veteran Phillie Frank Thomas. Thomas denies that there was anything smouldering to bring about the fight. "Nothin' was brewin,' " Thomas said. "It might have been brewin' with him to pick on somebody, but I don't know why it was me because we were the best of friends. Richie went to the manager and asked him to put me on first base because he wasn't afraid to throw the ball to me, because I could catch the ball barehanded and save him a lot of errors.

"The actual incident was a spur-of-the-moment thing. The night before I was in to pinch-hit with a man on first, the tying run on third with one out, and I tried to bunt down first to stay out of the double play and bring in the tying run. I eventually struck out. I didn't do the job. In the cage the next night, I'm taking my cuts, and then I'm finishing up and lay down a bunt towards first. Callison and Richie are down at third base, and Richie yells, 'That's twenty-one hours too late!' So I say, 'What are you, gettin' like Muhammad Cassius Clay?' So he says, 'Come on down here and say that.' I say, 'When it's your turn to bat, come down here and I'll be more than happy to tell you.'

"So I told him when he came down, then I walked away. And I said, 'If I hurt your feelings, I'm awful sorry.' I rubbed dirt on my hands, turned around, and I got bopped right on the chin. I did nothing, just walked away from him, and he hit me right in the face. I was spittin' blood like anything. And I don't remember what I did after that. I don't remember swinging the bat. Mauch told me if I'd hit him in the head I would have killed him, but I don't remember any of that. Afterwards I came up to him and said, 'Richie, regardless of what you did to me, what I did to you was wrong,' because I swung the bat at him and hit him in the shoulder. It was just a fit of anger where reflexes just took over at that particular time.

"Mauch put me in in the eighth inning. I hit a homer to tie the ball game up. Richie had probably the best game of his career, he hit two triples and three singles and drove in seven runs after this happened. And after the game was over, Mauch comes in the door and says, 'I want to see you upstairs.' So I go upstairs and sit down, and he says, 'We just put you on irrevocable waivers,' which means if another club claims you, we can't take you back. 'Gene, if it's because of the incident tonight, I think you're being unfair to me.' And his answer to me was, 'You're thirty-five and he's twenty-three.' And that was the end of the conversation. It's cruel, but that's the way life is.

"But it was an unfortunate thing that happened. Being traded was the bad part. In that light, I hold my head high. Because if you're going to punish one, you gotta punish the other. As I walked out of the dugout, I said to Wes Covington, 'I just lost my job.' And he said, 'If they do anything, I'm going to go on radio and television and tell them it wasn't your fault,' and he did do that."

While Thomas made a bid for public sympathy, the Phillies forbade Allen from explaining his side, and after the fight, the booing of Allen intensified. Thomas, a popular player, became a martyr, and Allen became Philadelphia's Public Enemy Number One. He had to start wearing a batting helmet in the field. "Do you know what it's like," asked Allen, "to have iron bolts thrown at you from the stands? Everyone just wanted to eat me up and leave my carcass for the vultures. That's the American way, especially where blacks are concerned. Management buys you, uses you, then throws you away. They don't shoot black players, but it's awfully close. I'm not a militant but people wanted to cut my heart out.

"The minute I stuck my head out of the dugout, people were yelling, 'Nigger' and 'Go back to South Street with the other monkeys,' " recalled Allen. "I expected to be booed, not stoned. The Phillies could have cleared everything up. They wanted to draw crowds, though. So they let me twist in the wind. It was one more betrayal."

In 1967, Allen was pushing a 1949 Ford up a hill with his right hand on the headlight. The headlight broke and severed the nerves and tendons leading to his ring and little fingers. "Things were sticking out like spaghetti," he said. In the emergency room while he was bleeding, a man asked him for his autograph, and another man shook his hand. They tied up the cables in his hand but it didn't work—he couldn't use his fingers.

Allen didn't move a muscle for four days, and then went on a two-and-a-half-month drunk. The Phillies gave him only a provisional contract. If he couldn't move his hand, he'd be sent home. He worked a construction job for no pay to get back the use of his fingers. He had to play first base because he couldn't throw very well anymore. He never did get all of his strength back, but nearly full use of his right hand returned in 1971. Still, he hit thirty-three and thirty-two homers in '68 and '69.

As his relationship with the Phillies deteriorated, Allen proceeded to do everything he could to get traded—skipping batting practice, missing games, coming to the ballpark smelling of liquor. When he was suspended for missing a doubleheader, he sat out for nearly a month and was fined $10,000.

Mauch was fired in 1968, and Allen again took the blame from the lunatic fringe of Philly fans who dumped a Confederate flag on his lawn, fired a BB gun at his house, and smeared his car with paint. He was clubbed by a Philadelphia policeman and four men in a car chased his wife through the city streets.

Allen countered the fans' taunts with graffiti he drew in the dirt with his feet. When he hit the ball over the Coca-Cola sign, he scratched "COKE" into the ground. He wrote "BOO" and the fans did. When the Phillies told him to quit the chicken-scratching, he wrote "WHY" and "NO." Then he wrote "MOM," explaining later that "she tells me what to do, not the man up there."

After giving the game of baseball everything he had, Allen wound up an isolated figure. He was traded to the Cardinals in 1970 for Tim McCarver and Curt Flood, a trade that Flood took to the Supreme Court, challenging baseball's reserve clause.

Allen then played the '71 season for the Dodgers and left the game until he was contacted by White Sox manager Chuck Tanner, a long-time friend of the family.

Tanner did what no manager had done. He made different rules for Allen, who could basically come and go as he pleased, and practice only if he was in the mood. Nobody ever carried a team the way Allen did in 1972, giving everyone a last glimpse of his true greatness, winning the American League Most Valuable Player award, and narrowly missing the Triple Crown.

He retired to tend his racehorses, having said on several occasions that he sees more profound virtues in horses than in men. Around the stables, he was reclusive in the extreme, earning the nickname "The Shadow." That's the way the cookie crumbled, but everyone has to agree that it was some kind of cookie.

Denny McLain was another of the game's superstars who didn't follow the rules laid down for his teammates. But he was in the midst of a thirty-one-win season, and about half of his teammates in 1968 felt that as long as he was winning, he could do anything he wanted. Tiger manager Mayo Smith had a laissez-faire policy regarding the running of a veteran ball club and felt there was no need for someone to crack the whip for the players. According to Bill Freehan, the Tigers' bed checks went this way: "Mayo would say, 'Hey, I got the GM on my case about you guys having parties and not being in by curfew. I'm gonna run a bed check tonight, tell the guys to be in.' "

McLain was the only one on the team who really took advantage of Mayo. But he had quite a number of extracurricular activities requiring his attention. He played the organ and wanted to head his own musical group, saying that his heart was really in music. "If it wasn't for baseball adding to my value as an organist," he said, "I would chuck the whole thing." He dreamed of being a big entrepreneur, running his own paint company, airline, and shopping mall, and also wanted to host his own television sports show. And in his free time he was simply blowing away the American League.

"Mayo and Jim Campbell have to take some of the responsibility for allowing Denny to be absent as much as he was during the '68 season," said Freehan. "We're players, and it became a joke: 'I wonder where Denny is today.' He was never there. It depended on whether it was a town on the road that he wanted to go to at the time. He told us one time he would buzz Tiger Stadium in his plane. We were standing there for the National Anthem, and a plane comes over and tips its wing. I'm not positive it was him, but in my heart of hearts I think it was."

As the Dick Allen and Denny McLain stories illustrate, sometimes the rules are suspended for players of uncommon ability. That was certainly the case with Ochiai, Japan's greatest home run hitter. Ochiai has won three Triple Crowns, two consecutively, with otherworldly numbers—fifty-two home runs and a .367 batting average in 1985 and fifty home runs and a .360 average in 1986. Once he was in his thirties, he said he didn't want to submit to the arduous infield practice and conditioning that is a mandatory part of Japanese baseball. He further departed from the traditional program by refusing to work with a hitting coach / guru, preferring to coach himself. In Japan they say Ochiai is playing by "the American style."

Ochiai also adapted the American style of going after some serious dollars. He changed teams and with the Chunichi Dragons became the first player in Japan to earn over one million dollars per year. I spoke with him when he was visiting the Dodger camp in Vero Beach, and he said, "Anyone can do what I'm doing." And yet he remains the only one who doesn't have to submit to the training program.

Ochiai is not built like a Sumo wrestler. He is about the same size as Sadaharu Oh, depending on timing to hit the long ball. He has no interest in the American superstars, and doesn't need to see Mattingly or Boggs. As a young man he studied a black-and-white photograph of Willie Mays's swing, but that is the extent of the American influence on him. He doesn't care either about being known in the West, and is extremely self-effacing about what he does so well. "I hit to eat," he says. With his salary, that's a lot of raw fish.

The Japanese baseball powers, meanwhile, are trying not to lose their disciplinary hold on their players. When American Randy Bass left the Hanshin Tigers to accompany his eight-year-old son to the United States for treatment of a brain tumor, the team thought he stayed away too long and released him. Presumably, since Japanese players aren't allowed a day off for births or deaths or family illnesses, management wanted to show that players could not walk all over them.

The Hanshin Tigers chief executive officer, Shingo Furuya, went to see Bass in California to negotiate with him. Apparently the rapprochement must not have gone very well, because Furuya, upon returning to Japan, jumped off his eighth-floor hotel balcony to his death.

Another extremely talented player who developed a reputation for being difficult to manage was pitcher Dock Ellis. When Ellis first reported to spring training with the Pirates, he got in seven different fights with teammates over racial name calling. Racial pride was a foremost concern for Ellis, who named his daughter Shangaleza Talwanga, which in Swahili means "Everything black is beautiful."

Pat Corrales managed Ellis with the Texas Rangers and never had any problem with him. "Usually the guys that Dock didn't get along with were the guys that didn't put out. He was very boisterous about that and Dock didn't hold anything back, but he wasn't a fighter. He'd put his chin out and say, 'Hit me, I'll sue you.' That was his motto."

Ellis had mellowed by that time. As a youth he had run with a tough gang in Watts, and "did a few things worse than stealing cars," but later channeled his aggressions into his mound work. Soon after he came up in 1968, Ellis established his reputation as a pitcher who would throw at a hitter if he had to reclaim part of home plate. At the time Orlando Cepeda was the biggest hitter in the league, so to Dock that meant he had to be hit. "From that point on," he said, "I had no trouble with the hitters. They were all running."

They were certainly running the night in 1974 when Ellis,

high on pep pills, tried to hit every batter in the Big Red Machine lineup. He had told people in spring training he was going to do it, but few believed him. Dock was genuinely distressed that his team was not as aggressive as the Reds, and felt that something had to be done. He hit Rose, he hit Morgan, and he hit Driessen, to load the bases. Perez was next but wasn't digging in too deep. Ellis, unable to hit a moving target, walked him. Bench came up hanging very loose, and Ellis threw at his jaw and the back of his head, barely missing him both times, and then was taken out by Danny Murtaugh, who had finally gotten wise to what Dock was doing out there.

Dock appeared in 1972 at Riverfront Stadium with a full Afro, and was stopped by a guard who thought he was a fan. He didn't have the proper papers and, when gentle persuasion wouldn't work, wound up getting maced. "Maybe I looked too wild to be a ballplayer," said Dock. "I just had my hair blown out." Ellis was also the first major leaguer to appear on a baseball field wearing hair curlers. He reluctantly gave up the practice when Commissioner Kuhn nearly had a coronary over it.

One of the more incredible legends from the career of Dock Ellis concerns his performance, on June 12, 1970, under the influence of the most powerful mind chemical known to man. "I was in Los Angeles," Dock explained to a Pittsburgh newspaper in 1984, "and the team was playing in San Diego, but I didn't know it. I had taken LSD at noon, thinking it was an off day. The girl I was with looked at the paper and said, 'Dock, you're pitching tonight.' She drove me to the airport at 3:30, I got to San Diego at 4:30, and the game started at 6:05."

Dock pleaded having a sore arm, understandably unwilling to take the mound when the whole ballpark was *melting* around him, but the Pirates had no one else to start what was the first game of a twi-night doubleheader. A desperate man, Ellis had trouble finding the plate, having no idea where the ball was going. But neither did the Padres' hitters. He begged to come out of the game after five innings, but was informed that he had a no-hitter going.

Ellis passed his own "acid test" with flying colors. He not only finished the game, winning 2–0, but got the no-hitter, although he walked nine and hit a batter. He walked off the mound looking like a man who'd seen God, eyes burning out of his head with that wild "lost look," a burnt-out, blown-out, psychedelicized zombie who had just thrown a no-hitter while scenes from unknown worlds unreeled in his mind's eye. When he tried to remember the night in question, everything was a tad blurry. "I can only remember bits and pieces of the game," he said. "I had a feeling of euphoria. I was zeroed in on the glove. But I didn't hit the glove too much."

TEMPER, TEMPER

Ellis demonstrated that he could pitch under duress without flipping out, but for many players, fits of temporary insanity are not unusual. In fact, it's the rare player who can bottle the frustrations of a game built on failure, where even the best hitters fail to do the job seven times out of ten. The Mets' Kevin McReynolds may be the most unflappable player in the game. It appears that nothing upsets him.

As Bill Robinson said, McReynolds has no problems with his disposition because he doesn't have one. His style of play mirrors his inner calm, as he seems to be on some kind of perpetual cruise control. He has the speed to steal bases (thirty in a row without being caught at this writing), and yet never appears to be running hard. He's an excellent left fielder, and yet seldom looks like he's making a difficult play.

Any attempt to get a rise out of him meets with his implacable indifference. In spring training, Len Dykstra placed a dead fish in McReynolds's uniform pants, and he just wordlessly tossed it aside and dressed. On one occasion in midsummer 1987 he hit a ball deep and John Shelby of the Dodgers went over the fence to steal a homer from him. Lee Mazzilli watched him intently as he sat back on the bench, figuring that there had to be some reaction from him now; he had to blow. And what he saw was the most you will ever see from Kevin McReynolds. He shook his head, staring off into space, and said, ruefully, but without raising his voice, "Damn."

McReynolds is an exception. Most every player finds some way during the long season to vent his frustration in a cathartic way. The California Angels even set up a punching bag in the runway, so players can beat the hell out of it instead of injuring themselves.

But every year there are several players who break their hands punching a brick wall. Letting off steam is a time-honored tradition in the game of baseball. The great manager John McGraw, after a defeat, would go into a saloon, quickly down four or five shots of whiskey, and throw bottles against the wall. Then he would hand the bartender a fifty-dollar bill and walk out.

Not being able to let loose can be worse than giving in to a full-bodied fit of rage. As Dave Winfield said when the Yankees were in the midst of a horrendous stretch, "You'd like to go home and break all the lamps. But you can't because they're all imported."

Mike Heath amazed Ed Lynch in Tucson in 1979 when he combined a temper tantrum with an unearthly calm. "Mike had a terrible game," recalled Lynch, "and afterward I saw him systematically destroy the team's soda machine. It wasn't like he got a bat and whaled on it until he cooled down. He took his time and used a screwdriver. After he got enough screws loose, he picked up his bat and *wham!* The front of the machine fell off. Then Mike picked up his screwdriver, loosened more screws, put his tool down, grabbed his bat, and *bam!* Another part of the machine fell off. I was amazed at how a guy could have a tantrum and be so systematic."

After one bad outing, Dan Quisenberry tried to drown himself in the shower, taking in water until he vomited. Quiz learned to roll with the punches and take these things in stride, but for some players, throwing a major tantrum is part of their makeup as a player.

When it came to wild displays of temper, pitcher Mark Lemongello, who came up to the Houston Astros in 1976, rated with the very best. After a defeat, his teammates would scurry to the clubhouse so they wouldn't miss the show. In the minor leagues once, he threw himself headlong onto the buffet table and laid there covered with condiments for about a half hour. Another time he was so mad that he bit his shoulder until it bled. He would frequently injure himself breaking mirrors or kicking soda machines, and while he became known for his creative displays of temper, he was also good at the basic, destroy-everything-in-sight conniption fit, and could make a clubhouse look like it was in the Dresden bombing in about two minutes.

Lou Piniella is fondly remembered by many of his teammates for the extremes of emotion he would display when things were not going his way. Piniella was a terrific competitor, and a good enough hitter to have very high standards to maintain, hence the frequent tantrums (.220 hitters don't usually go nuts when they strike out). When he was in the minor leagues, Piniella had a chance to blow the game open with the bases loaded, and took a called third strike. A huge rain barrel that was used for drinking water stood next to the dugout, filled with chunks of ice. Lou threw his glove into the water barrel, and it sank to the bottom. Now he had nothing to play the outfield with. He leaned over the barrel, reached in for his glove, and lost his balance on the wet turf and fell headfirst into the icy water. They tried to pull him out by tugging at his knees but the barrel tipped over and the water ran all over him. He sat there on the ground, coughing, soaked, as the fans roared with laughter. And the obligatory fat fan stood up and bellowed, "When I yelled for you to soak your head, I didn't really mean it!"

Lou mellowed with age, but even when he reached the big leagues, he was still liable to snap at any time. He was known for his brilliant execution of the flying double-foot stomp on his own batting helmet. Once, playing for Kansas City, he resumed his frequent attacks on the water cooler. He looked at it lying there, dented, and decided to buy it. He had it shipped to his home in Tampa where he could give it a good kick every once in a while in the off season, just to keep in practice.

Buck Martinez was Lou's teammate in Kansas City and recalled how Lou would furiously rip all the buttons off his uniform, and then turn to the trainer, meek and polite as could be, and say, matter-of-factly, "I need a new uniform." Martinez once saw Piniella go into a long tirade that included every curse under the sun. He had just finished when infielder Jackie Hernandez, who spoke little English, came into the clubhouse and innocently asked Lou how it was going, "¿Cómo está?" Piniella leaped to his feet and repeated the five-minute tirade for him in Spanish.

Perhaps it is this fiery drive to excel while doing the most difficult thing in professional sports, hitting a round ball traveling at ninety miles per hour with a round bat, that leads to losing your mind. That is one way to explain the classic winkouts of Hall of Fame–bound George Brett. Brett has always been known as a fierce competitor who hates to lose. "If a tie is like kissing your sister," he once said, "then losing is like kissing your grandmother with her teeth out."

Brett awes his Royals teammates with his tempestuous outbursts. "He's the best," says teammate Jamie Quirk. "One day at Royals Stadium, George made an out and charged into the tunnel where you could hear him beating a trash can with his bat. Then there was silence. I didn't know what the heck was going on so I went to investigate. There was George inside the trash can and all you could see was his head sticking out. Finally, he climbed out and played the next inning with trash all over him."

Brett recalled what he termed "his greatest snap" with perfect clarity. "I had just struck out for the third time in two days and I had to find a release, so I went into the dugout runway and then I threw my bat. Then I saw a gallon paint can. First, I kicked it and then I threw it up against the wall and it just exploded and paint went all over the place. I picked up the can and saw there was still paint in it. I was going to pour it over my head but I chickened out at the last minute. I always wonder what would have happened if I had poured it over my head and then gone out and played. Right now, I wish I had done it."

I talked with George Brett in Winter Haven after he hit two home runs that left the park like howitzers. While the game finished up, he sat out in left field in the brilliant sun. One would think that he would be pleased with his day, but in baseball, even being a hitter the caliber of George Brett is to worry about the transitory nature of any success. "I've hit five balls hard in three weeks of spring training and three of 'em were today. I might talk to you about hitting and not get a hit for another three weeks. Don't get me wrong, I'm happy with my performance. I made great strides. Maybe it'll carry over to tomorrow, and by April fourth I'll be ready."

While Brett is one of the most scientific-looking hitters of his generation, he doesn't lean toward theorizing about it. "It's pretty easy when you're seeing it good. Everything is so natural. You don't have to think about what you're doing, your subconscious mind takes over. All you do is get out there and relax and concentrate on seeing the ball and your body reflexes do everything else, whereas there's times that you go up there thinking 'Okay, I gotta keep my hands back, swing through the ball, I gotta get my arms extended, I gotta have a weight shift, I came off that pitch, I'm gonna look for this pitch.' That doesn't happen when you're swinging good. You stride, you see the ball good, you react to the ball in and you react to the ball away and you hit it hard. It's that simple. I think what a lot of people do is get too scientific. I'm not scientific. I'm a high school graduate and that's where I want to stay. These guys that tell me they can see the seams on the ball, I don't know if I can, and I don't give a shit. I work on fundamentals that I've learned over the years in batting practice, and then in the game, I just try and relax, see the ball, and hit it hard. It's worked for ten out of fourteen years."

I asked him how he thought Charley Lau, his hitting instructor and long-time friend, should be remembered, but he didn't think that was at all important. "I know how I remember him and that's all I care about. Everybody else has already formed his opinion, he's been dead for five years. It happens whenever someone dies, they become ten times better than they were. Presidents, everybody. When Nixon dies, they'll say he was a great president. Whoever dies, they forget how much they dislike the person, they forget what an idiot he was, and they have nothing but nice things to say about them. I have my own opinion of him, what the man meant to me and what he's done for me over the years. He was like a father figure to me."

Brett is quick to point out that he was far from Lau's only star pupil. "Ever hear of a guy named Hal McRae? Ever hear of Joe Rudi? Harold Baines and Greg Walker, all these guys on the Red Sox that Walt Hriniak teaches? Where do you think Walter learned it from? Charley Lau. Where do you think Mike Lum learned all his stuff? Charley Lau. Where do you think a lot of these guys learned it?

"He studied, he had films and videos, he studied hitters, he talked to hitters, he listened to hitters. He found out what all good hitters have in common and he put it on paper. I don't know how many hitting coaches get out an old film of Babe Ruth and say, 'Watch this swing. What does he do? It looks like when he makes contact his hands are extended and he has a weight shift.' Yeah. 'Now let's watch this guy, watch Johnny Bench hit a home run in the World Series, what's he do? Looks like he has his hands extended and a good weight shift. Now let's watch one of your swings. How come you hit that ball good? Looks like you had a good extension and a good weight shift. How are we going to get that to happen more often?' "

In the spring of 1988, Brett was healthy, and very eager to remind all the people talking about young stars in the game like Eric Davis and Jose Canseco that he hadn't retired yet. Brett was a man on a mission, and his anxiousness to see what he could do was just oozing from every pore. Maybe that's why he gave the impression of being wound very tight, but that has always been one of his trademarks.

Two days after I spoke with Brett, he threw a photographer's camera against the wall in the clubhouse over some old disagreement, obviously getting ready for a regular season that would include a fight with Willie Wilson on the team plane. Spend some time with George Brett, and you experience all the coiled intensity of one of his at-bats. I got the impression that the raging bull who came running out to throttle the umpire the day of the famous pine-tar incident in Yankee Stadium is not buried too deep below the surface.

Spring training was also an anxious time for him most of all because during the spring his father, Jack, faced open-heart surgery. Jack told his youngest son George that there was only one thing he wanted to do before he died, and that was to go back to Cooperstown to see George inducted into the Hall of Fame. His father recovered from the surgery, and an inspired Brett was able to look toward the coming season with a new perspective.

"I think for the first time in my life it made me realize the importance of what I do, not only to myself, but to other people— how happy it makes him when I have good games, how happy it makes my three brothers, how happy it makes my friends." By mid-season of 1988, he was making a lot of people very happy, hitting around .330 at the break and making the All-Star Team at first base over Don Mattingly.

✪

EGGHEADS AND GOZZLEHEADS

After talking with George Brett for a while on that day in spring training, he asked me, "Are you doing a book about hitting or a book about how stupid this game is?" Of course, any excursion into the realm of characters in the game of baseball will plunge you into a deep morass of monumental stupidities. Even the greatest philosopher the game has yet produced, Casey Stengel, is known as much for being impossible to understand as he is for his considerable profundities.

As anyone who has been there will tell you, an anti-intellectual atmosphere persists in the major leagues today. The erudite catcher Ted Simmons, an art collector sitting on the board of a museum in St. Louis, said that "most ballplayers read the sports pages, but I'm sorry to say that in most cases that's all they read." As a case in point, one day Dodger second baseman Steve Sax noticed his manager Tommy Lasorda reading *The Wall Street Journal* on the team bus, and asked to borrow the sports section.

This is not to single out Sax as a bonehead, but just to help put things into perspective. At least some players have an excuse. John Kruk of the Padres led a sheltered life before he came to the big leagues. He grew up in Keyser, West Virginia, hanging out in moonshine country with a bunch of barefoot guys in overalls with serious dental problems. These are his people, who strongly resemble the guitarists in ZZ Top. His first year in the minors was "the first time I ever had to talk to people I didn't know." On his first trip to Chicago he saw Lake Michigan and asked "What ocean is that?" Later he said, "I know it's Lake Michigan now. I thought it was the Mediterranean."

Franz Lidz of *Sports Illustrated* was probably right when he wrote that "all a ballplayer has to do to be considered an intellectual is read Kurt Vonnegut or own a Billy Joel album." Jim Bouton said that when he played, if you started reading a book on the bus, your teammates would immediately start calling you "professor."

That's what they called Jim Brosnan, a relief pitcher from 1956 to 1963 with the Cubs, Cardinals, Reds, and White Sox. None of his teammates had any idea that Brosnan was working on a diary of the 1959 season that he spent with the Cardinals and the Reds. His book, *The Long Season,* was published in 1960, and marked the first time a ballplayer wrote an inside account of a major-league season without the aid of a ghostwriter.

Broz wouldn't have it any other way. He was unusual in having serious aspirations of being a writer. While he sometimes wore a beret, smoked a pipe, and wore glasses, Brosnan was not the stereotypical highbrow. "I value Ross Thomas and Robert Parker as much as Mark Twain and Vladimir Nabokov," he said. "All I ask for is style and entertainment."

Brosnan was the bullpen ace for the Reds in 1961 when they won their first National League pennant since 1940, and got the final out of the pennant-clinching game. His singular fascination with language is most evident when he recalls his biggest thrills in baseball—"I can tell they're thrilling," he says, "by the horripilation."

After publishing his book he was persona non grata with the Reds, who traded him away. In fact, every general manager he ever played for tried to discourage him from writing, citing a clause in the major-league contract that says you cannot publish without the consent of the ball club. But Brosnan would not be deterred, and at present he has written several drafts of a yet-to-be-published first novel.

Of course today the celebrity sports biography, with various degrees of kissing and telling, is a staple of the publishing industry. Shane Rawley, Phillies left-hander, has even written a few scripts for the television show "Miami Vice." Several young players, such as the Mets' David Cone, wanted to be sportswriters in college until they discovered they could throw a baseball ninety miles per hour. But there don't seem to be many real poets around the locker rooms today.

Jim Bouton said, however, that there is no mistaking the fact that today's major leaguer has a lot more on the ball. "Guys today aren't so stupid. We were really dumb. The owners told us not to talk to each other about our contracts, so we didn't. The owners told us not to talk to the press. We did everything they told us to do. When they told us we were getting paid a lot of money, we believed them. We were really dumb."

But after Marvin Miller came on the scene and educated players about their worth, good business sense became the norm in baseball. Rob Murphy, the fine setup reliever for the Cincinnati Reds, illustrates the kind of player who uses his ample free time as a major-league ballplayer in a fashion more financially constructive than devising New Wave pranks to play on his teammates. On the frequent flights to various National League cities, while his teammates are plugged in to their Walkmans, Murphy has his lap-top computer booted up.

His extracurricular business is operating M375 Thoroughbreds, specializing in the computerized selection of winning racehorses by pedigree. While many owners, executives, and players have become involved with horses over the years, nobody in baseball has ever become involved the way Murphy has.

Interest in horse racing runs deep in the Murphy family. His mother's father, Frank Ashley, was a track announcer for thirty-five years in Kentucky, Arkansas, and Illinois. His mother's mother worked for *The Daily Racing Form.* And his father's step-father, Freddy Smith, was a jockey who rode Bimelich to victory in the 1940 Preakness and Belmont Stakes. His father, Bob Murphy, is a general contractor who kept a stable of horses as a hobby while Rob was in high school.

In Florida, admission to the racetrack is forbidden under the age of eighteen, so Murphy didn't go to the track until he was sixteen, but he remembers the date—November 13, 1976. In his senior year in high school in 1978, he took a computer class and for his senior project decided to write a program for handicapping the Triple Crown. His teacher said that was fine, but that he would be judged on how the Kentucky Derby finished.

The program picked Affirmed, Alydar, and Believe It, horses that finished one-two-three. This auspicious beginning led Murphy and the friend with whom he wrote the program to test it out at the track with their own money. They picked the tenth race Trifecta all six days they were there and collected $15,000.

To say the least, Murphy was encouraged, but his interest soon turned to how one could objectively select winning thoroughbreds based on their pedigree. He took nine computer science classes in college, the key course being one in systems analysis. He was working by himself now, and had taken on an awesome task.

"There's so much subjectivity in the selection of a racehorse," he said. "Jockeys say, 'I rode this horse's grandmother,' but it doesn't mean a thing." The much ballyhooed Dosage Index doesn't impress Murphy, because you can't breed a horse for dosage. When he was signed with the Reds two months out of college, he was in the midst of an exhaustive search through the American Produce Records—13,000 pages detailing the pedigree on every yearling sold between 1975 and 1983. What he was looking for were the characteristics that distinguished good race-horses from the run-of-the-mill.

He examined thirty-one points on each stallion, then went to the female side and broke down the families of horses to nine. He found finally that three of these nine families have produced three-quarters of the greatest horses of all time. Of the 26,129 yearlings he researched, only 433 were approved by his program. One hundred seventeen of these 433 were stakes winners, or 27 percent, well above the 2.5 percent industry average.

He looked back at the horses that his program dictated should have been bought when they came up for sale as yearlings. Seattle Slew was part of a sale of 202 horses, one of two approved by Murphy's program. If you had bought both for $24,700, it would have been a wise investment, considering that Seattle Slew is worth $100 million today.

It's a big game for big stakes. If you had bought all 433 of the horses approved by the program that went up for sale from 1975 to 1983, it would cost $70 million, with a $400-million return on the investment. Some of the horses that Murphy's program targets for purchase are expensive, and some go for relatively small amounts.

In February of 1984, he spoke with an investor for a few minutes and was authorized to buy a horse for him. The horse, Artillerist, won a race and showed great promise, but the owner ran the colt seven times in eight weeks, and Murphy decided he would prefer to buy horses that he can manage himself. He now has twenty-four clients in racing and breeding partnerships. He has no plans to publish his program, and it's not easy to get onto his computer disk, for which you would need a code that has 11 trillion combinations.

When Murphy was getting so involved in racing as a business, he wasn't sure he would even have a baseball career. His arm was out of shape when he showed his pitching coach Harry Dorish what he could do in 1981 in A Ball. He was throwing a sixty-mph fastball and a curve that didn't break, and they made him into a knuckleball pitcher. "I wasn't a prospect," he says. "I was a suspect."

Bruce Kimm, now the Reds' third-base coach, told him that he wanted to make him a reliever, and taught him a slider. He came up to the Reds in 1986 and has been an integral part of one of the best bullpens in the National League for several years now. His girl friend of twelve years, Kimberly Stratos, serves as his agent for his baseball contracts.

In innings six through eight, he is ready for manager Pete Rose to give him the call. While he doesn't walk many batters, he says "the irony of it is that I don't know where I'm throwing the ball. I can't hit the glove. I aim right down the middle for every pitch. If I throw for the inside corner, I'm liable to either hit the guy or throw it right down the middle and it's a double."

Relying on his natural ball movement is like offering his pitches up to the Gods of Pitcher's Luck. Even with his high-tech, ultra-modern business approach, Rob Murphy retains the ballplayer's superstition. Every time he comes into a game he goes through the same routine, standing behind the mound à la Hrabosky to get himself together, and then goes for the Good Housekeeping Seal by lining up the resin bag with home plate, precisely. He is, after all, a left-hander. For good luck, he always wears, underneath his Reds uniform, a pair of black bikini briefs. In 1988, however, Murphy set a major-league record when he appeared in his seventy-third game without getting a single victory; maybe he should change his underwear.

Big leaguers with off-field interests such as Murphy's are still a rarity. While baseball requires years of training, a balance of relaxation and concentration, and the ability to perform under pressure, it doesn't require a penetrating critical intelligence. As Dizzy Dean said upon being inducted into the Hall of Fame, "The Good Lord was good to me. He gave me a strong body, a good right arm, and a weak mind."

An egghead is always out of place in baseball, like a pearl onion sitting atop a banana split. Red Barber must have been at the end of his intellectual rope the day he asked fellow announcer Joe Garagiola what he had done during the day, and Joe replied that he had gone with some of the guys to a movie. Barber couldn't resist chiding Garagiola. "A movie, huh? Have you ever been to an art museum, Joe? Read a book?"

Brainy ballplayers are always the exception in baseball, and are usually given a wide berth. Ben Oglivie used to amaze his teammates on the Tigers and Brewers with his ability to do the *New York Times* crossword puzzle in fifteen minutes. Oglivie, a Panamanian, would drive long stretches in his car while reading Jean-Jacques Rousseau, and was also known for frequently leaving the shower running in his room because he was engrossed in some intellectual conundrum.

Even more than the goofballs and superflakes, the super-smart players are the ultimate oddballs in the world of baseball. The most fascinating of these was the extraordinary catcher who came out of Princeton in 1923 to join the Brooklyn Dodgers, Moe Berg, who became known as baseball's greatest intellect. Joe Cronin called him "a living university" and to Casey Stengel he was "the strangest fellah who ever put on a uniform."

Berg was a pure scholar, who learned voraciously because he loved it, and it became his principal momentum in life. He was an expert in many fields, but the study of languages was his greatest passion. He would buy a dozen or more foreign newspapers a day, and had a strange quirk about them—before he read them, the newspapers were "alive," and nobody could touch them before he was finished with them. If somebody violated one of his newspapers, he would walk through a snowstorm, if necessary, to buy a new one. He would even bring books into the bullpen. If the pitcher for that day went the route and Moe didn't have to warm anyone up, he would hit the books and sometimes give tutorials. But usually he just tried to fit in when on the ball field, intentionally spicing his language with double negatives and other grammatical gaffes.

In 1934 he accompanied an All-Star team that included Ruth, Gehrig, Foxx, and Gehringer on a tour of Japan. The ballplayers were greeted by more than a million people and the Americans coached the Japanese college students on the fine points of the game. This tour did a lot to further the cause of baseball as a national sport in Japan. Moe played a crucial role in this transfer of information because he spoke fluent Japanese.

But Moe had other fish to fry on this trip as well, because he was working as an undercover spy for the State Department. He skipped out of one of the games, and on the pretext of visiting a woman in a hospital, went up to the hospital roof and took out a concealed movie camera. His film of industrial complexes, armament plants, oil refineries, and railroad lines would be used several years later by American military intelligence in the massive air raids against Tokyo in World War II.

Berg was chosen by the intelligence services because of his knowledge of languages, his quick mind, and the fact that he was tightlipped and comfortable living alone, all the requisites of the ideal agent. When the Americans and the Germans were involved in their race to the atomic bomb, Berg was a top atomic spy for the United States, working for the OSS (Office of Strategic Services, the wartime predecessor of the CIA) under Wild Bill Donovan. Berg studied the principles of physics so that he could attend a lecture by world-famous German scientist Werner Heisenberg and determine if Heisenberg was close to the development of an atomic weapon. If that was the case, Berg was instructed to assassinate Heisenberg. As it turned out, Heisenberg did not directly discuss the atomic problem, much to Berg's relief.

Berg was a warm man who knew people from all walks of life. When he was traded to Washington, he danced frequently at embassy parties and was one of the few players to regularly have a tuxedo hanging in his locker. He kept his distance from his teammates, though, and in fact his team usually did not know how to reach him because he changed apartments so frequently. Throughout his career he remained a mystery to those with whom he played.

Berg's life was certainly unique in the annals of baseball, but he was not the only player to be proficient with languages. One of the most brilliant of pitchers was Ken Holtzman of the Cubs, A's, and Yankees. Ken was a French scholar and read the seven volumes of Proust's *Remembrance of Things Past* in the untranslated original. On the A's he was known as "The Thinker," and was teased by his teammates about being an intellectual, but Holtzman didn't care, most of the time keeping to himself.

When Holtzman played on the Yankees amid the "Bronx Zoo" of the '70s, who did he hang out with? Why, Mickey Rivers, of course, who was rumored to have an IQ no higher than that of an ice cube. Holtzman and Rivers, who was known as "The Gozzlehead," were inseparable pals, strange bedfellows who played gin rummy while the superstars around them preened, quarreled, and won back-to-back championships.

Mick the Quick was one of the fastest men who ever played the game, but when he walked up to the plate he looked like an arthritic seventy-year-old man in pain. As Sparky Lyle put it, it looked as if Rivers "walked on coals for a living." He told one manager that he wasn't going to steal more bases because if you hit that ground a hundred and fifty times a year, "you got to be painin' at the end of the year." Mickey was known not to run out grounders if he was in a bad mood.

Rivers reportedly asked to be traded from the Rangers because the only thing to bet on in Texas was the cockfights. Jay Johnstone said the funniest thing he saw while he was with the Yankees in the late '70s was in the Yankee parking lot, where Mickey was driving in circles in one car while his wife, having found out about one of Rivers's peccadilloes, chased him in their Mercedes. They bashed in nearly a dozen cars in their very own version of Bronx bumper pool on wheels.

Rivers has since left the game, but samples of his wit and wisdom still reverberate around the big leagues. "I might have to commute. You know, left field, DH, wherever." Or: "My goals are to hit .300, score 100 runs and stay injury-prone." And then the capper, which made many wonder if Rivers could be serious when he asked, "What was the name of that dog on 'Rin Tin Tin'?" Jim Kern, who played with Rivers on the Texas Rangers, said that Rivers was actually a pretty sharp fellow, and made these plant-like declarations mostly for effect. Mick the Quick's fondest wish when he was in Texas was to return to the Yankees where he had his best days, and be reunited with George Steinbrenner and Billy Martin. As Mickey explained, "George and Billy and me are two of a kind."

Some baseball players just have that special talent for meaning one thing while saying another. Jim Gantner of the Milwaukee Brewers, who his teammates call "Gumby," has the gift. He is a master of the mixed metaphor, the non sequitur, and the nonsensical. One time he forgot to show up for a radio talk show, and explained it by saying, "I must have had ambrosia." Since then, his Brewer teammates have been compiling a list of what they call "Gumbyisms."

When asked to describe his off season, Gantner said, "I mostly stayed around the house, but I did take a hunting trip to one of those Canadian proverbs." He said one of his favorite players was "Sandy Manguillen," meaning Manny Sanguillen. And when he saw A's infielder Donnie Hill throwing right-handed and left-handed in warmup, he pointed out, "Hey, look at Donnie. He's amphibious." As teammate Robin Yount said, "You say to him, 'Do you know what you just said?' and Gantner replies 'Aaww. You know what I mean.' "

Gantner is a definite comer, and so is Triple A reliever Mike Smith with the Expos farm club in Indianapolis. Smith is a fire-balling reliever who comes up with some doozies, ordering "neu-trons" on his salad instead of croutons, and picking "Mario Mandretti" to win the Indianapolis 500. But they all have a long way to go before they can make you think twice the way Yogi Berra can.

Berra takes a stripped-down, existential view of life's dualities. When asked about a popular restaurant, he said, "No one goes there anymore. It's too crowded." Someone asked him what time it is, and he said, "You mean now?" It's easy to get lost talking to Yogi, and that's why he's always maintained, "You've got to be very careful if you don't know where you're going because you might not get there."

His insights into the difficulties of the game he played so well are by now legendary. "I ain't in no slump," he once said. "I just ain't hitting," not to mention the old chestnut he delivered, after striking out, "How can you think and hit at the same time?" His all-time classic is now a part of sportspeak everywhere—"It ain't over till it's over." He went out of the game the same way he came in, on Yogi Berra Day stepping up to the mike to say, "I want to thank everyone who made this day necessary."

Yogi is now a coach with the Houston Astros, but in his latest incarnation he appears on sixty-four television stations as a film critic on "Yogi at the Movies." He's the kind of straight-from-the-hip movie reviewer who leaves no doubt about where he's coming from aesthetically. "I like a good Western. I like a good war movie. Rin Tin Tin was my favorite dog actor." He found that the film *Biloxi Blues* touched off some old memories. "It reminded me of being in the Army, even though I was in the Navy."

At times Yogi can mix up people's names so thoroughly that he achieves something noteworthy. He saw the action flick *Above the Law* and was asked about its star, Steven Seagal. "He could be another Cliff Eastwick," he replied. What a coup, apparently mixing up Clint Eastwood, Rawly Eastwick, and somebody named Cliff—Cliff Johnson? Montgomery Clift? Only Yogi knows, and he's probably not too sure about it himself.

Baseball is a repository of some classic malapropisms that spew from the mouths of many an announcer. Jerry Coleman, the voice of the San Diego Padres, has come up with some amazing play-by-play descriptions, such as: "There's a fly ball deep to center field. Winfield is going back, back, he hits his head against the wall. It's rolling back toward second base. This is a terrible thing for the Padres." Coleman really paints a picture for any listener who can figure out what a "sun-blown pop-up" is, or what a player looks like when he's "sliding into second base with a stand-up double."

Ralph Kiner, the Mets' broadcaster now for a quarter century, continues to delight listeners with his fluffs of names, turning to introduce his broadcasting partner Tim McCarver as "Tim McArthur." After Gary Carter's first game as a Met, which he won with a tenth-inning homer, he went on Kiner's Korner and Ralph was so excited that he called him "Gary Cooper." Over the years, his classic gaffes have included calling Dan Driessen "Diane Driessen" and Dann Bilardello "Don Bordello." But everyone gets mixed up occasionally, especially when sufficiently jet-lagged to open a telecast from Los Angeles by informing the audience that it was "7:30 P.M. Pacific Coast League Time."

When Harry Caray was convalescing from his heart surgery, a number of guest announcers filled in for him. Longtime Cubs fan and actor Bill Murray took the mike one day for a game against the Expos. When Floyd Youmans was ejected for arguing, Murray said, "You hate to see that sort of thing happen, especially when we're hitting him so well." After Cubs outfielder Chico Walker took a big swing and missed, Murray said, "He was trying to tie this game up with one swing of the bat, which isn't easy when your team is winning 7–0." He wrapped up the telecast by complimenting Rick Sutcliffe on his work that day. He was particularly pleased "because frankly, he owes me money."

Bob Uecker has been working in the radio booth for the Milwaukee Brewers for many years now. He originally signed with the Milwaukee Braves for $3,000. "That bothered my dad at the time," he said, "because he didn't have that kind of dough to pay out. But eventually he scraped it up."

Uecker was and is the master of self-deprecation. He was well aware that he was lacking in natural tools. "Anybody with ability can play in the big leagues. But to be able to trick people year in and year out the way I did, I think that was a much greater feat."

What is all but forgotten is that Uke did have a great arm and was a capable catcher, but it is nonetheless true that he could not run at all. Even the president of his fan club admits that he ran like a batting cage with a flat tire. "I had to compensate with a few tricks," Uecker said. "One was to knock my hat off as I ran down the first base line to make it appear I was really moving."

The way Uecker tells it, his checkered career as a backup catcher was all part of a great master plan. "I mean, if a guy hits .300 year after year, what does he have to look forward to? I always tried to stay around .190, with three or four RBIs. And I tried to get them all in September. That way I always had something to talk about during the winter."

He was on the 1964 pennant-winning Cardinals but didn't see action in the World Series, unless you count what happened before Game One. One of the bands on the field took a break, so Uecker grabbed the tuba, put it around his neck, and began trying to catch fly balls with it. Several hit the rim, denting the instrument, and the tuba's owner sent the Cardinals a bill for damages, which amounted to all the statistics he had for the Fall Classic.

On "The Tonight Show," he told Johnny Carson (who dubbed Uecker "Mr. Baseball") that he had made a major contribution to the Cardinals' pennant drive by coming down with hepatitis. When Carson asked how he caught it, Uecker replied, "The trainer injected me with it."

Giants manager Roger Craig used to room with Uecker. He told me that after one long road trip they got off the plane and Uecker met his first wife and said, " 'Honey, I gotta tell you something. When I was out on the West Coast I stayed with Roger's wife a couple of nights, we've been doin' some sharin', so I'll see you in a couple of days,' and he walks off, and his wife was standing there with her eyes glazed, like 'What?' She really believed it for a few moments. He was a funny, funny man."

Uecker has kept every club with which he's been associated loose. On a team flight, he'll impersonate other announcers such as Harry Caray or Bob Elston, and sometimes, just as the plane is about to touch down, Uecker will come over the intercom: "This is your captain speaking. Please remain seated and keep your seat belts fastened until the plane has hit the side of the terminal building and come to a complete stop."

Buck Martinez, whom Uecker used to call "Dr. Martini," was a member of the Brewers and recalls another announcement of Uecker's when the team flew into Seattle over Mount St. Helens the day after it erupted. On the bus to the hotel, Uecker told the team that they were going on a little field trip to the edge of the volcano. "Just remember," he advised over and over, "to stay in your groups."

Boog Powell already knew Uecker when they started taping the Miller Lite beer commercials. He recalled the last commercial they did, the one where the spaceship comes down while the Miller Lite All-Stars are sitting around the campfire. "Before the taping we were in the dressing room, and Uke comes out and he's got this pair of chaps on and no pants underneath, and all he's wearing is a jock, so his raw ass is hanging out, and you really can't tell if he has anything on from the front, because these chaps are hanging there. A girl was going to interview me for 'Entertainment Tonight,' and before I do it Uke comes over and says, 'Hey, Booger, when you get over there doing the interview, tell her to look over here.' So I'm gettin' ready to go on and do the interview, and I said, 'God, look at Uke, he's really signing autographs over there,' and she looks and he's bent over, and he is mooning her. He walks around acting like nothing's wrong. He must have gotten fifteen people that day."

Powell says doing a Lite commercial is just like being in a clubhouse, like being in a locker room. "Most of the guys have been in team sports, with the exception of 'Doll,' and I think the Doll wishes that she could have been in the clubhouse, too. When we first started doing the things, she was hesitant to get involved in it, but as we went along she realized that we weren't going to change, so now she has a great time along with us. She came out one day with a jock on and a hot dog hanging out of it."

It would appear that the Doll has become acclimated to baseball humor, which no less an authority than Uecker himself described as "crude and shameless and irreverent. It is army humor, with more sweat."

Jim Bouton wrote in *Ball Four* of the time utility infielder Ray Oyler was warming up a pitcher in the Seattle Pilots bullpen during a game when he missed a sinker, which hit him in the cup. Oyler, unable to make a sound, crawled weakly toward the dugout on his hands and knees, and then vomited over the railing. Manager Joe Schultz laughed like it was the funniest thing he ever saw. Things haven't changed much in that regard. When Eric Davis got hit right in the cup with a fastball from Pascual Perez, he went down on his knees in pain, and Pete Rose came out to see if he was all right and couldn't hide his laughter.

A lot of Doug Rader's classic escapades are X-rated. It's one thing to organize nude swimming relays in the Astros' hotel pool, but it's quite another to videotape it and broadcast it over the hotel's closed-circuit TV system.

Norm Miller, now a Giants coach, was Rader's roommate. "I roomed with him for two seasons, but I got tired of him giving me airplane spins over his head. You could never turn your back on him." Miller and his wife once made an unannounced visit to Rader's home. When Rader saw the car pull up, he stripped and greeted the couple in his birthday suit. "Even as well as I knew

Doug," Miller said, "I wasn't ready for that. And my wife obviously wasn't."

Rader was nicknamed after the cartoon character he most resembled—Foghorn Leghorn—hence the name "Red Rooster." He played on the Astros for nine of his eleven years in the big leagues, and for the last two he was the team captain. He was a steady player, but may have stayed in the majors so long because he also had the ability to keep things loose, do the unexpected.

He would sit on the bench during a game eating baseball cards, to absorb the statistical information on his opponents. In the locker room he would switch the contents of the mouthwash and the after-shave lotion. He once drove a motorcycle into a brick wall on purpose. He was a certified crazy and a leader of men, which someone must have recognized, because he later became a big-league manager.

It is generally acknowledged in baseball that having fun goes hand in hand with winning, and that having a free spirit or two on a ball club can be quite beneficial to all concerned. Tug McGraw was always known as the type of individual who could entertain himself in a stalled elevator. He had a name for each of his pitches. The "Peggy Lee" was when, after batters swung and missed, they asked, "Is that all there is?"; the "John Jameson" was "straight, the way I like my Irish whiskey"; the "Cutty Sark" was a pitch that "sailed." McGraw also named pitches after celebrities. His "Frank Sinatra" was so named because "after they connected, it was 'Fly Me to the Moon,' and his "Bo Derek" had "a nice little tail on it."

Tug's gems were scattered freely throughout his baseball career. He was frank with his fan club, telling them they could better devote their time and money to helping the American Indian Movement. When asked what he thought of Astroturf, McGraw said he didn't want to play on anything he couldn't smoke. And, after winning a World Series with the Phillies, he was asked what he did with his World Series earnings. "I spent half of it on booze and broads," he replied. "The other half I just wasted."

The National Pastime continues to spawn its fair share of comic philosophers. Larry Anderson, currently a middle-inning reliever for the Astros, is fond of creating the impression that relief pitchers have too much time on their hands. He's out there in the bullpen pondering the riddles of the universe. "How come 'fat chance' and 'slim chance' mean the same thing? How do you know when invisible ink is dry? Isn't it an incredible coincidence that both Washington and Lincoln were born on national holidays? What do they call a coffee break at the Lipton tea company?" It's not as if Anderson is advertising that he's strange. He just happens to wear a T-shirt that reads, "Roses are red/ violets are blue/ I'm a schizophrenic/ and so am I."

Dan Quisenberry parlayed an offbeat approach to the pressures of being a late-inning closer into a very successful career. His underhand delivery was unique, and so was his outlook. He was the first to admit that his view of baseball and life was slightly skewered. "I'm off the wall," he said, "for a double."

He told me that he originally started giving reporters wild responses because he didn't know what else to say. But he has always used humor to get him through the bad times, "probably so I can live with the memory of letting down another pitcher, the manager, the pitching coach, the GM, and thirty-five thousand fans."

When he doesn't do well, he's honest about it, and uses the post-game interview as a wondrous release. After one miserable outing, he said, "I was Drāno out there—right down the drain." After getting knocked out of the box in back-to-back games, he abandoned his forkball by saying, "I stuck a fork in it and decided it was done." But when he broke his slump by making a change in his pitching motion, he explained that he had found "a delivery in my flaw."

One time a reporter asked him if the night's loss was the worst way to lose. Quisenberry gave him a veritable stream of consciousness of worse ways to lose: balking a runner home from first base, that would be worse; if an earthquake hit just as Amos Otis settled under a fly ball, that would be worse; and on and on.

Quis was no power pitcher. His deliveries never made the catcher's glove *pop!* It was always more like a *poof!* But Quisenberry had extraordinary control and worked fairly quickly, so his fielders would always be ready to make a great play behind him, which they did with uncanny frequency. "My infielders have to be alive," he said, "if they want to have kids later on."

He's an expert on the working conditions in the bullpens of the American League. He likes a good bathroom, preferably heated, because he always like to relieve himself right before coming into a game. In the early innings, he likes to get his fellow relievers going, so they can entertain him and keep him loose. A few of the bullpens are underground, so being in there is like being in a submarine. "The bullpen is a closed environment, but I like it better than the dugout or the clubhouse. I guess I just like being locked in a closet taking a lot of verbal abuse from hostile people."

When I spoke to him at the Royals spring training complex in Baseball City, he was still in limbo, no longer being used by the Royals in a save situation, and then as the '88 season began, not even being used in the middle innings. The difficulty in moving him to another team was Quisenberry's lifetime contract tied in to real estate holdings and estimated to be worth more than $40 million. Still, what gnawed away at him was this purgatorial state of not being allowed to pitch. He was hopeful in the spring that he would get another shot at being the closer, but as the season wore on, he said, "I'm not a short man, I'm not a long man, I'm a dead man."

In July of 1988 he was released by Kansas City and picked up by the St. Louis Cardinals. The National League was a strange, brave new world for Quisenberry to explore. For one thing, he got to bat for the first time, after hiding behind the designated hitter in the American League his whole career. "My first at-bat was surreal," he said. "Maybe Salvador Dalí could paint it, but I can't talk about it." What does the future hold for Dan Quisenberry? He once pondered that very question. "I have seen the future," he said, "and it is very much like the present, only longer."

We don't find many Dan Quisenberrys anywhere, but only in baseball do players so often express their personalities and idiosyncrasies in the playing of a game. Maybe that is why baseball is the one major sport in America that has created a literature and a lore all its own, an aura of legend and a style of humor, and a cast of such remarkable characters. There should be a shrine somewhere dedicated to the characters and pranksters and all-too-human happenings that are really not a sidelight of the game, but part of its very fabric.

I can imagine what would lie, hermetically sealed, in the glass-enclosed trophy case of such a gallery, so that future generations can wax nostalgic over the hallowed, Lloyd's of London–insured contents. There is the reconstructed urinal that Billy Martin smashed (a collector's item signed by Billy); a cake sat upon by Sparky Lyle; a bottle of whiskey emptied by Babe Ruth; a few choice masks from the collection of Roger McDowell; and the rope which Jay Johnstone used to tie Lasorda in his office. Among the tonsorial treasures are Joe Pepitone's hair dryer, Dock Ellis's curlers, and even a lock of Al Hrabosky's hair circa 1975. And set off on the highest plateau is a gold-inlaid mahogany box displaying some of the freeze-dried rotten vegetables, rocks, chicken bones, bullets, firecrackers, and various kitchen utensils thrown by fans at Jimmy Piersall and Dick Allen, as a reminder that the players aren't the only monkeys in this zoo.

Baseball's original flake: Hall of Fame pitcher Rube Waddell, renowned for his drinking and chasing of fire engines. (*National Baseball Library, Cooperstown, N.Y.*)

Moe Berg, the "living university." A gifted linguist, Berg spoke many languages, gave tutorials in the bullpen, and worked as a U.S. spy in his spare time. (*National Baseball Library, Cooperstown, N.Y.*)

Mark "The Bird" Fidrych (right) and Tiger teammate Dave Rozema in the days when they were flying high.
(*Detroit Tigers*)

Roger McDowell's Upside-Down Man stalks Dodger Stadium in June of 1987.
(*AP/Wide World Photos*)

Oriole manager Earl Weaver had no choice but to put an American League pennant in the hands of this man, Don "Stan the Man Unusual" Stanhouse. *(Baltimore Orioles)*

Rick Dempsey's favorite rain-delay pantomime was the one he did in Milwaukee of Robin Yount's two homers against Baltimore in the last game of the regular season in 1982. *(AP/Wide World Photos)*

Jim Kern, "The Amazing Emu," when he pitched in the Texas Rangers bullpen known as "The Cuckoo's Nest."
(*Texas Rangers*)

May 29, 1978. Things got a little hairier than usual for Al Hrabosky when umpire Bill Kunkel would not allow the Mad Hungarian to psych himself up behind the mound.
(*AP/Wide World Photos*)

Bill Lee meets with reporters at the ACLU in 1979 after Bowie Kuhn fined him for saying that he had used marijuana since 1968. Kuhn said that Lee's remarks were "not in the best interest of baseball."
(UPI/Bettmann Newsphotos)

Luis Tiant, who had several major comebacks in his career, savors the last one, a no-hitter for the Portland Beavers in 1981.
(UPI/Bettmann Newsphotos)

Right: Jim Piersall gets the bugs out in
Detroit, 1960.
(*UPI/Bettmann Newsphotos*)

Dennis "Oil Can" Boyd, truly one of
baseball's greatest characters, whose
career is now threatened by recurring
blood clots in his arm.
(*Boston Red Sox*)

Stormin' Norman Cash, one of the
great good-time players of the '60s,
near the end of his career.
(*Detroit Tigers*)

The author talking with Al Kaline in Lakeland. (*Barry Oreck*)

This picture really *is* worth a thousand words. In the spring of 1988, a beaming Billy Martin holds aloft a photo of himself with the man who hired him for the fifth time and would fire him yet again, and the man who would replace him, only to be fired himself at the end of the season. (*UPI/Bettmann Newsphotos*)

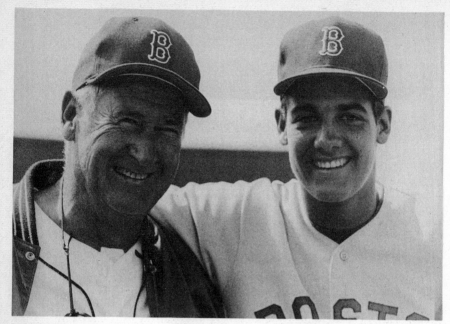

Ted Williams and his only
son, John Henry, in Winter
Haven.
(Steve Connolly/SCI-Sports)

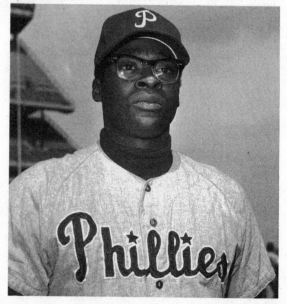

A troubled superstar:
Dick Allen in 1967.
(UPI/Bettmann Newsphotos)

PART TWO

DIAMOND VOICES

Stormin' Norman

*I*t is not that unusual in baseball to see players on the field that make us think we are seeing them at their most authentic, that they are most themselves in their playing. I think of the enthusiasm of a Mays, the pride of a Clemente, the dignity of a DiMaggio, the arrogance of a Williams or Reggie Jackson, the cool fire in an Aaron or an Al Kaline. It seems that many of the great players have succeeded by exaggerating something in their personalities, self-becoming to the nth degree.

It's not like there are great performers in baseball and then other guys who are the flakes and personalities. Many of the greatest characters in the game have been the greatest of players, like a Babe Ruth, and in some cases I believe that is part of the reason they became great players.

Baseball is unique in that it's played every day. You can't succeed at it by pumping yourself up to be the Incredible Hulk once a week like in football; you have to be yourself to be successful. In a game as difficult to play as professional baseball, each player has to adapt somehow to the nagging frustrations of the game itself. It's about finding yourself, finding the best ways of concentrating, relaxing, and letting off steam, a mental approach that works for you, and that's the only person it's got to work for.

What worked for Norman Cash, the Detroit Tigers' first base-man from 1960 to 1974, would not work for all players. But Cash knew that he played his best and his hardest by enjoying himself on and off the field. He was a prankster, a cowboy honky-tonker, what some would call a hard liver, and he performed well enough and long enough to hit 377 career home runs.

Norman Cash arrived in a big league spring training camp for the first time in 1958 with the White Sox. He had been playing for the Army at Fort Bliss the previous two years, and now accrued enough leave time to work out with the team that had signed him in 1955. Cash was thrilled, and sought out manager Al Lopez to thank him for the opportunity to train with the White Sox. Lopez smiled graciously. "It's good to have you down here, Joe."

To the White Sox brain trust, Cash was just a guy named Joe. He sat on the bench in 1959 when the Sox won the pennant, hitting .240 in fifty-eight games. Bill Veeck, then owner of the Go-Go Sox, didn't like Norm's wooden swing, and sent him to the Indians as part of a seven-player trade. In the spring of 1960, he didn't impress Cleveland's general manager Frank Lane, and Trader Frank showed Norm how he got his name.

Lane called the Detroit Tigers general manager Rick Ferrell to offer "Cash for Steve Demeter." The Tigers were momentarily confused. "You mean cold cash or Norm Cash?" Cash was part of the famous deal that sent Rocky Colavito, homer champ, to the Tigers for Harvey Kueen, the batting champion.

Norm arrived in the Tiger camp in Lakeland in the spring of 1960, walked into the lobby and almost got knocked over by Tiger players on their way to a party. It was Freedom Day, when wives, family, and others went back up north, and the team was having a big dinner at a local VFW Hall. Hank Aguirre told Norm to just drop his suitcases right there, and two days later, his bags were still sitting in the lobby. As Aguirre recalled, "It was a hell of an introduction to the ballclub."

Norm played part-time in 1960 and managed to hit eighteen

homers, catching the attention of Tiger manager Bob Scheffing, who wanted to see what Norm could do over a whole season. The following spring, Scheffing tried to take the pressure off Norm by telling him flat out, "You're my first baseman." Scheffing had a strong feeling that Norm Cash was about to break out. When photographers were taking pictures of Kaline and Colavito, Scheffing scolded them for ignoring Cash. Who's that, asked the photographers. "Oh," said Scheffing, "he just might be the next American League batting champion."

Cash responded to Scheffing's confidence with the kind of year that few players have ever had in the last forty years; only a Williams or a Mantle hit for that kind of power and average. He hit line drives to all fields, betraying no weakness whatsover. Pitchers tested him, knocking him down, and he got up and hit four-baggers. Detroit fans hung banners in the stands—"Who Needs Money? We've Got Cash!" For a while it looked like it might be a Triple Crown season, until Maris and Mantle pulled away in the home run department.

In June of '61, Cash made an appearance in my suburb of Oak Park, Michigan, at a small shopping mall where he and Al Kaline signed baseballs. The Tigers were hot, they were neck-and-neck with the Yankees and about to go to New York for a midsummer series. In 1961, before the Beatles, I was not accustomed to being part of a surging youth mob. The little mall was so overrun with kids that a plate glass window almost caved in.

After a near-suffocating hour wait, I met Kaline and Cash. They were tan, trim, crew-cutted, in glowing mid-season form. I thought that they looked like the astronauts. Norm was friendly and seemed to be enjoying himself a great deal.

Demands on him were tremendous for personal appearances that season, and he tried to meet all of the requests. One afternoon he went to a bowling alley, a pizza restaurant, a drawing for a color TV set, and when he arrived at the ballpark, he had blurred vision. Kids rang his doorbell from dawn till dusk. Norm just couldn't say no, and that's why some think he didn't hit as well that year at home as on the road. He hit .331 in Tiger Stadium, a hitter's park, but hit .388 on the road!

He did love hitting in Tiger Stadium. In 1961, he hit his first of four lifetime shots completely out of the park, over the right field roof and onto Trumbull Avenue. And the fans responded to the roof shots, exciting as they were. He was dubbed "Stormin' Norman" and liked the nickname as much as hitting the ball up on the roof. He hit a changeup from the Red Sox' Don Schwall that wound up striking a police tow truck. It was a longer home run than any ever hit in Tiger Stadium, farther than the shots of Ruth or Gehrig or Williams or Mantle. (Only Reggie Jackson's blast in the '71 All-Star Game might have gone farther, but it hit a light tower.)

I was in attendance for one of the roof shots, this one hit off of Eli Grba, the Angels right-hander with the oversized glasses that made him look like a Kafkaesque bug. The noise is what I remember the most: there was no crack of the bat; it was more like an explosion. At Lakeland, I asked Al Kaline where Cash's power came from. "He had big huge hands, monstrous hands, Arnold Palmer hands," said Kaline, "really wide and thick fingers, you just shake hands with him, it was like grabbing a log or something. He was just an awful strong person. He had the short arms. You look at his body and he was put together like a rock."

There is no doubting that Norman Cash was one strong son of a gun. At six feet tall and 185 pounds, he was drafted as a halfback by the Chicago Bears after playing at Sul Ross State. But it wasn't playing football that toughened him up. Cash developed his wrists working a hoe. His father, Bandy Cash, had a farm in Justiceburg, Texas, a town sometimes referred to as a wide place in the road near Lubbock.

"My dad's life was hard work and it was my job to help him," Norm said in looking back. "He had 250 acres of fertile land and we grew cotton on 200 acres. I drove a tractor from the time I was ten. Sometimes I drove it ten to twelve hours."

For the 1961 season, Cash's final numbers were 41 homers,

132 RBIs, and an eye-popping .361 average. (The Tigers wound up winning 101 games but the Yankees hit 240 team homers and won 109.) "I remember having dinner with Norm the last day of the season that he won the batting title," Kaline said, "and what a great year it was, the greatest I've ever seen. But I went through it myself (Kaline hit .340 at the age of twenty), and I said, 'Norm, it's going to be a lot different next year. They'll be more conscious of you.' He said, 'No, I'm a good hitter and I'll always be able to hit.' I said, "I know you're a good hitter but you have to be ready for next year.' "

What Norm would find out is that unless your name is Ted Williams or Stan Musial, it's a dangerous thing to hit .361. "It was a dream year, '61," Cash would later acknowledge. "I knew it was a freakish year and so did everyone else. I accepted that fact but although a lot of people said they did, they really didn't. They expected me to do it again every year since then, or at least come close to it."

As the '62 season began, Norm hit a bunch of homers, but the base hits weren't falling, and his average plummeted. He wound up with thirty-nine homers, but only hit .243, the biggest average drop ever for a batting champion.

"I think Norm definitely changed his philosophy on hitting after his first year," Kaline said. "He wanted to be a home run hitter. He liked the attention that he got from hitting the ball up on the roof and hitting long home runs. And he liked that nickname, Stormin' Norman. He got off to a bad start and he just said, 'Well, I'm going to hit thirty homers and that'll be good enough.' "

Considering the ease with which he powered forty-one homers by swinging to all fields, Cash had geared up for better power numbers. "I guess I remembered how Roger Maris hit sixty-one," Cash reflected. "I guess I figured I might take a run at the record. It was a mistake."

Mistake or not, it was the kind of hitter that Cash developed into, a dead-pull hitter. By the time Bill Freehan joined the Tigers in '63, he almost never saw Cash hit to the opposite field. "He couldn't hit the ball on the other side of second base," said Freehan. "I never saw him hit any shots to left field by design, it was only because his bat was slow that day. The trouble is Tiger Stadium can get you like that, the same way Fenway can."

"I think part of the problem," said teammate Jim Northrup, "was that they didn't give him much of a raise for the batting championship, at least according to him. And then he figured, well, if they're going to pay for the home runs and not the batting average, that's what I'm going to go for, and that's exactly what he did. I know he told me that. I asked him why he tried to pull so much when he could hit the ball everywhere, and he said, 'Hey, they don't pay for average, they pay for home runs. If that's what they want, that's what they're going to get.' That's what they got, but it's a shame, because Norman was a better hitter than that."

Whitey Herzog played on the Tigers in 1963 and he said Norm was taking pitches on the outside corner that he used to swat for doubles and come back to the bench muttering about pitches being on the black. Cash himself knew it was true because his father told him he was taking too many pitches, and his father, according to Cash, "didn't know squat about baseball."

It was in that trying 1962 season that Cash suffered through a few of the hitting slumps that would dog him throughout his career and initiate the full-throated booing of many Detroit fans. His being prone to slumps and striking out a lot had something to do with the booing, but at times the catcalls got very intense. Cash was booed like few players of his stature, probably more than any Tiger in recent history except for Willie (now known as Guillermo in a last-ditch change of identity) Hernandez, who had his own dream year with its attendant problems. People who think you can walk on water stop throwing you the life preservers.

There was another curious element to the booing—Cash's facial expressions. Cash had that chipmunk grin with apple cheeks (they used to call him "Melvin" in the clubhouse) and when he struck out, the home fans around the plate area and dugout would see him grimacing and thought he was laughing about it. Team-mates Kaline, Freehan, Dick Tracewski, and Mike Rourke all said the same thing, that the fans near home plate and the dugout thought he was laughing about striking out.

At Kaline explained, "Norm would joke around on the field, and he had this funny look, where his teeth would always show, and they thought he was laughing when he struck out. I think people didn't understand him and thought he wasn't trying. But that was just his normal look."

Sometimes it got to Cash, when he would smash his bat in splinters on the top of the dugout, or bow to the crowd in a savage parody of himself under the hail of boos. Then he would press in front of the home fans and lose all resemblance to a big league hitter. But for the most part, he kept his feelings about it inside. "He never let it show," said Kaline. "My locker was right next to him every year he was there, and he kept it inside of him. Norm's hearing wasn't so good, so maybe he didn't hear it a lot of the time." In fact, Norm maintained that when 50,000 people boo, he didn't really hear it. "But when one or two guys get on your back, they drive you nuts."

Bill Freehan used to watch Cash come back to the bench after being punched out in the midst of a long slump. "When a guy is struggling, it's interesting to watch how he'll handle it. None of us are ecstatic when you screw up in front of 80 million people. Cash would fire his bat down and sit down next to you, you're really feeling for him, and he says, 'You know, I was lookin' at my wife comin' in here, and even she was booing me.' He was always on the lookout for taking himself too seriously."

But he didn't slough off all the slings and arrows so easily, according to Freehan and Northrup. Detroit sportswriter Joe Falls wrote an article about Cash's demise as a ballplayer in 1962, and Cash saved it. "Norman was beautiful," recalled Freehan. "He kept an article by Falls pinned to the inside of his hat for two or three years. He kept it in there as a reminder. He didn't speak to Falls for a year."

"Joe Falls," said Northrup, "is the guy that turned the fans against Norm Cash and got the fans booing. He jumped all over Norman and criticized him heavily because of the year he was having and Norm didn't speak to him for a number of years. They didn't like each other very much, and Norm thought it was unfair."

It was hard to put a damper on Cash, one of the great characters of '60s American League baseball, who in later years became a bona fide favorite of the Detroit fans. Ernie Harwell remembered Norman wearing his oversized battery-operated wiper-blade sunglasses. In the field, Cash would run after a ball yelling, "I got it . . . I hope." Others recalled the time he stole second base during a rain delay. Once he signaled time out when he was caught hopelessly in a rundown. (They always show Willie Stargell doing this in Major League Baseball's video clips, but it was Norman who did it first.)

The classic Norm Cash story is probably the time he came up to bat with two out in the ninth as the last man when Nolan Ryan was throwing his first of two no-hitters in 1973. Cash took a leg off a table in the clubhouse and came up to the plate with it. Umpire Ron Luciano didn't notice at first. So Cash had to ask him if he could bat with this here table leg, considering he couldn't hit Ryan with a bat. Despite this profound attempt to break his concentration, Ryan got the last out.

Cash admired the great standup comedians, and fancied himself as an entertainer who liked to give the fans a little something extra. While he was always quick with a homespun quip, he was at his best as a physical comic, a man in perpetual motion. You could see him either tap dancing in his spikes on the dugout floor, or bouncing his bat on the ground and catching it like Fred Astaire would his cane. Running, he resembled a fire hydrant on the loose, and his swaggering bow-legged walk brought to mind both Gary Cooper and Popeye.

As pitcher Gary Peters remembered Cash from his days with Chicago, "He just enjoyed life so much." Peters used to go with Norm on hunting trips with Joe Horlen and Dave Nicholson. Norm also fished, golfed, fenced, water-skied, and rode horseback in addition to being a fine dancer and ukelele player. As Whitey Herzog put it, "There was nothing Norm Cash couldn't do."

Freehan remembers joining the Tigers, having grown up in downtown Detroit and never having heard country-and-western music, and being thrown in the middle of all these guys on the team from Oklahoma and Texas. "Cash and Frank Lary used to take out their guitars and I never had so much fun in my life." Lary used to go up onstage with Eddie Arnold at the Grand Ole Opry when he was near Nashville, and Cash could sing like Johnny Cash with adenoids.

Norm's philosophy in a nutshell: "If you can get somebody to laughing, it gets their mind off what's bothering them. It makes them a better ballplayer, it makes them looser." Norm could keep you loose all right. Once, during a trip to California, Cash arranged to have seventeen ballplayers steal a P-51 fighter plane, decorated with the trademark gaping mouth and ferocious teeth, from the front of an art museum. They were spotted running the plane down a side street, trying to start it up.

Later in his career, Cash realized that he was one of a vanishing breed. "I think that's one thing baseball has lost," he observed. "When I broke in in 1959 we had the Jimmy Piersalls, the funny guys. The fans used to come out just to see what funny thing they'd do. I think they get a big kick out of some of the things I do. I know I hear a big roar when I do something funny sometimes, so they must enjoy that type of thing. That's just my makeup. You can't be standing out there in the bottom of the ninth with the bases loaded thinking 'I hope he doesn't hit it to me.' You can't think that way. If you catch it, you catch it, and if you miss it, you miss it. You can't worry about things like that."

"I've had the same attitude all my life," Norm used to say jokingly, " . . . bad." When he wasn't hitting, people would think he wasn't taking the game seriously, but everyone has their own way of ridding themselves of nervous tension, and Norm's way was to have a good time. He always said that when the game wasn't fun anymore, he would quit.

Norm Cash liked to drink now and then. He was close with

the Butsicaris brothers who ran the Lindell Athletic Club, and for a time he received his mail at the legendary Detroit sports bar. Whitey Herzog roomed with Cash one season, and he told me that he just roomed with his suitcase, he never saw him. "It was just like having your own room," he said.

Cash liked the macho image of the hard-living player who could tough it out and play no matter how he was feeling. The Tigers, being like any other major-league team, had their share of heavy drinkers on their roster. Freehan and Aguirre both talked about two Tigers who used to polish off a bottle of vodka between them after every game. But Kaline maintained that Norm was "a moderate drinker at best. He used to fool everybody. He used to drink a lot of orange juice. He would nurse his drinks for quite a while. Even though he'd be at a party for a long time, he wouldn't drink that much. He'd always have a glass in his hand, but it wasn't necessarily always a drink. Norman was a lot smarter than people gave him credit for, he took better care of himself than people thought. He liked the impression of being a macho type guy who could play when he wasn't feeling good. Norm always said, 'If you're gonna dance, you gotta pay the fiddler.' Norm loved to play the game. I was amazed sometimes to see that Norm was able to play the following day."

Jim Northrup agreed that Cash's drinking was overrated. "I don't think Norm drank as much while he was playing as everybody said he did. He loved having the reputation of being a party boy who was always ready to party, and he was a honky-tonker, he loved going to c-and-w bars, but he wasn't a drunk. He didn't get sloshed drunk so that he was bobbing and weaving. Norman monitored his drinking very well."

General Manager Jim Campbell called Cash "one of a kind." "He could beat on that body of his and still come out and play. Norm was the kind who could bounce back." "Pain was nothing to Norm," Kaline said. "He just felt that he had to be in the lineup. That was what he was paid to do and he didn't want to let his teammates down." This is what teammates like Kaline and Tony Taylor really appreciated—that Norm could have a broken finger and still go out and give it everything he had.

The fact that he was a great competitor was obscured somewhat by his reputation as a clown, but Cash worked very hard at the game of baseball. When he first came up, he was not a good fielder, but took so many ground balls that he wound up leading the league in fielding percentage. He developed a unique way of catching foul pops behind his head, a style others have adopted. He did the little things like pulling his foot masterfully just as the throw reached him at first, perfecting the first baseman's sweet cheat the way Gil Hodges and Keith Hernandez did. I was there one day when he pulled the hidden ball trick on the Indians' Chico Salmon.

Cash was always looking for a little edge, a search that led him to corking his bat. He told few about it, but he knew in that era that his friend Kaline was not about to be traded to another team, so he let him in on his bat tampering. "Norm showed me," Kaline said. "He said, 'Look at this, they can't even tell. I had somebody check my bat, they couldn't even tell.' Norman would come in and say, 'You want me to do one for you? Man, that ball really jumps off your bat.' I'd say no. He had tools and everything to work with. He had someone else at Tiger Stadium do it for him originally, and then he learned how to do it himself. He would use the corked bat if he got on a hot streak with it, but didn't do it all the time. He liked corking because it made the game more fun for him, and he liked getting an edge, he was very competitive." Umpire Ron Luciano said that Norm tapped his bat on the plate one day and the end fell right off. But the umpires liked Norm, and none of them said anything.

Cash didn't change his approach to the game when he got to the World Series with the Tigers in 1968. He was the last strikeout victim in Gibson's seventeen-strikeout performance in Game One. Afterwards he said, "Where would Gibson be without me? I'm the one that broke the strikeout record for him. Hell, I knew that if I let him get me in the ninth, I'd get my picture in every paper in the country as the guy he struck out for the record."

Cash tried to keep the team loose, but when the Cardinals went up 3–1 in the Series, it was Cash, according to Kaline, who was walking around saying, "We won a lot of games in the ninth this year, let's get 'em to the seventh game, and we'll beat 'em. These guys are loose now, but if we get 'em to the seventh game they won't be quite as loose, and we'll beat Gibson."

The Tigers won in a fabled comeback in Game Five, then broke Series records with a ten-run inning in Game Six, during which Cash tied a World Series mark with six consecutive hits. The Tigers got their seventh game meeting with Gibson, which went scoreless into the seventh inning when, with two out and none on, Norm Cash started the decisive rally with a single. He wound up leading the Tigers with a .385 average in the Series.

When I asked Al Kaline what the World Series meant to Norm Cash, he said, "What meant the most to Norm was all the guys getting together and having a bunch of laughs. Norm liked to have a good time with all the guys, he was a party guy and he just liked to have everybody around."

Jim Campbell is frequently asked to compare the '68 World Championship with '84. "A ball club was different then than it is now," he said. "There were a lot of close friends on that club. Nowadays guys pretty much go their own way. They're married, and have their agents. When they ask me what was sweeter, the '84 Championship or the '68 Championship, you just get to know the '68 guys better. The group of guys now, their agents don't want them to come to the office, and they don't even mingle with each other, I don't think. They might think they're close to each other but they don't know what they're talking about, because I've been there and seen it. Back in those days, they ran together more, you might say."

As Norm Cash moved closer to the end of his playing days, every slump became a crisis where he would be written off as washed up. "Every year they wanted to replace him," Jim Northrup recalled, "but every year they were talking about replacing thirty to thirty-five home runs and eighty-five to a hundred RBIs no matter what his average was, and they looked at the talent that they had, and nobody could do it. So it was a big joke in spring training that he supposedly had to fight for his job."

Cash knew that as long as he didn't lose the reflexes in his wrists, he could still play. He was one of those players who swore they would have to tear the uniform off him. "I'm not going to quit baseball to go to work," he said. Billy Martin came to manage the Tigers in 1971 and became close with Cash. That was the year that Cash won his second Comeback Player of the Year award, causing him to wonder "How many comebacks can there be in one career?" But he was proud, at the age of thirty-seven, to beat out Harmon Killebrew and Boog Powell for *The Sporting News* first-base slot chosen by the players. His last goal before retiring was to hit 300 home runs, and he wound up with 377.

In 1972, he knew the end was near. "It's wonderful to have been able to do what you love and get paid for it. It's a great life— the fun, the money, the games, the friends. It'll be over one of these days, I know that."

In 1974, he was honored at Norm Cash Day, there with his children and his second wife, Dorothy. According to Dick Tracewski, Cash met her the night of the Tigers' pennant-winning celebration in Dearborn, and they married a few years later. His first wife, Myrta, whom he married in 1954, had been Norm's opposite, quiet, a schoolteacher. "Dorothy and Norm were very compatible," said Al Kaline. "They liked to laugh and have a good time. They liked to play golf, go out fishing, go dancing to c-and-w bars, I guess they were very happy."

On Norm Cash Day, Cash went 0–4. He would have loved to hit one out, but he got a chance to make the crowd laugh once more. When he walked out to the ovation from 43,000, he pretended to trip over the foul line. He broke out in a big grin when the Detroit writers gave him one of his own bats, drilled full of holes as a reminder that the thirty-eight-year-old Cash had struck out more than any Tiger who ever lived. But Mantle struck out a lot, and so did Reggie Jackson. Cash stepped up to the mike and told the crowd that he never expected the Tigers to give him a day "unless it was a day to get out of town." He made it very clear how he wanted to be remembered by the fans, as a guy who made them laugh once upon a time, way back when.

Cash seldom blew his own horn as a player. "I'm not the kind of ballplayer that has to read about himself to think he's doing a good job. I know when I'm doing the job." When he was through, only Hank Greenberg and Al Kaline had hit more home runs for the Tigers. Between 1961 and 1972, he hit twenty homers in eleven of twelve seasons. He was a four-time All-Star, but there were subtle reasons that he was, as Kaline said, "the most underrated player I ever played with."

Cash did have a reputation as a guy who liked to have a good time. Jim Northrup thought a lot of people misunderstood that Cash had fun playing baseball, and that it didn't mean he wasn't putting out as much as anyone else. Another reason for Cash being neglected is that he played somewhat in the shadow of Kaline. Some would cite his low batting averages, but when Cash hit .263 in 1968, the league was only hitting .233. (Being thirty points over the league average today makes you about a .290 hitter.) Plus, although his power numbers were plenty impressive, he produced despite only 400 or so at-bats because of injuries and drawing a lot of walks.

When Cash finished his playing days, he became a representative for auto parts suppliers and did very well for a time, although he yearned to get back in baseball. He had a short fling as a color man for ABC's "Monday Night Baseball," but only lasted a year. He suffered a stroke in 1979, but recovered and joined Hank Aguirre as color announcer for ON-TV, broadcasting home Tiger games on cable television. ON-TV folded in 1982, but Tigers owner John Fetzer started PASS-TV to broadcast Tiger games. Cash wanted that job badly, but was passed over.

When the auto industry was turned upside down by foreign

competition in the late '70s and early '80s, Cash experienced a down time financially. When times were hard, he kept to himself, not wanting to burden anyone with his problems. On Saturday night, October 11, 1986, Cash left a bar on Beaver Island in northern Michigan, returning to his boat to spend the night. When his wife couldn't find him, she enlisted some help in looking for him and on Sunday morning one of them spotted a human form lying face up on the lake floor where the water was fifteen feet deep, twenty feet away from his boat, the *Stormin' Norman*. The glasses he wore were still on his face, and he was still wearing his cowboy boots. There was no evidence that he had hit his head, only that he fell from the dock and couldn't pull himself out of the water.

As sorry an end as this was, it was compounded a few months later when Norm's adopted college-age son, Jay, committed suicide by eating rat poison. "He was a great kid," said Jim Northrup. "I saw him at the funeral and thought he was doing really fine. Jay was always a nice kid, and fun to talk to, and he knew my children real well. We had a long discussion about the kids, and who was doing what, and less than a month later, he was gone. It was a big surprise to me. I never knew he had any problems of any kind. He didn't seem to be depressed or despondent to me."

Before and after the funeral, Jay had stayed with the Kalines. "He was really a strange kid as far as getting something out of him," said Kaline. "He left school because he wanted to do some other things. He got in late the night of the funeral and I stayed up because I didn't know whether he'd be able to find my house at night, and I sat up and talked to him. He said he hadn't seen much of his father in the last year or so. And the last time that he saw Norm wasn't a happy time for him. I guess they had an argument. He said he loved his father a lot and wished he could have been a lot closer to him. Jay was a very quiet kid, he kept a lot inside, maybe too much inside."

Cash's wife Dorothy asked Al Kaline to give the eulogy. Despite being a broadcaster for the Tigers, Kaline doesn't like standing up in front of people to begin with; for him it was the hardest thing he had ever had to do. As Jim Northrup summed it up, "Kaline and myself and Freehan and Stanley, we were all very close to Norman, and it was a big loss for all of us. Very sad." Many came to the funeral, former teammates and a lot of fans who felt that they knew Norm Cash. Kaline spoke of the good times they had together. "When people see first basemen running down the first base line and catching the ball over their shoulders," he said, "I hope they'll remember Stormin' Norman Cash."

Remembering Bird

*S*o many amazing stories in baseball, as in life, begin with a knock on the door. That's how it started for Mark Fidrych, who was home watching television that day in 1974 when he answered the door, not knowing that his very own Magical Mystery Tour was just beginning. At the time he was pumping gas in Worcester, Massachusetts, a job that agreed with him because he didn't have to get a haircut.

The scout, Jack Cusick, had seen Fidrych throw one pitch. His high school coach had moved Fidrych in from the outfield to pitch to one batter. Fidrych threw a slider and got a ground out, and on the basis of that pitch, the scout told Fidrych that he'd like to sign him for the Tigers. That was on a Saturday, and Fidrych left his job at the gas station and was in Florida on Monday.

He got $10,000 and a $3,000 bonus, enough to pay off a loan his father took out for him, with a little left over to get himself a good stereo. He was ready to enroll in college in New Mexico, having found a school that didn't ask to look at his SAT scores, but his father Paul advised him that he could always go to school in a year or two if things didn't work out in baseball.

He was sent to Bristol in the Appalachian League, where he was 3–0, worked his way through the Florida State League, the Southern League, and then in the American Association at Evansville he sparkled with a 4–1 record and a 1.59 earned-run average in 1975.

In the minors, Fidrych was doing all the things that would later create a sensation in the major leagues, including talking to the ball before he went into his windup. He was actually talking to himself, but it looked strange, and brought forth some bench jockeying. But, as his minor league manager Stubby Overmire noted, even then it became friendly wisecracking, because the players on the other teams grew to enjoy watching him pitch.

He came down with the Tigers for spring training in 1976. To make pocket money he got permission to set up a car-wash strip in the parking lot. He made the roster five days before the season when the Tigers' starting staff fell apart. On the night he found out he was going north with the team, he celebrated by taking a girl onto the field at Joker Marchant Stadium and having intercourse with her on the side of the pitching mound, to show her where he worked.

Fidrych at that time was, by his own admission, a "supergrub," and Tiger general manager Jim Campbell had to take him to get some clothes so he could dress in something more than T-shirts and cutoffs. They finally settled on a compromise, where Bird could wear a T-shirt if it had a print on it. Campbell didn't really want to change him in any way. While Campbell generally turned up his nose at anything flashy, from the first time he saw the Bird, he said, "Boy, I hope no one ever changes his style, I hope he doesn't change a thing."

The first time Fidrych came into a major-league game he only threw two pitches before he hung a slider and Don Baylor beat him. Then he got his first start in May of 1976 against the Indians, and pitched no-hit ball for six innings, finishing with a two-hit, 2–1 win. That would have been enough, but he was also down on his hands and knees manicuring and landscaping the mound, running around to congratulate fielders after they made a good play, and catching stray hot dog wrappers. And of course he did appear to be talking to the ball.

That afternoon at Tiger Stadium, which steadily filled up with fans who heard what was going on by radio and were lured to the park, Fidrych was surrounded by the kind of excitement born of being witness to a very special event. He sprinted on and off the field between innings and after every out he strutted around like a mad stork on the balls of his feet, long curls bouncing as his head bobbed like an excited turkey, calling for the ball back. He had his own style, and was into his own moves, which were definitely ornithological. When he got in a groove, he would flap his arms and shriek like a bird, a gawky display resembling a punch-drunk pelican trying to take wing.

As he continued to pitch that year, assorted idiosyncrasies would come to light. For one thing, every time somebody got a hit off the Bird, he discarded the offensive ball, throwing it back to the umpire. "In my mind, if the ball has a hit in it," he said, "I want the ball to get back in the bag and goof around with the other balls, I want it to talk to the other balls, let the other balls beat the heck out of him and smarten him up, so the next time he comes out he'll be a pop-up."

The Bird was not trying to be a hot dog or a showoff, he was just so young and unaffected and focused on the task at hand that he appeared almost childlike. He went out to warm up one time and realized he hadn't put on his protective cup, so he just dropped his drawers in front of the crowd and put it in place, like a kid would do in a sandbox.

Fidrych won seven of eight decisions, and the Tigers, a pretty woeful club at the time, were coming off a moderately successful West Coast road swing when they came home to play Billy Martin's first-place Yankees in a game to be telecast on ABC's "Monday Night Baseball." Thurman Munson of the Yankees heard about the Bird's antics and called him bush: "Tell that guy," he said, "that if he pulls that shit in New York we'll blow his ass out of town." At the time, Fidrych only cared that his teammates didn't think he was bush, and besides, he really didn't know who Thurman Munson was, anyway.

Before the telecast, producer Don Ohlmeyer was going to open the show with pictures of the Yankee starter, Ken Holtzman. Warner Wolf told him that he was missing a giant story in Fidrych, but Chet Forte and Ohlmeyer were just not aware of him. They caught up with the story in due time, because this was the Bird's date with destiny.

The Tigers took a 2–0 lead in the first on a homer by Rusty Staub and the Yankees made it 2–1 in the second on a homer by Elrod Hendricks. It was the last ball the Yankees would hit hard off the Bird all night, and one of the few they got out of the infield. It was a totally virtuoso and exciting performance, a game that made Fidrych into a national folk hero. What came through the cameras and spilled into living rooms all over the country was the sight of more than a fine young pitcher. Here was someone who pitched not because he could make $350,000 a year doing it, but because he loved doing it.

"The Monday night game, that's what made him. What was so impressive," recalled his manager Ralph Houk, "was that he didn't disappoint anyone. He went out there and showed a lot of courage. He very easily could have succumbed to the pressure. The Yankees were all on him the whole game, hollering 'showboat' and all that, until about the fifth inning when they realized they weren't going to hit him like they thought they were. When they found out that he was for real, that's why they liked him."

For the Detroit fans, Fidrych's games became more like rock concerts than baseball games. After the endless chants of "Go, Bird, Go," and the final out, the whole crowd would stay and chant and stamp their feet until he came out of the dugout. Fidrych tried to get the team to go out with him, but finally one night after beating Baltimore, two security guards grabbed him and pulled him out in full view before a capacity crowd, and they responded with a long standing ovation.

It became customary after the Bird's starts in Detroit for him to circle the field acknowledging the crowd. What has become a rather perfunctory "curtain call" in the major leagues today began on those nights with the Bird, when it was magical, electric, emotional, and even partly religious—that's how deep the communion and involvement that he inspired was. All the Bird could say was, "I'm loving it, I'm just loving it."

"It's exhilarating being out there when he pitches," said Rusty Staub. "It's hard not to be up. There's an electricity he brings out in everybody. Everyone can see the enthusiasm in Mark. He brings out the exuberance and youth in everybody. He's the most exciting thing I've ever seen. I've never seen a city turn on like this. I've seen Tommy Seaver go out there and mow 'em down but I've never seen anybody electrify the fans like this."

"It was exciting for me when I knew it was his time to pitch," said Houk. "It was one of the most exciting things I'd ever seen. For a night game, I'd get there at two o'clock, and there were all those people lining up for tickets and selling birds and all those wacky things. It was a great thrill. I can't say too much about it."

In Fidrych's twenty-nine starts, he pitched in front of over 900,000 fans. Houk would get letters and calls from general managers asking when he was going to pitch in their park so they could sell out, too. But Houk wouldn't change Fidrych's pitching day, every fifth day, and so he inevitably got some people mad.

The Tigers were grossing six times as much money every time he pitched than they were paying Bird for the entire season, which didn't bother Fidrych. "I don't care about that," he said. "Why change something when it's going good? It's great just to be free like this, not worrying about money." But the Michigan State Legislature was worrying about it, and passed a resolution that his salary should be raised above the major league minimum.

It all happened at warp speed. As Brooks Robinson said, "The first time we came to Detroit no one had heard of Fidrych. When we came back they were ready to make him the mayor." Fidrych's fame grew so exponentially that many looked for reasons beyond his being a talented, lovable, and funny young guy.

Detroit itself was experiencing a real down time with all of its major sports teams, and the Bird was one of the few things the city's sports fans had to cheer about. Nineteen seventy-six was the Year of the Free Agent, featuring widespread lawsuits. In a season of obvious professionals, he was the obvious amateur, a kid who got the national spotlight turned on him and said he wanted to drive a truck for a living. And, unlike Bill Lee, the Bird was a safe, nonpolitical kind of flake who alienated no one. He was a phenomenon.

Everyone in the media rushed to capture on videotape and in print the charm and naivete of the Bird, and he handled this onslaught one day a time with a naturalness that was just amazing. Fidrych didn't have a phony bone in his whole body, and that's a big reason that his impact was so immediate, and why he was voted the most popular person in the world in a Bicentennial poll. As Bill Veeck told Ernie Harwell, "If someone had tried to stage Fidrych, they would have fallen flat. It would have looked artificial." Vida Blue, who went through a media blitz of his own, said, "He seems to enjoy the attention. I didn't. He'll make it because people think he's crazy. They knew I was serious."

By the All-Star break, Fidrych was 9–2, with ten complete games in eleven starts, and a 1.78 ERA. In both of his losses, the Tigers were shut out. By the end of the year he had won nineteen games for the Tigers, more than any Detroit rookie in sixty-eight seasons. His ERA of 2.34 was the lowest in both leagues for starting pitchers. He completed twenty-four games out of twenty-nine starts and had a 1.000 fielding percentage as well. He was naturally voted the Tiger Rookie of the Year by Detroit sportswriters and broadcasters, and finished second in the Cy Young Award voting behind Jim Palmer.

Fidrych was so successful as a pitcher because everything he threw was down, down, down. George Brett said the first eight times he faced Fidrych, he didn't see one ball above the waist. "I wouldn't call him a power pitcher," Ralph Houk told me. "We didn't really keep guns in those days, but at times he threw close to ninety. It wasn't his overpowering fastball, though, it was his control and the movement on the ball. His ball always did something. It usually sank. He had a little slider that wasn't too bad, and he would spot it. But his control was unbelievable. He could throw a ball in an area of about a foot, and you just couldn't lay off of it, and when it would sink it was almost an unhittable pitch.

"But he was an amazing young man, and in some ways much different than people thought he was. People thought that he just went out and pitched, but he was a very serious man during the ball game, and very serious on the day he pitched. He'd come into my office and discuss the hitters, which ones have power, which ones liked to run, but I never messed with Mark about how to pitch a hitter, because he only had one way to pitch.

"He didn't know what pressure was. When he got to that park, he knew everybody expected him to have a big day, and he usually had one. And I think our ball club played better behind him, because they thought every ball was going to be hit, because he just threw strike strike strike strike. He never tried to set hitters up, he just went after 'em. He very seldom went to three balls on anyone. For a young pitcher, he was a great finisher. You don't find many that when you get into the eighth inning, you know that you're going to win."

Success didn't change Mark Fidrych. He was still pumping his own gas, checking his own oil. He lived austerely in an apartment with no phone. "Sometimes I get lazy and let the dishes stack up," he said. "But they don't get stacked up too high. I've only got four dishes." He would get home and find people waiting on his doorstep, or there'd be a girl singing outside his window, so he had to move to another building with twenty-four-hour security, but somehow he took it all in stride.

He would go out on the town with friend and teammate Dave Rozema, who remembered Bird as a caution on the dance floor.

"He could go on for hours," said Rozema. "We'd go out dancing and he did the wildest, weirdest dancing I'd ever seen in my life. No rhythm, just go out there and start dancing, drink beer on the dance floor, and dance with some girl who was dancing with someone else, just say, 'I want to dance with her.' "

Fidrych and his buddies had invented a dance step back in Massachusetts called "The Fried Egg." "We lay down on our backs and roll back and forth and bump into each other," said Fidrych. "The people clapped and thought it was great, but the bouncer asked us to leave."

Rozema remembered how in spring training the Bird would open up his room to the team at the Holiday Inn in Lakeland, and bring in davenports and chairs and grill up fish and steaks and his prized steamed vegetables. "He liked his vegetables and he liked his beer," he said. "He got a stereo that covered a whole wall of his apartment, and he'd get out his frozen mugs for the beer and just be space truckin'."

When the 1976 season ended, Tiger owner John Fetzer awarded Fidrych a substantial lump-sum bonus, and then, in the age of agents, six-figure salaries, and heated, drawn-out contract debates, Fidrych and his father hammered out a three-year contract with Jim Campbell in less than half an hour. "I looked at my father," said Fidrych, "he gave me a signal that it was okay, and that was it. An agent probably could have gotten me more money but maybe then I wouldn't have been happy. I got what I wanted. Hey, I'm happy.

"Up here," he explained, "I've got more spikes than I know what to do with, and I don't even have to buy them. Same with my gloves. You know what's really neat about playing in the big leagues? It's playing on all these good fields. In high school I played on fields that had weeds in the infield. Here they cut the weeds. It's neat to see fields that are kept up like that."

In February of the following year, Fidrych was in spring training shagging flies in the outfield with Rusty Staub when he hyperextended his knee. Ten days later, he underwent surgery at Henry Ford Hospital to repair a torn cartilage in his knee. Ten days after he returned from the disabled list, his right shoulder popped, and the nightmare began.

In the next few years he would try doctors, osteopaths, chiropractors, hypnotists, and psychologists. He took long rests and at other times tried to pitch through the pain. He gulped aspirin and anti-inflammation pills, and rubbed all sorts of strange concoctions on his arm. He proved a couple of doctors wrong by continuing to pitch, but most of the next six years were spent in the minors. The last year and a half was spent on Boston's Triple A team in Pawtucket under Joe Morgan, who said Bird was the same at the end as he was at the beginning. "He never complained," said Morgan.

Morgan recalled the night that Fidrych pitched against Righetti, Pawtucket against Columbus, and that night Fidrych won and ended the game with a three-pitch strikeout of Butch Hobson that made Morgan wonder, as many had, why he couldn't throw like that more often. The maddening part of his arm trouble was that there were these glimmers of hope. But his control and velocity remained inconsistent, and in June of 1983, about to be given his release, he retired.

The difficult adjustment that all professional athletes must face was, in Fidrych's case, compounded by dreams of what could have been. He had bought a farm in Northboro in 1977, and went to live there year-round with his parents. There were many times when he unavoidably wondered "Why me?" going through the dark nights of the soul that would turn anyone into a philosopher. "Life is a mystery," said Fidrych. "If you knew how things were going to turn out, it wouldn't be life." A few years ago, he married a local waitress and runs his farm and tends to his animals, although he is reluctant to describe himself as a farmer.

There are several theories on what happened to the Bird. Dave Rozema maintains it was the strain of the way he pitched that did him in. "Everybody's always saying, you should have seen that guy four years ago, he was throwing ninety-five. But when you throw so hard for so long, in high school and college and A ball, when you get to the big leagues, your arm just can't take it, it explodes, it just wears down.

"I say the man started twenty-nine games, he completed twenty-four. That's got to be one of the reasons, throwing so many innings, especially the way he threw. I'll throw a fastball, then I'll waste a pitch, not put too much on it. Forget wasting a pitch, he didn't have time to waste anything. Man, he was coming at you hard to get you out. I don't think the people would let him. If he got 2–0 on somebody it was like, 'C'mon, Mark, let's go.' From inning one to inning nine it was 'Go, Mark, Go,' and do that for a hundred pitches a game. The energy that people brought to it . . . I know why he probably had arm trouble, because people can pump you up so much that you overthrow, you get so involved."

Jack Morris first met the Bird in spring training of 1977. When the Bird was having his big year, Morris was pitching in the minors. "Ironically," said Morris, "he was the reason I got to the big leagues. When he got hurt the second time, in June of '77, I got called up, and I got my chance to pitch in the big leagues. Then he came back at the end of the year.

"He certainly did throw a lot of innings in his rookie year. But that leg injury had to hurt him. I've never had leg injuries, but I know there's no way you can pitch with bad legs, especially if you were a power pitcher the way the Bird was. Even though he threw sinkers and sliders, he still threw hard. And anytime you do that, you push off the mound very hard, which puts a lot of stress on the pushoff leg and the landing leg. I'm sure he favored his arm considerably when that happened, which is the reason he hurt it.

"The real question is why he didn't come around. I hurt my arm myself in 1977 and we went to three different doctors. I had the exact same thing, it was diagnosed exactly the same, as bursitis, tendinitis, and the rotator cuff injury. And I went to Puerto Rico the winter of '78–'79 and Bird was sent home to rest, and my arm came back. I was introduced to a weight program and I got some strength back in there and I was able to pitch through it.

"The biggest part with him was he never got over the pain. His mind never let him consciously pitch through the pain. In other words, I was in a state where I was hurtin', and your mind tells your body, 'Don't do it,' and you've got to eliminate that and pitch through a pain area until your arm builds strength, and then the pain goes away. I think in Mark's case the pain just never went away. Consequently his arm hurt so much that he couldn't pitch anymore.

"I have a tremendous amount of respect for the guy. I can understand what he was going through because I was going through the same thing. I remember those days—it's hard enough to pitch when you're healthy, when you're hurt it's almost impossible. You've got to concentrate more on the game than your body. And Bird worked as hard as anybody I've seen in the game to date. He did every bit of weights and he was in tremendous shape. He was a strong, strong person. People don't realize how strong he was. That's why it was a little disheartening for a lot of us as teammates, because we saw the desire he had to do everything he could to work through it, but his body just told him something else."

Ralph Houk doesn't believe it was the leg injury that led to the arm trouble because Bird threw several ball games after the leg injury and "he was the same old Fidrych" until his shoulder popped. Unlike Morris's arm injury, they never did find out what was wrong with Fidrych's rotator cuff. "If anybody could pitch through the pain," said Houk, "Mark would have. He got through the pain, but he just lost all his control."

Ten years after the arm trouble that Morris and Fidrych had, Morris has won more games than any pitcher in baseball in the 1980s, and for that Morris thanks his lucky stars. "Let's face it," said Morris, "if he was healthy he would still be pitching here today. And I would like to have been on the same rotation with that guy. We would have had some great pitching staffs. But it never happened.

"I liked the guy, he loved the game of baseball. He made the game fun. He was the first guy who was really a phenom, something different in the game. Fernando Valenzuela for one year had a taste of it. Dwight Gooden for one year had a taste of it. Roger Clemens never has, I know I've never had a taste of that. He had the whole city and the whole country excited about not only him but the game of baseball. It would be exciting to pitch in front of that many people, yeah, it would be great. In his case, it was a thing that really got him pumped up, and he knew he was the show, even if he didn't act like he knew."

Prince of Wales

*T*he first time I saw Jim Walewander, he was about to step into the batting cage at Lakeland, and I confessed that I really didn't know that much about him except for the fact that he liked the post–punk rock band called the Dead Milkmen. He took a swing and then said, "Neither do I."

More and more people are finding out things about Jim Walewander. He's been featured in *Sports Illustrated* as "Detroit's Frostiest Flake," and the Letterman people have called about his appearing on the show, although they didn't call again. The young man they call "Wales" is no publicity hound, but a few things he has said and done in his brief major-league career have garnered a fair amount of attention. His first quote to go national was uttered on the occasion of his first home run in the major leagues. The whole episode was like a fractured fairy tale.

Walewander listens to a lot of rock bands, some of which can be described as hardcore, Chicago bands like Green and Big Black, as well as more mainstream groups such as the Pogues and REM. (He saw REM in 1982 and especially enjoyed their rendition of "The 'Barney Miller' Theme.") He mentioned the Dead Milkmen to a reporter who knew he was interested in new music, and a relative of the Milkmen saw it and informed the band.

So when the Dead Milkmen were in town, having heard that Walewander was twisted enough to be one of their fans, they left tickets for him to catch their act in a Hamtramck lounge. Walewander reciprocated by inviting them to come to Tiger Stadium as his guests, a motley crew wearing fatigues with spike haircuts and rings in their ears and noses.

The Milkmen gave Wales an autographed album, and wrote on it, "To Jim . . . Satan is our master." The ever-affable Sparky Anderson met the Milkmen and just said, "Don't take no prisoners." Walewander was not supposed to start the ball game, but Lou Whitaker had a stiff back and he was inserted at second base. He had not been thinking about when he would hit his first major league home run, because he never expected to hit one. But lo and behold, that day he hit the facing of the second deck in right field off California's Willie Fraser. Moments later a long banner unfurled in the center field bleachers reading "Jim Walewander Fan Club." After the game, Walewander was kind of choked up. "The Dead Milkmen, my fan club, and my parents were all here. You couldn't ask for anything more."

After his epic homer, the Tigers allowed Walewander to put anything he wanted on the clubhouse stereo, so he pulled out the Dead Milkmen's album "Bucky Fellini" and treated his teammates to a few mellow selections such as "Bomb the Sewage Plant" and "Take Me to Your Specialist." (Soon his teammates were calling him "little David Bowie" or Sid Vicious, after the Sex Pistols' lead singer who OD'd.) Walewander now wears a Dead Milkmen T-shirt, which features a drawing of a smiling cow, with its eyes crossed. He says his apartment now resembles "a shrine to the Dead Milkmen," and the band, in turn, goes from town to town carrying around their new totem—Wales's baseball card.

Walewander took the game ball from his first-homer game and put it in the glove compartment of his car, with his first-hit ball. "When the glove compartment's full," he said, "I'll be able to buy a new car." The next day he was still being interviewed about his homer, as the national media became aware of the rare emergence of an eccentric new personality in the game. "I haven't been on TV that much since I was on 'Bozo the Clown' in sixth grade," he said. "But I never got the bean bag in the third hole."

Walewander was already a near-legend in the Tigers organization. After Kirk Gibson was down with the Triple-A Toledo team on injury rehab, he returned to the Tigers and told the ball club, "Wait 'till you meet this guy. He uses tin foil for drapes." (Someone who read about this sent him a much-treasured fan letter written on tin foil.) In Toledo, all Walewander had on the floor of his apartment was a blanket and a pillow. He ate his morning cereal from a dog dish. "I also had a nine-inch TV," he said, "but it had a bad picture tube and I could only watch it for five minutes at a time."

He developed a reputation for being flaky by playing eighteen holes in a celebrity golf tournament wearing combat boots and carrying only two clubs. He shot a 78. It's not like he has to try hard to court the bizarre. Things just seem to happen to him. He was sitting on the bench one day in the minors during a rain delay in Florida, just watching it pour by himself while his teammates huddled in the clubhouse. "I was leaning up in the corner against the drinking fountain, because it was the only dry spot in the dugout, and lightning hit and shot through the fences of the field and went up the drinking fountain and hit me in the back. I felt a pretty good shock. I ran into the locker room and said 'You guys are not going to believe this!'

"I've done stupid things," he freely admits. "There was a minor-league all-star game and it started to rain so me and this guy went to McDonald's to get some burgers and we came back and the game had started. Kevin Seitzer was playing third in that game so they had to move him to second base where I was supposed to start. Everybody knew where we were, but they couldn't get a hold of us. I had to run on the field half-dressed. The manager was pretty steamed."

Most of Wales's managers, however, have fallen in love with

the guy. Sparky Anderson certainly has. Sparky is fond of saying that Wales can't hit or play. When asked if there's a player he reminds him of, Sparky thought a while, and then said, "Me. I couldn't hit either." "Sparky sees a little bit of himself in me," acknowledges Walewander. "That's his problem, not mine."

But Walewander did put up some serious numbers throughout his high school, college, and minor-league career. A native of Harwood Heights, Illinois, he played high school ball at Maine South, and could never get enough of the game. He turned himself into a switch-hitter by using the play toy at home called "the Johnny Bench Batter," where you smack a ball around a pole on a tether. He also was a waterbug-style guard in basketball and a great dribbler who made the state championship game as a junior (he once played against Isaiah Thomas). But baseball was always his first love. In high school he batted .380 and stole 100 bases in 102 attempts.

He chose Iowa State University because of their highly competitive baseball program and their coaching staff. He had his speed going for him. Walewander was clocked at 3.8 seconds going to first base, and in his sophomore year set a Big Eight stolen base record by swiping forty-six bases, and only being thrown out twice. When he came to Iowa State, he only weighed 135 pounds. Weight lifting strengthened him, and in his junior year he hit .388 and only struck out twice in 162 at-bats.

Tiger scout George Bradley was attending the Big Eight playoffs in 1983 when he noticed Jim Walewander. Walewander stole second base three times. The fourth time he came up, the pitcher was a little annoyed and hit him in the knee. Walewander limped around home plate for a while, but now he was ticked off as well. He went down to first base and stole second again.

This gave George Bradley a gut feeling about Walewander. The Tigers selected him in the ninth round of the draft and offered him $7,500. Walewander tried to ask for more, but before he could get the words out of his mouth, they said he could take it or leave it, so he took it. "I could tell they wanted me real bad," he said.

In Walewander's first professional season, with Bristol in the Rookie League in 1983, he hit .319 and stole thirty-five bases. He was named the team's most valuable player. He played two years in Class A before moving up to Double A in 1986 at Glens Falls, New York. He got hurt there, recovered, and then found it odd that he wasn't playing much.

"I couldn't figure it out at first. I was ready to play but the manager, Bob Schaefer, wouldn't put me in any of the games. Then I realized that he thought I was one of the funniest guys in the world and kept me on the bench next to him during games so I could make him laugh. I finally just stopped talking to him, and I started playing again.

"I was in Double A and hit .246, which will get you nowhere fast. I was hurt the whole year, that's the reason they didn't release me. I had a bad hamstring and broke a finger. I hurt my back." Then Walewander got his big break in 1987, partly because he played golf. "The next year I was ready to go back to Double A. But the Triple-A manager, Leon Roberts, liked the way I ran, and I played golf, and he wanted a golf partner. So I made it to Triple A because I could play golf. I was supposed to be utility in Triple A but a guy got hurt right away and I started playin' and I was playin' real good, and I got called up May 30th."

When he got the call to the major leagues, he was lying on the floor of his apartment (he still had no furniture) reading a book. He remains an avid reader. When he was in college he loved science fiction, having read Isaac Asimov's imposing *Foundation Trilogy* and Frank Herbert's *Dune*. (He cites the film version of *Dune* as "one of the major disappointments in my life.") His tastes now are eclectic, meaning that if he likes the cover, he'll buy it. He browses through thrift stores and finds books on sale. "I'm into reading books by authors who are alive, so they can appreciate the fact that I'm reading their books. I mean, if I read something by Thoreau, he's not even around to care." (He did make an exception for Sartre's *Nausea*, which he bought in a thrift store, and was reading in mid-season '88. The Tigers were in first place, and Walewander was reading about the existential quagmire of Sartre's Roquentin.)

So Jim Walewander, who could have been mistaken for the batboy (some have compared his looks to a grownup Opie from "The Andy Griffith Show"), joined the Tigers. The first big-league game he was supposed to start was rained out. The next day he faced Mark Langston and got two hits, two runs batted in, and stole a base. He was asked after the game how he found Langston, one of the hardest throwers in the American League. "I took a left at the on-deck circle," he said, "and there he was, on the mound."

He said the only difference between the minor leagues and the majors was that he had "fewer bugs in my apartment." Apparently he had no trouble adjusting. The hotels were nicer, the food was better, and it was just more fun playing on a team that good. But the clothes he wore left a little to be desired. On his first trip with the Tigers, Dave Bergman (also an alumnus of Maine South High School) asked him what size coat he wore, and a few days later he left two sports coats in Walewander's locker. Sparky Anderson tried to help out by sending him to his personal haberdasher.

No one ever tried to school him in good grooming in the minors. "They'd just say things like, 'You iron that shirt with a rock?' or 'You dress in a closet this morning?' " But there just aren't a lot of major-league players who acquire most of their wardrobe from thrift stores and the Salvation Army. Jim Walewander has been wearing that stuff for years—old pants, skinny ties, a whole range of clothing so far out of style that it's obsolete.

"In the minors, I liked to wear a collared shirt underneath my uniform, you know, when button-down collars were big. I said, 'If I'm gonna play like a pussy, I'm gonna dress like one.' " The truth is, Walewander could dress like a corporate executive in pinstripes and still be considered a tad unusual. As Dave Bergman said, "Some players are flakes from the outside in, Jim's a flake from the inside out."

When he has a free moment, he still hits the thrift stores. His latest acquisition is a shark he bought for sixty-five dollars that is now mounted in his apartment "to make the place feel more like home." It's not only aesthetically pleasing to him, it's functional, as he uses its large mouth for his loose change.

Walewander plays behind Lou Whitaker on the Tigers, so he has little gripe with not being a regular. His limited role on the team was even glorified in a rhythm-and-blues song called "The Walewander Blues." The fans love him, the players love him, Sparky loves him, and he's in the big leagues. "I can die happy," he says.

It's also a great thrill for Walewander's father, Lee, who had his own aspirations of being a major leaguer. "Every father dreams of his kid doing what he couldn't do," he says proudly. Lee Walewander was bitten by the baseball bug early. "I used to sell papers around Wrigley Field. After I sold my papers, I'd buy myself a box of popcorn and sit up in the stands. And I looked at the vines and the beautiful infield, and I said to myself, 'My, wouldn't that be a nice thing to do, what these guys do.'"

Because of his commitment to play as a professional, Lee Walewander never smoked, since he did not want to cut down on his wind—he already had too much going against him. Although he was very fast, he only weighed 125 pounds. At that time, ballplayers didn't lift weights. Lee Walewander drank milkshakes, tried everything, but couldn't gain very much at all. Still, he played in the Brooklyn Dodgers farm system in the 1940s under the name Windy Wanders, until an elderly woman asked him why he wasn't fighting instead. He enlisted in the Marines after one year of pro ball. "It's ridiculous," says Jim. "Who listens to old ladies, anyway?"

Ironically, Lee Walewander played ball in the service just about wherever he went. In the Solomon Islands, once the island was secured, they would look for any ballplayers so the Marines could play the Army and Navy teams. After the service, he got his bachelor's and master's degrees from the University of Illinois and became a high school chemistry teacher, which he's been doing for thirty-five years.

"I had my kids close together," he said, "and I always wanted a keystone combination. I had three sons, and I would take them all out and hit them grounders. We'd all go back in the house, but Jimmy would come and drag me off the couch, begging me to hit him more grounders."

Jimmy and his brother Bob were already such good fielders that they were turning double plays at the age of seven. And both had inherited from their father great speed afoot. "I never realized how fast Jimmy was until we took him to a Fourth of July picnic at Oriole Park," his father said. "There were about two hundred kids there and they had a one-hundred-yard race. I'm watching the race and I see this skinny little kid in a green T-shirt come racing out of the pack blowing everyone away and it was Jimmy." His sons finished 1–2 in the race, as they did the following year.

Jim Walewander just kept coming out of the pack, until he found himself playing a key role in one of the most memorable pennant races in the history of the American League between the Tigers and the Toronto Blue Jays. Although Walewander only hit .241 in fifty-four at-bats for the season, he scored twenty-four runs. The Tigers made their pennant drive behind some older players such as Darrell Evans and Bill Madlock, for whom Wale-wander would pinch-run in the late innings, and that is where he made his biggest contribution. It became a theme of the Tiger season, and everyone on the club knew it and used to joke about it—"Let's get Wales on," they all would say, "and we'll win it." They kept saying it, and it kept happening, right through the final two series between the two teams.

First there was a four-game set in Toronto, and the Jays took the first three. A fourth win would set the Tigers four and a half games back, and the Jays led in the ninth inning until Kirk Gibson tied the game with a one-out miracle homer off Tom Henke. The game went into extra innings, and with Walewander on second base, Gibson hit a pop-up into no-man's-land in center. Shortstop Manny Lee came out to get the ball on one bounce, whirled, and threw to catcher Ernie Whitt, who came out to get the ball as Walewander made a beautiful headfirst slide to the foul side of home.

It was the winning run and kept the Tigers alive for their three-game series in Detroit. The Tigers won the first one, and then Walewander scored the winning run Saturday afternoon on Trammell's bases-loaded shot through the legs of Manny Lee, clinching a tie of the pennant for the Tigers. "I don't mind being a lucky charm," he said, "as long as they don't put me on a key chain."

When the Tigers won the pennant the next day, Wales joined Jack Morris, who was in his underwear, and a few other champagne-soaked Tigers to cavort around in the infield. Then they went across the street to a bar to throw beer and champagne on a throng of delirious Tiger fans.

Someone asked Sparky Anderson if he was bothered that Wales didn't play winter ball after the '87 season. "I wouldn't want to put Wales in a foreign country," he said. "He might start a civil war. You've got to keep Wales locked up at home in Chicago."

To start the '88 season, Walewander was not given a major-league contract, despite the big runs he scored down the stretch in 1987. He went to spring training as a non-roster invitee, and when I spoke to him down there after his wind sprints, he wondered if his role on the club was less secure now that Bill Madlock had left to play in Japan, since Madlock was the player he pinch-ran for the most. "I might be pinch-running for him in Japan," he said sardonically.

But he made the team, and Sparky Anderson now insists that he has a job as long as he can run. "A role player such as Wale-wander can be appreciated by teams who win," said Anderson. "A struggling team couldn't afford to keep a player on the roster who pinch-runs and fills in on defense. His job is safe because Jimmy knows what his job is and he does it well."

Still, it's hard for Walewander not to hold his breath whenever they make a roster change or someone comes off the disabled list. Sure enough, at the end of August in the 1988 season, when the Tigers needed to add a pitcher to their roster because of an injury, it was Walewander who was sent to the minors, making him ineligible for post-season play.

On September 1, when the major-league rosters can be expanded, he was brought right back up, and soon found himself the starting second baseman after Lou Whitaker injured himself. Whitaker, while dancing with his wife at a friend's wedding, did the splits, twice—the second time he popped a ligament in his knee and was sidelined. Whitaker's mishap thrust Wales into the American League East pennant race as a starter during the outmanned Tigers' collapse in September. It was another lesson in how unpredictable the game can be. For players like Walewander, readiness is all. "All I care about," he said, "is packing for the next city."

Loo-ie!

I met him at an old-timers' game in St. Petersburg. He was standing at one end of the dugout in his Red Sox uniform, chaw of tobacco bulging from his cheek, lips pursed, chewing and spitting—Luis Tiant. He looked pretty much the same as his glory days. The mutton-chop sideburns had a touch of gray, but he was not much heavier than in his playing days. He never had the svelte, classic build of the long and lanky power pitchers, Gibson and Blue and Palmer and Gooden. He always had that stocky frame.

From the moment I saw him, most of my reporter's reserve melted away, because I had lived in Boston in the '70s, and I had seen Luis on those nights in Fenway when you just simply had to be there. I made a beeline for him and told him I had a trivia question for him. "Say, Luis, do you know what pitcher held hitters to the lowest batting average for a season?" And he gave me a playful look, eyes wide, and then started nodding his head like one of those springy-necked dolls, chewing furiously. "I know," he said. "It's me. Somebody told me last year."

We sat down in the dugout and talked about the night in 1975 when he beat Palmer 2–0, when Rico and Fisk homered and the

"Loo-ie" chant became a long, drawn-out, yearning incantation that rolled around the park continuously for the last half of his masterful shutout. Face to face with Luis, it was somewhat hard to believe that it was thirteen years ago, the night was so vivid—the sounds, the Fenway bleachers (admission was $1.50), the taste of the Schaefer beer, and most of all the sight of Luis whirling and twirling on the mound.

He spit and nodded, remembering the night very well. "Palmer never beat me," he said, pitching his voice even higher than usual. "Not in Fenway, not in Baltimore. In Baltimore, he told me, 'Tell your manager not to pitch you against me anymore. I can't beat you.' I win 1–0, 2–1, 2–0, he make a little mistake, somebody take it out and he lose. He was pitching good games, you know, he's a pretty good pitcher. Fuckin' baby, though. He's a baby. He can't take the shit."

The Red Sox' '75 dream year was part of a long love affair with the Boston fans which started in 1972, the year after Luis had joined the team, and continued into the mid-'70s. I spoke with Dwight Evans at the Red Sox training camp in Winter Haven about what it was like to play behind Luis in those years. "The one thing that really impressed me about those games—and Luis was really the one behind that whole Red Sox era—as soon as he was done warming up and that lever came up from that gate, there was dead silence, and as soon as that latch opened he got a standing ovation all the way to the mound. It was exciting for us to see that, and it got us going, too. It was a tremendous thing."

The Tiant Cult really began in the stretch of the '72 pennant race, when Tiant came back from four years of arm trouble. Tiant was in the process of winning thirteen of fifteen, and about to pitch in Fenway against the Orioles' Mike Cuellar. He finished his warmups, slung a jacket over his shoulder, closed the bullpen gate behind him, and began the trek across the outfield on his way to the Boston dugout. The noise started in center field in the storied bleachers, spread along the right-field line, and grew to a crescendo as he reached the dugout. His teammates, to a man, were thrilled by the tribute. Some had tears in their eyes.

Boston sportswriters wrote that they had never heard such an ovation, except for the last time Joe DiMaggio went to bat in Boston, or Bob Cousy's final game. Carl Yastrzemski, who had heard a few cheers in his own career, said, "I've never heard anything like that in my life, but I'll tell you one thing: Tiant deserved every bit of it."

Luis won 4–0 that night, sealing his pact with the fans. Luis didn't let it go to his head, he had been booed when he first joined the Sox and didn't have his rhythm, and had heard the Boston fans boo Jim Plunkett and Phil Esposito and even Yaz. But the night in '72 was nonetheless very special to him. "It made me feel funny inside. I kept thinking it was the biggest night of my life. It made me want to cry out there."

Why did the notoriously reserved Fenway faithful love this man in such a special way? I think it was really several things—that he was a class individual, a great competitor, and a warm, funny, human being—but without question one of them was the singular way that he threw a baseball. Nobody who watched him pitch will ever forget it.

Luis's motion began with a pivot and an almost complete pirouette that showed his back to the batter as he looked out at the center-field bleachers. From there, he balanced on one leg, seeming at times certain to fall over backwards, and would begin a series of contortions. He looked something like a cement mixer on the fritz, or a hippopotamus trying to wriggle into a girdle. At various times his delivery resembled someone trying to pitch underwater, or a man trying to kick off his left shoe, and sometimes he just went into convulsions, as if hit by lightning as he released the ball.

During the season of 1988, much was made of what constitutes a balk. Tiant's motion from the stretch position was a perpetual balk crisis, as he wagged the glove seven or eight times before coming to a "discernible stop." The American League umpires got used to it and he was never called for a balk until the World Series, when the National League ump wouldn't buy it. But that was the only time he was ever called for a balk, and then he picked that guy off. "They never caught me," he laughingly boasted.

But balks were not the half of it. Some claimed that Luis's regular windup with no one on base was an illegal motion. He was walking the fine line of a delayed delivery, and in 1965, after he beat the Senators, manager Gil Hodges claimed that Tiant was using an illegal motion. "Half the time he throws that changeup," insisted Hodges, "he stops his motion. It's just like Satchel Paige's old hesitation pitch."

Tiant had five basic pitches, and threw them all from who knows how many different deliveries, giving him quite an extensive repertoire, all of it legal, by the way. He told me that he didn't throw a spitter because his wouldn't do anything, and neither would the forkball that he tried to learn from his friend and fellow Cuban, Orlando Pena. One time a new delivery had the writers in Cleveland demanding a rational explanation, and Luis accommodated them. "I call it 'The Jaw Breaker,'" he said. "My head stops seven times. Once it looks up; once it looks down; once it points the jaw at second base; once it points it to third; once it points it at the scoreboard; once it points to behind my back; and then just before I let go of the ball, it points the jaw upstairs to where Gabe Paul is sitting."

Bill Lee likened a Tiant performance to a concert. "The orchestra comes out and everything starts banging and it shakes the place. Then it comes to the middle part of the symphony and things get very calm and sweet, and you want to kind of fall asleep. Then, all of a sudden, you sense that the end is coming. Everyone starts getting noisy again. The whole gang is letting out with all the instruments. Then, boom! The whole show is over. That's Tiant! Hard at the start, a little sweet, slow stuff in the middle, and then the big explosion at the end."

Of course, being so flamboyant, some labeled Tiant a hot dog. To Luis, it was just doing his job. Tiant was a showman, but he didn't put in all these extras just for show. It was to keep the hitters off balance, which he did for many years. Yastrzemski, later to become a teammate and friend, had troubles with Luis when he faced him. "Speed," he said, "plain speed, doesn't usually bother hitters. At least I know it doesn't bother me. But Luis comes at you from all angles and throws your timing off. There's no zone you can look for and know that's where the ball will be coming from. The guy who is herky-jerky, who can completely hide the ball and then deliver it at the last split second, he's the guy who bothers you most of all. Luis is the only guy I can think of who kept me guessing every minute."

That night in St. Petersburg, the rain refused to let up. Most of the old-timers wouldn't even get to play a little catch. It became more and more apparent that I would be Luis's old-timers' game, the thing that he suited up for. It was the first time that I was happy that a game was rained out. As Luis chewed and spit for punctuation, we talked about the games and the hitters, the friends and the pranks, the fights and the disappointments. Then the rain came down harder, and all the other players joined us in the dugout, everybody's talk echoing loudly. Luis talks very fast, and not very loud to begin with. I was determined not to miss a thing, and therefore got two inches from his face, which as it turns out is a quite comfortable distance for Luis to speak with you.

From the time he was very young, people were telling him that he would injure his arm because of the unorthodox deliveries that he used. But being tricky was perhaps inbred in Luis, whose father was one of the craftiest and most celebrated athletes in Cuban history. From 1926 through 1948, when his son was too young to remember watching him perform, the senior Tiant was a supremely talented left-handed pitcher whose exploits were as legendary among Cubans as Babe Ruth's feats were among Americans.

At the time when Cool Papa Bell was supposed to be the fastest man in the game, Tiant Sr. would respond to that reputation by intentionally walking Bell on four pitches, just to set up their classic base-stealing duel. According to one famous anecdote, which many others are quick to confirm, the elder Tiant's pickoff move once resulted in a remarkable mixup play. The batter swung at his move for strike three and the man on first was out, too.

Like many a legendary incident, there are various versions floating around. One version goes that the funniest part of it all was that the batter started insisting he had fouled off the pitch, which was never delivered. I asked Luis about it and he gave me his version. "One time this guy's hitting against my father, and he goes through his motion and he throws to first base. The batter swings and misses. He says, 'I know I can't hit the son of a bitch. Now I can't see him.' Everybody's going *Woo!* And he looks at the umpire and says, 'What happened?' And the umpire tells the batter he threw to first base. He says, 'You're shittin' me.' "

Like the classic father and son in the Pulitzer Prize–winning play *Fences*, the elder Tiant did not encourage his son to pursue a career in baseball. "I think my father still had bad feelings about his own career. The colored leagues never paid him much money, and the major leagues didn't want him because he was black. He went through so many bad things like that. I think he was afraid I would have bad luck, too. But I tried to tell him this was 1959 and things were different now. He didn't care. He still wanted me to go to school."

Tiant Sr.'s batboy was Bobby Avila, who won a batting championship for the Indians and later brought Looie to the attention of the Cleveland organization. After leaving Cuba in 1959, Luis pitched three years in Mexico, because it was the only place he was able to play, and then came the call from his parents not to come home to Cuba, that it would be too difficult to get out after Castro's takeover.

Soon after that he came to America to star in the minors. The only English word he knew was "chicken," and that's all he ate for three months. He was brought up to the Indians in the summer of 1964, along with Sudden Sam McDowell. His first roommate in the big leagues was Chico Salmon. "Chico Salmon crazy," he said excitedly. "My first roommate. Son of a bitch Chico come home on Saturday night, he was a utility player so he would stay out late, but I have to pitch the next day, he comes in four in the morning, puts the fucking lights on, wakes me up. We're talking and shit, and as soon as I start talking to him, he starts snoring, he goes to sleep. So I really got mad. I didn't like that boolcheat, boy. You know what I do to him? I go to the fucking bathroom, get a glass of cold water, throw it right in his face. He wakes up, and I say, 'I'll be damned you son of bitch wake me up when I'm pitching tomorrow. Fuck you, you're gonna stay up with me all night.' And me and Chico became good friends." He was also close with Chuck Hinton on that ball club, laughing at the memory. "All day, every day, we fuckin' around, we laughin'. When we got going, we got going."

Within a few years he was dominating the American League. In 1968, they used to give away a suit to anybody pitching a shutout. It wasn't long before Luis was the best dressed man in town. He had forty-one strikeouts in three games, with nineteen in a ten-inning game. He wound up 21–9, most wins by anybody on the Indians since Bob Lemon and Early Wynn had twenty-three apiece. His ERA of 1.6 was the lowest in the American League since Walter Johnson's 1.49 in 1919. And he set the record for holding hitters to the lowest batting average for a full season. People remember Denny McLain for his thirty-one wins and Bob Gibson for his 1.12 ERA that year because both pitched in the World Series. But that season Luis Tiant, with a good team, could well have won thirty games himself.

But Tiant developed serious arm trouble and the Indians gave up on him, trading him to the Twins with Stan Williams for Chance, Uhlaender, Bob Miller, and the key figure in the deal, Graig Nettles. When he joined the Twins he made an instant impression on everyone. As Tom Mee, the Twins' director of public relations, said, "I'll never forget the first time I saw him walk into the showers with a cigar in his mouth. The whole team cracked up. We thought he forgot it was there. Then we found out he always smokes while taking a shower. He became our clubhouse comedian right away."

The Twins won the divisional title in 1970, and Luis was the happiest face in the celebration pictures. But there were fewer laughs with the Twins as his arm trouble continued, and he was released. His friend and teammate Stan Williams called Ed Roebuck and got him a tryout with Richmond, the Atlanta Braves' Triple A affiliate. They gave him a month to get himself together, but it wasn't enough time, and El Tiante found himself out of baseball.

It was in this state of baseball limbo, after the Indians, Twins, and Braves thought he was washed up, that he was given a chance by the Red Sox. The rest, as they say, is history, as Tiant became the ace of the pitching staff. But he became more than their number-one starter. As Dwight Evans told me, "Whatever frictions there were, Luis was above it, he was the glue that held the team together. . . . If you play this game long enough, you know that the bus rides and plane rides along the road are vitally important, and Luis knew exactly when to turn a bus ride into something out of 'Saturday Night Live.' "

Tiant had pet names for most of the Sox. Petrocelli was "Pinocchio," Jim Rice was "Mandingo," Fisk, with his erect posture, was "Frankenstein," and Yaz was "Polacko." Yastrzemski carried his stuff on the road in a brown paper bag and wore ratty raincoats, which didn't pass Luis's notice. "Hey Polacko," he would ask, "did you clean the bus in that raincoat?" In an unending battle to destroy Yaz's coats, he would set them on fire or throw them in the garbage. "I had fun with Yaz," Luis recalled. "He wore that raincoat, it was an ugly motherfucker, he looked like Columbo. Yeah, we opened the window one time and threw it out."

His most outrageous pranks on the Red Sox were reserved for outfielder Tommy Harper, who was a teammate of Tiant's on the Indians. Harper had acquired a reputation as moody and sullen, until Luis made him the butt of his pranks. "Before I go fooling with people," Luis stressed, "I study them. I think I'm pretty good at that. That's why no one gets mad at me. Before I do anything to someone, I make sure I know what his reaction will be."

Harper would come into the locker room with a new hat, and minutes later he would find a fish, wearing his hat, grinning at him. Someone had stuck tongue depressors inside its mouth to make it look like it was smiling. Harper didn't have to ask who did it, but Tiant would swear he knew nothing about it.

Luis would follow a set routine with the Red Sox. He would come into the clubhouse, take off his clothes, wrap himself in a towel, and talk a while. Then he'd grab a newspaper or magazine and head into the bathroom. Nobody ever paid any attention to this until one day they heard him yell, "Bye Tommeee!" and then flush the toilet. Of course it got a tremendous laugh, and got to be a daily routine.

Harper remembers it very well. "Day after day he'd go in there with his papers and pretty soon the players would hear that silly high-pitched voice going 'Bye Tommeee!' You'd think after a while it would seem ridiculous. But not the way Luis did it. He made it funnier every day, then he'd walk out and give me a foolish grin. . . . Luis never let me alone. It seemed I became the butt of every joke in his book. It's funny, but I really didn't mind it. In fact, it kind of made me feel good. To most people, I suppose all of these things don't really seem funny. But when you've got twenty-five guys together day in and day out for seven months, you have to find ways to break the tension. And nobody ever found more ways to do that than Luis did."

Harper and Tiant became close friends, like brothers, really, but Luis let him know what would happen if the Red Sox ever traded Harper. "If they ever trade you," Luis warned Tommy while the rest of the Sox laughed, "don't you ever try to steal on me. First of all, you probably wouldn't even get a chance unless I walked you because you can't hit me. But don't ever try to. You know what I'll do?" Tiant reached over and poked his forefinger into Harper's mouth. "If I ever pick you off, I'm going to walk right over to first base and hook you by the mouth, just like this, and say 'Get your ass out of here. You are out!' "

This was a move Luis had perfected when he was with Cleveland. The Indians' young slugger Tony Horton was in a miserable slump, and after popping out to the pitcher, Luis came out to get him, hooked him by the mouth and led him back to the dugout, saying, "A man with a family hit de ball like that. What a fucking shame."

In fact, Harper was traded, and played first base against the Red Sox one day and kicked a grounder. He knew Tiant was going to be all over him, and tried not to look into the Red Sox dugout. When he lifted his head up, he couldn't believe what he saw. Tiant was wearing a chest protector, batting helmet, shin guards, and had gloves taped to both of his feet, dancing out in front of the dugout. "Here, take these," he yelled, "you need them!"

"I like meeting people that you can joke with anytime," Tiant told me. "A lot of guys, they're good when they're going good, but when they're going bad they don't want to talk to nobody, they're angry, they want to fight you. I don't go for that shit. You should be the same person all the time. . . . Sports are funny. When you're winning it makes no difference if you're fat or skinny, if you're funny or quiet, if you do things in a certain way or not. But once you lose, no matter what the reason is, everybody starts looking for an explanation. And I think that's stupid."

Before Tiant was going to pitch, he would prepare himself before coming to the ballpark, and then jabber in the clubhouse even more than usual as a way of working off nervous tension. And after a game, if he lost a tough one, he wouldn't destroy a clubhouse. He rarely lost his temper if someone pulled a boner that cost him a ball game or ruined a shutout for him. He would just light a cigar and go home.

Managers and teammates marveled at his composure under fire. Anyone who played with him came to know he was a great competitor with a burning desire to win. Red Smith described him, with his black Fu Manchu and sinister countenance, as "looking like Pancho Villa on the mound after a tough week of burning and looting." Both Dwight Evans and Yastrzemski said that if they had one game to win, Tiant was the pitcher they would want to have on the mound.

While he was a fighter on the hill, he was out of place when he found himself in the middle of some of the famous Yankee–Red Sox wars of the '70s. In 1976, Boston took first place and played in May in Yankee Stadium. Bill Lee was losing 1–0 when Piniella tried to score on a single, but Evans uncorked a perfect throw to the plate, and Piniella tried to knock Fisk down with his cleats and knees. Fisk applied a vicious tag and then came up swinging. The benches emptied as Lee came charging in from the mound, firing punches.

Luis rushed out to help and got sucker-punched. "Every time I try and get into it, I get hurt. It's the guys who don't do anything who get hurt. Because there's guys who come in from the outside and hit guys. You're in a pileup and somebody comes up from behind and hits you, you don't know who hit you, you know, they're hiding, *boom*, somebody hits you, it's no good."

When he was with the Red Sox and Munson and Fisk had their epic fight, Luis ran into the fray again. This time Ralph Houk spiked him in the shoe. "He got me *twice!*" He didn't have any better luck with the Yankees. "One time in Milwaukee somebody threw at Reggie, and I'm sitting on the bench with Ron Guidry. So I go storming out, and I miss the top step, and I crash my shin into the cement. I'm on the floor, holding my leg. So Guidry gets back and sees me, he's laughing. I said, 'You son of a bitch, you help me!' I had to see the trainer. I thought it was broken."

As a Yankee he was now teammates with Rivers, known for his cheap shots, and when a bench-clearing brawl started, Rivers came up behind somebody and started to kick him. "I pulled him out," said Luis, "and he said, 'What the fuck are you doing?' I said, 'You don't hit people that way!' "

Tiant has his own code. Knockdowns were not a part of his

game. "Somebody hit a home run, I don't throw at the next guy. What does that fuckin' guy have to do with it? I think that's chickenshit. When a pitcher throws at a hitter, I think that's boolcheat. Hitters today, you pitch 'em in, they want to get married, they want to come out and kiss you. They used to tell you, 'Knock him down, stick it in his ear.' You don't do that, you go home. But a guy like Frank Robinson, at the meeting they would say, 'You knock him down, we fine you.' Those were the only guys you didn't want to hit, Frank Robinson and Reggie Jackson. You knock those sons of bitches down, you better make some fuckin' pitches after that. Because they're gonna get up and hit you deep! But that's the way it should be. You don't have to throw at nobody in the game."

Tiant's code touches on another facet of the man. Besides being the funny man, and the competitor, Luis is also a devout man. In 1973, he made a personal religious commitment. For a whole year, he wore nothing but white—shoes, socks, everything. The only exception to this dress code was his Red Sox uniform. There's a room in his house that few people ever see, which is almost like a little shrine or chapel. He had selected this time in his life, as a Roman Catholic, to devote one year to thanking God.

As Luis explained, "I been way down in this game. I been in, what you call it, the big box. Yes, the coffin. But I got out. So many good things started happening to me. It was no accident. Like the way I came back when everybody was saying I was all through. God was good to me. I just wanted to pay Him a tribute. That's all."

The moment for which Luis was most thankful was the first game of the 1975 World Series, because throwing out the first pitch was his father, whom he had not seen for fifteen years. Luis had tried for a long time to help his parents get out of Cuba, but nothing had come of it. Senator Ed Brooke of Massachusetts became involved, and then George McGovern spoke to Fidel Castro about it in Cuba on a night when Castro was returning from the Cuban baseball championships. Shortly thereafter, the Tiants were allowed to come to America.

Tiant Sr., a thin old man wearing a Red Sox cap, accompanied by his namesake, walked to the mound as the crowd cheered. Tiant Sr. removed his jacket and handed it to Luis, who stood beside him, covered with goosebumps. He went into a graceful motion and fired a pitch low and outside. Not satisfied with the pitch, he called for the ball again and this time split the middle of the plate and made the mitt really pop, and the place erupted.

Then his son took the hill for the first game of the World Series, shut out the Big Red Machine and even scored the first and winning run, as in a fairy tale. Their reunion was finally too good to be true, and Luis's father died that winter, and his mother a few days later, presumably of a broken heart. An only child, Luis buried them on the same day.

The Red Sox traded him to the Yankees in 1978. Yastrzemski said, "When they let Luis Tiant go to New York, they tore out our heart and soul." Luis's main goal in finishing up his career was to have the most wins of any Latin American pitcher who ever lived. He wound up with 229, fourteen less than Juan Marichal.

For all the adversity and personal trauma that he has endured, Luis Tiant does give thanks for everything. "I enjoyed the game, all the years I played. If there's another guy younger than you, he's making a lot of money . . . but I was lucky to play when I did. I love to be here today. Forget about playing baseball and all that shit. I'm glad to be here, because if I was still in Cuba, maybe they kill my black ass already, or maybe I be in jail now." (Luis had met Castro once, but after getting out of Cuba in 1961, he didn't know if Castro was a fan of his or not, and didn't care, having no plans to return to Cuba.)

There are things about how the game has treated him since his retirement, however, that rub Tiant the wrong way. Since 1983 he has not been able to find a job in baseball. "I apply for a job for a pitching coach, nobody give me a fucking job, they say we already got it, they don't have a place for me, it's boolcheat.

"I'm upset because I can't see no reason why I can't get a goddamn pitching coaching job. I can be dumb, but I know I'm not stupid. I may be stupid, but I know I'm not dumb. All I can say is, you pitch seventeen years in the big leagues, you don't last that long pitching in luck.

"I know I get along good with the young kids, I know I can teach, and they don't want to give me a good job, fuck 'em. They tell you they want you to play in the big leagues, then they won't hire you. It's boolcheat, it's not fair. Every fucking year the same thing, over and over and over. How much can you take of that shit? I don't need them, I got a good job, I work for the treasury in Massachusetts, public relations. I got that job last July."

Neither is Tiant thrilled about how the Hall of Fame voting has gone. Seeing Don Drysdale skate in ahead of him when he doesn't hear his own name even come up rankles him. "I got a better ERA than Drysdale, I got more shutouts. . . . But why they put in the other guys? I got a better record than Catfish Hunter, and the first time he comes up, they put him in, and they aren't talking about me. That's not right. That's a mistake! Because I should have more credit, I've got to have more credit than them, because most of the time I'm pitching for horseshit teams, and they were on good teams.

"Orlando Cepeda, he gotta better record than Willie McCovey, he's got a better record than Billy Williams, and he's not in because he got caught with the dope. You know, anybody can make a mistake. And they don't put in Orlando. He make a mistake, he paid for it. Ferguson Jenkins, because he had a little problem in Canada, he's not in, that's boolcheat. You make a mistake, and you pay for it, and then it should be over. You can't do shit about that.

"These guys, they been to the fucking police station, they're taking dope, I never had nothing like that on my record, I'm a regular citizen. You know what the fucking problem is? They want the guy who is, you know, the Mona Lisa, the guy who doesn't do shit, who looks good. Like now, some of the things, like taking the beer from the clubhouse, they don't let the players take the drugs from the street, what are they talkin' about? They been doin' that shit for 130 years. They want to make a better player today, so they say no drinking in the clubhouse, so they're drinking in the bar. That's stupid to me. We used to go, Yaz, Doug Griffin, myself, we stay there, we have a beer, we talk about the game, drinking the beer, now everybody leaves when the game ends. I think it's one of the things that we're losing in the game.

"They're talking about how the kids are gonna look at you, they're wrong, because I say you've got your own child, and you have to train your kid at home. You're gonna have your kid looking at me instead of making a man out of your kid, if you have to do that. . . ."

The rain in St. Petersburg finally abated, and hundreds of fans stayed through the long delay, even after the game was called. They let the fans on the field and in the dugouts and Tiant signed every last autograph request. As he joked with Mudcat Grant, "When they don't want your autograph no more, you might as well go home and break your ass in the toilet!"

In May of the 1988 season, an old-timers' game was played in Fenway Park, pitting the Red Sox Old-Timers against the Equitable Old-Timers. Luis came into the locker room with his trademark big cigar, and greeted Yaz, George Scott, the Boomer himself, Bernie Carbo, and Dick Radatz among others.

Tiant came to do more than sign autographs and have his picture taken. During batting practice he courageously played third base while a slimmed-down Frank Howard pulled shots down the line. When it was his chance to hit, he went for the Wall in earnest. Then he tried to lay down a bunt, and Paul Blair almost hit him, initiating a full round of agitating back and forth.

When they took the team picture in center field, Yaz kneeled down next to Luis. "I'll go here next to him so I'll look good," he said. In the dugout before the introductions, Yaz asked Tiant how he did against the Boomer when he was with Milwaukee. Boomer recalled the one home run he hit off Luis, and Luis recalled the numerous times he fanned him. "Phht. Phht! Phht! Good-bye!"

The players were introduced, and Walt Dropo fell as soon as he got to the top step. The rest of the introductions went smoothly. Tiant came out and then Yaz, the man they save for last in New England. He's hatless, acknowledging the cheers, and then grabbed Luis's hat to wave to the crowd. Tiant covered his bald spot in mock embarrassment, as the crowd laughed and cheered at the same time.

The top of the first, with Luis on the mound, was thirty minutes long. They were all dink hits, and Tiant, despite instructions in exhibitions of this nature to lay it down the middle, threw Paul Blair a mean slider, and then a big changeup, and the Sox in the dugout cracked up.

On a solid hit by Manny Sanguillen, the relay came in to Johnny Pesky, who turned and watched as the run scored from first. In the dugout, someone could not resist saying "He held the ball again. He's still holding the ball," this a fairly cruel joke about the seventh game of the '46 Series when Pesky received a throw from the outfield and hesitated while Enos Slaughter scored from first on a single to win the Series.

Boomer was worried during the long first frame that he was not going to get up to bat. Finally the inning ended and Tiant walked into the dugout after giving up four runs. Everyone was waiting for his comment. "That was some weak shit," he said, and everyone exploded. A few teammates started rubbing his arm. Is your arm warm? they asked. "My arm is fine," he said, turning his rear end to his teammates. "Massage this."

The game had its moments. Piersall executed a perfect drag bunt. Boomer went in to pinch-run, looking like there was another player in his uniform, and then started limbering up his legs as if getting ready to steal. Tiant went crazy, laughing and pointing at Scott's prodigious spare tire. "Look at him, he's got two Michelins."

Yastrzemski wouldn't play in the field. "I can't stand out there for that long," he said, a remark that Tiant would not allow to go by. "Hey, Polacko," he shouted, "I know why you won't go out there, you're afraid to get hit in the fucking nose."

Bill Monbouquette took the hill for the Sox Old-Timers and threw a slowball to the plate. Radatz said, "Hey, Monbo's fastball's got a hump in it!" The Monster then got his chance to mop up. In the last inning, the Red Sox Old-Timers mounted a final rally, with the Monster rooting them on. "Give me seven," he exhorted his teammates, "I need the W." So Bernie Carbo came up to hit, and they made the pitching change from the seventy-year-old Bob Feller to the still-imposing Bob Gibson. Carbo looked deadpan into the dugout as the switch was made and got a loud hee-haw. As always, Tiant laughed the loudest and longest.

After the game I walked into the press room, where by coincidence Stan Williams was charting Roger Clemens as an advance scout and adviser for the Yankees. In Yankee baseball's continuing game of musical chairs, Williams would be named the Yankee pitching coach after the June firing of Billy Martin, only to be replaced a month later by the always-willing Clyde King. Williams was one of Tiant's closest friends in the game, his teammate with Cleveland, Minnesota, and the Red Sox, and his pitching coach in Boston and New York. When Williams was traded to Minnesota from Cleveland, he said he wouldn't go unless Luis was in the deal. "I love the guy," he said, unabashedly and without reserve.

"He was a master, he really was. He had great stuff and he had the ability to throw the ball where he wanted to. The reason I liked him so well was mainly because of what a fierce competitor he was. I remember in the '75 Series he started stomping around the mound in around the sixth inning in Cincinnati. He was fighting like hell, but he was struggling. I went out there and he was pissed off that Darrel Johnson had somebody warming up while he was pitching. He said it was breaking his concentration. 'It's my game,' he said, 'and I want to pitch it.' "

Now when Stan Williams says someone is a great competitor, we must examine the source. It was Williams who said that if hitters dug in on him like they do today, "I'd step off the mound, tell him it was a nice hole he was digging, and tell him to make it at least six feet deep, because he was going to be buried in it."

Early in his career, Williams hit Hank Aaron in the helmet with a fast ball, dazing him. After the game, Williams apologized to Aaron. "I meant to hit you in the neck!" he explained. Williams used to keep a picture of Aaron hanging near his locker so he could throw baseballs at it to keep game-sharp. So when this man says you are a competitor, we're talking big-time competition.

"At the end of his career," Williams said, "Luis got a little cynical. He was always a very sensitive man. But when he was at Cleveland, he was unbelievable, one of the funniest people I ever met. I used to call him the Cuban Cantinflas. He kept you loose. He didn't care much for flying. When we'd start taking off he'd start chattering and hollering, 'Yi! Yi! Yi!', and holding on to the luggage rack. That'll do you a lot of good to hold on to that if the plane goes down."

Tiant used to call Williams "the Mullion," a term now in common usage in the big leagues. Precisely translated, it means "big ugly motherfucker." "He'd always get on me," said Williams, "especially people he liked. That was an endearing phrase coming from Luis. He was always joking to relax himself. He always carried on more before a game."

As we drank coffee out of styrofoam cups, Clemens continued to blow away the Seattle Mariners on the TV screen. "I think Luis should definitely be in the Hall," Williams said. "Drysdale had a couple of good years, the fifty-eight-inning string. But he was mostly a .500 pitcher. Luis should definitely be considered. He was the greatest right-handed pitcher that I ever played with, and I played with Drysdale."

Earthman

*B*ill Lee, presidential candidate of the Rhinoceros Party, came from a conservative background. His father worked for the telephone company and was a supporter of Barry Goldwater, little knowing that one day his son would become renowned as a master of space, time, and the slow curveball.

There were plenty of baseball genes in Lee's family. His grandfather was an infielder in Los Angeles in the early 1900s. His brother was a two-sport player and his aunt, Annabelle Lee, pitched the first perfect game in the history of the Women's Semi-pro Hardball League.

Lee attended the University of Southern California, again a traditionally conservative school, where he played for legendary college coach Rod Dedeaux. Pretty soon he was showing his true colors, shagging flies in the outfield in his jockstrap. But he could pitch, and when he left USC he had the most wins by any pitcher there, with a 38–8 record. Still, Al Campanis told him at a party, "Lee, you'll never pitch a day in the majors."

In the minor leagues he infuriated his manager, the late former Pirate third baseman Don Hoak, when he started a game-ending double play by catching a grounder behind his back. It was Lee's theory that his follow-through made this play mandatory, but Hoak didn't see it that way, as he explained to Lee while chasing him out of the ballpark and through the parking lot.

Bill Lee was auspiciously given number 37 by the Red Sox, a number worn by Casey Stengel and his predecessor on the Sox, Jimmy Piersall. The Red Sox never had a player like Lee. If some classic southpaws-at-heart seemed to dance to a different drummer, Bill Lee was perceived as being tuned in to a whole different orchestra. At times he did seem to be receiving messages from a distant star system, and thus his moniker, "The Spaceman." He became known as "Spaceman" when he was doing a radio show in 1969 and talked more about the moon shot than baseball.

To put Lee's career in perspective, it should be noted that the Red Sox have been one of the most strait-laced organizations in all of professional sports. They were one of the first to institute a no-liquor rule on team flights, and the last by far to have a black player on their major-league roster. They were even reluctant to have their players form-fitted in knit uniforms.

Lee was a most effective pitcher for the Red Sox, in fact the most successful left-handed pitcher they had since Mel Parnell. But although he won seventeen games for Boston three years in a row, his pitching would never garner as much attention as his off-the-wall behavior.

Sure, Lee wore onto the field such accoutrements as a gas mask, a Daniel Boone cap, and a beanie with a propeller, but he doesn't think he did anything all that weird. "I consider the world flaky," he said. "I'm one of the few people with his feet planted firmly on terra firma. People perceived me as flaky because they didn't understand me."

Lee was a baseball traditionalist who loved the rhythms, sights, sounds, and smells of old-time baseball, even the springtime ritual he described as "unlimbering the body and snorting the new glove." Exploding scoreboards and frisky team mascots weren't the things that turned him on about the game. "In baseball, I was really a conservative, because I wanted day games and real grass and pitchers who hit. And it was the *owners* who were the liberals, because they were always tampering with the planet, but nobody saw it that way."

Lee never thought of himself as any kind of spaceman. "I never wanted to put on that spaceman's uniform for the *Sports Illustrated* cover in '78, and it's on the cover of my book, too. I'm not a spaceman, I'm an earthman. If they want to show the real me, they'd show me in my flannel shirt and Levi's, chopping wood. Johnny Appleseed."

Shortly after joining the Red Sox, Lee was holding court in the Boston media on such earthly topics as Zero Population Growth, the rape of the planet earth, and the relationship between baseball and mysticism. (Lee said a Tibetan priest could make a baseball disappear and then materialize again in the catcher's mitt. *"There,"* he said, "is my idea of a relief pitcher.")

Lee could also expound on such subjects as extraterrestrial life, Pyramid Power, and the Bermuda Triangle. He took ginseng before he pitched and read *Rolling Stone*. "In baseball, I was different, but in real life, I was basically normal. I was a product of the sixties, and that's why I got such a strong following, because there were a lot of other people thinking the same way out there." Indeed, to the college population in Massachusetts, Lee became a genuine folk hero.

He once explained that baseball was a very simple game, because "All you have to do is sit on your butt, spit tobacco, and nod at the stupid things your manager says." But Lee was and is one of those people who has to speak his mind. "I was elected as the player rep, I was supposed to have a conscience, but that's something that's not looked on as an asset anymore."

He ruffled a lot of feathers while in Boston when he said that busing was a pretty good idea and that the Boston fans who disagreed with him were bigots with no guts. After Lee defended the decision of Judge Arthur Garrity, Lee was none too popular in the Irish bars of South Boston. When he received an angry, misspelled letter from city councillor Albert O'Neil, he wrote back to warn the councillor that "some moron" was using his stationery.

Just about everything Lee did had a little spin on it. Even when he egged on his opponents, he didn't deliver the customary comments. Before pitching against the California Angels, he said they could take batting practice in the hotel lobby and not chip a chandelier. He could also be strangely cryptic, as when, after beating the A's, he said they were "emotionally mediocre, like Gates Brown sleeping on a rug."

On one of his greatest days, he started a double play while sitting on his rear, and clowned around in a downpour throwing blooper balls. After the game he said, "When I'm through, I'll end up face down in the Charles River." Perhaps he had received a precognitive flash of the role he would play in the 1975 World Series.

Lee started the Series with vintage aplomb. He was pitching in Game Three when there was a rain delay. With the Series tied at one game apiece, and the score 1–1, he was asked his perception of the Series so far. "Tied," he replied, with a consummate deadpan delivery. Lee lost the game in the ninth inning.

Lee was chosen to pitch Game Six of the World Series, and when asked if it was the biggest game he'd ever been asked to pitch, replied that it was nothing compared to the 1968 College World Series. "That was real baseball. We weren't playing for the money. We got Mickey Mouse watches that ran backwards."

Another reporter asked what he would do if he won and forced a seventh game, and Lee replied that he would declare an automatic forty-eight hours of darkness so Tiant could get another day's rest. "That's what Zeus did when he raped Europa. He asked the sun god, Apollo, to stay away for a few days."

It rained for three days, and Tiant started Game Six, which the Sox won on Fisk's memorable twelfth-inning homer. And so Bill Lee, philosopher and iconoclast, maverick and agitator, pitched the seventh game. He carried a lead into the seventh inning. Earlier in the game he had gotten Tony Perez with one of his floating "leephus" pitches and couldn't resist the opportunity to throw it one more time. The looping pitch with its elongated parabola was belted by Perez over the Green Monster and the lead was gone by the time Lee hit the showers. "Hell, I live by that pitch and I'll die by it," he said after the game. Immediately after the Series, he left for China, where he saw every person in Shanghai out in the street for the three-day funeral of Chou En-Lai.

The Red Sox' chief rivals in the mid- to late '70s were of course the Yankees, and Lee usually pitched well against them, although he continually riled the Yankees by referring to them as "Billy's Brown Shirts." In one of the games he pitched in 1976 there was a famous brawl caused by a home-plate collision between Piniella and Fisk. Lee's reputation as a Yankee-hater made him fair game, and in the ensuing melee Mickey Rivers pounded away at Lee under a mountain of bodies. When Lee was able to get up, his arm was already shot, and then Graig Nettles punched Lee, picked him up, and dropped him. Lee fell on his shoulder, suffering an injury that incapacitated him for most of the season.

Increasingly, he rubbed the baseball establishment the wrong way. His continuing problems with Red Sox manager Don Zimmer reflected the schism in the culture at large, the traditionalist versus the free thinker. Lee was part of a faction on the Red Sox that ridiculed Zimmer, known as the Loyal Order of Buffalo Heads, which included Bernie Carbo, Jim Willoughby, and Ferguson Jenkins. Zimmer didn't care for the Buffalo Heads, but Lee thought he disliked all pitchers, citing the metal plate in his manager's head from two beanings. "If you've been beaned and nearly killed twice, you're gonna wanna make pitchers live in fear."

Their relationship was further strained when Lee called Zimmer a "puffy-cheeked gerbil." The last straw for Lee was when his friend Bernie Carbo was sold to Cleveland. With Carbo gone, there would no longer be anyone on the Red Sox who would buy an extra plane ticket so his pet gorilla could sit next to him. Lee took it hard, calling Zimmer "a front-running son of a bitch." He said the owners were gutless, and that he would be much happier working on his grandfather's walnut farm than pitching for the Red Sox. He also said he felt like the character in *Network* who was shot on the air. He later returned, "on behalf of future ballplayers yet unborn."

He was just days away from becoming a ten-year man who could veto any trade when the Red Sox traded him to Montreal. For his Canadian incarnation, he grew a long, Ahab-like beard. It took him just a few days of spring training to become embroiled in another controversy.

The first time the Expos played Boston in spring training, the writers flocked to Lee and one asked if there was a drug problem on the Red Sox. "You mean alcohol, nicotine, and caffeine? Yeah, the entire team used that stuff far too much." One writer said, "No, Bill, marijuana."

"Oh," Lee said, "reefer madness, hemp, doobies. I've been using that stuff since 1968. I never had any problems with it. It's the other stuff that really did me in."

The next day the headline was LEE SMOKES POT. A man named Art Fuss, a former drug enforcement official in the Nixon administration, then working for the commissioner's office, came to see Lee. Fuss asked Lee about his smoking marijuana, and Lee pointed out that the article doesn't mention his *smoking* pot. "I don't smoke pot," he said, "I use it. Very early when I get up. I have these organic buckwheat pancakes and I sprinkle about a half ounce of marijuana on top and I eat 'em. When I run my five miles to the ballpark for spring training practice, I'm impervious to all the bus fumes."

Fuss took this all down dutifully. "Yeah," he said, "I can see that. I think Bowie will buy this." And Lee replied, "Ask him if he wants to buy a bridge, too." Kuhn did not think that this constituted the breakfast of champions and said Lee's remarks were not in the best interests of baseball. He fined Lee $250, so Lee donated $251 to an Eskimo charity.

He later admitted that he had taken the mound under the

influence of hashish. He rose from a meditative, relaxed state with a burst of energy and proceeded to pitch very well under the influence. Lee claimed that "I could see every play in my mind moments before it actually occurred."

He was the Expos' best pitcher in 1979, their top winner at 16–10. In Montreal, he got injured when he was hit by a car while jogging, complained about the scapegoating and trading of teammate Rodney Scott, and was eventually released. Expos owner John McHale personally told Lee in his office, "You'll never play another day in the major leagues," and he hasn't.

In his final year, Lee had a 2.93 ERA and never relinquished a lead, even though he was hurt for much of the year. Bill Lee has good reason to believe that he has been blackballed from baseball by McHale, who "put his name in the computer with Shoeless Joe, Al Capone, and Jack the Ripper." He thinks that teams are afraid of him because of his brutal honesty. "The last thing they want in baseball is anyone who's brutally honest."

Lee is not invited to any Red Sox functions. While his weird and wonderful teammates like Carbo and Tiant are invited to play in old-timers' games, Lee isn't. The Equitable people who make the rosters for the old-timers' games told Lee they didn't know where he was, which is funny because they get a check from Lee four times a year for his health insurance. "They know how to send the bills," he confirmed.

When he is contacted by Triple A teams to pitch an exhibition, so they can get on their feet financially, major-league teams have to okay everyone on a Triple A roster, so it always falls through. "There's only one guy who's disliked more by major-league baseball, and that's [former pitcher] Mike Marshall. But he was nasty." Lee already has a title for his next book—*Just Because You're Paranoid Doesn't Mean They're Out to Get You*.

Lee had so much fun playing the game that he always felt guilty about being compensated so richly for it. He always said he would play for free, and now he does. For several years now he's been pitching in semi-pro leagues for teams like the Moncton

Mets. Even though he feels somewhat isolated by being frozen out from the game he loves, he said he likes being an amateur ambassador. "It doesn't help me in the present to do what I want to do, but it makes me consistent with my fans."

He still throws eighty-five miles per hour, and will always have that changeup. Last week he lost 3–0, pitching a six-hitter, but two weeks ago he threw a two-hitter and struck out fourteen. He watches pitchers like Tommy John, Frank Tanana, and Jerry Reuss continue to get people out the way he would, and just knows he could still pitch in the major leagues. "Nothing like pitching off a great mound with great defensive players behind you." But apparently no major-league team needs a guy who used to walk around with "Friendship First, Competition Second" on his T-shirt, even if he has a good curveball.

"We love baseball," he said, "because it takes us out of time and puts us in a unity of peace and time outside of the nuclear age. A ton of fans see baseball as an alternative to thinking of 100,000-megaton blasts all over the planet. We're actually a race of people who have their heads buried in the sand. We're no different from the group of people living on top of the land in perfect bliss in H. G. Wells's *The Time Machine*, who are sent down to the mines as food for the Ewoks on their twenty-first birthday."

It is not so unseemly that somebody with Lee's planetary concerns should become involved in the political arena, although how he became the presidential candidate of the Rhinoceros Party happened mostly by chance. "The party got me cornered. They asked me what I was doing for the next five years and I couldn't say I had anything planned, since I never plan anything beyond the next day."

Lee is out there pressing the flesh as an alternative to the progressive conservatives and conservative liberals, a candidate who describes himself as "a Fred Harris populist, a Ralph Nader consumer advocate, a citizen of the world, an Indian, a Zen Buddhist, a Roman Catholic in the purest sense of the word."

The party is using the campaign slogan of "No guns, no butter." ("Too much cholesterol," he explained.)

Lee has always felt that there is a group of like-minded people who are interconnected but were never meant to come in contact with each other, "a karass" as Vonnegut called it. Now, as a politician, he is meeting a lot of them, people who become active participants in speaking out against the two-party system. "People are confused and angry, they'd just as soon not vote as do anything. Bill Cosby did a spot on voting, that it's the greatest thing in the world, and here's a big corporate man who will sell anything, pudding pops, and there's a lot of people out there who just say it's not really worth it. Being a Rhinoceros means you don't vote for a Republican or a Democrat because you realize that neither is going to push the planet in the right direction."

Hunter Thompson was proposed as his running mate; the Rhinos thought he would be a great vice president because of his expertise in the field of vices. But at an appearance in Cambridge, Massachusetts, he introduced Dick "The Monster" Radatz as his veep. Lee sat on a stool sipping beer in his Jack Kerouac T-shirt, and answered questions fearlessly. When someone asked him about the issue of drug testing, he took his typical hard-line stance. "My position on mandatory drug testing? I've tested mescaline. I've tested 'em all. But I don't think it should be mandatory."

Joking aside, the psychedelic drugs were a turning point for Lee at one time. Regardless of all those who have abused controlled substances, Lee remains a staunch advocate of the altered state. Psychedelic use in the '60s, he said, gave people true conscience. "Once you went that route, you weren't going to vote Republican again. With the advent of knowledge, you reach another level of consciousness, and you can't ever go back again, as Thomas Wolfe said."

I asked Lee, a self-described product of the '60s, what he thought happened to the best and brightest hopes of his generation. "A lot of people went back into the stock market and started playin' the game. You can't bow down to the economic machine. If you get stuck in that, you're just as guilty as those depleting the rain forest in South America or destroying the ozone, it's as if you're holdin' a gun to the planet's head. On my gravestone, I don't want it said that I was responsible for the death of the late, great planet Earth."

The Can

*O*il Can Boyd was labeled a hot dog on his very first day in the big leagues. He pitched on Opening Day against the Yankees in Yankee Stadium and first baseman Bill Buckner made a diving stop behind him. So Boyd ran over and shook his hand excitedly, as Mark Fidrych, the Bird, used to do. Boyd's actions rubbed his opponents the wrong way, and hitters especially didn't care for his habit of pumping his fist after he got a big strikeout.

But that was the way Dennis Boyd learned to play the game growing up in Meridien, Mississippi. It was there that he got his nickname. "Oil," in the local slang, was the word for beer, and Boyd could throw down six-packs like it was nothing. Before he became a pro, it was nothing for him to drink prodigiously before the ball games.

No matter how much he eats or drinks, he doesn't gain an ounce. He stands six feet one and still only weighs 145 pounds. Inside his strong, scrawny frame are bundles of nervous energy; he has always been temperamental and high-strung. When he used to pitch as a teenager, a hitter would hit a homer off of him, and he would get so "burned up" that he would have to tear off his uniform.

Exhibiting that kind of behavior on the major-league level will cause people to ask questions about you, and Boyd came under close scrutiny in the middle of the 1986 season. When he wasn't named to the All-Star Team despite a fine first half, he started tearing up the locker room, and left the team. Considering that the Red Sox were leading the division at that point, some thought his outburst strange, wondering if Boyd's erratic behavior was caused by the use of controlled substances. (Boyd took a drug test to quell the rumors and passed it.)

Just about everything in Dennis Boyd's makeup—the showboating, the confidence, the pumped-up intensity and will to win, the blowups—can be traced to his baseball upbringing, for Dennis Boyd learned the game in a world far from that of the big leagues. For him it was a family recreation, a way of having fun and a way of life as well.

I met Dennis Boyd in Winter Haven in the spring of 1988. He had been hit by a line drive a few days earlier, but it proved not to be serious. Coming off a 1987 campaign that he lost to recurring injuries, he knew very well how much the Red Sox were counting on him to team with Clemens and Hurst as the backbone of the pitching staff, and was committed to showing everybody his newfound maturity.

I had never heard Boyd speak at length about anything, and frankly didn't know what to expect, but he bowled me over with his sincere kindness as soon as I told him I wanted to talk about growing up in Mississippi. I knew Dennis Boyd had stories he had never told, having pitched from the same mound as Satchel Paige, and having a father, Willie James Boyd, who played for the Homestead Grays.

We sat outside the Red Sox clubhouse in the warming sun, after the morning workout. Boyd wore his new wire-frame glasses that made him look quite studious. (The day after I left, I read that Boyd had shaved his head, which would make him the spitting image of Malcolm X in his prime.) It wasn't long before he got on a wondrous roll—in his rhythmic voice was all the enthusiasm and reverence for the game of baseball one could ever imagine.

"My dad's dad was Johnny B. Boyd, my mom's dad was a reverend, Benny McCoy. I never got a chance to see my mom's dad. My parents' mothers are living, but both of my grandfathers are not alive, and my dad's dad died when I was fourteen years old. From what I can understand, they were both very strong men, but from my dad's side of the family is where my baseball came from.

"My grandfather played and my great-grandfather played ball. My great-grandfather was ambidextrous. He pitched with both hands, a big man, the way I understood it, a Lee Smith type of pitcher, but bigger, that would be my granddad's dad. He played in the early days, with the original Homestead Grays, out of Mississippi. The Grays still exist in Mississippi, as a semi-pro sandlot kind of thing, and a lot of reminiscing goes on about those early days.

"My father probably has talked to me more about Satchel than any other man. He saw him pitch a lot. My dad's younger brother got a chance to travel with the Kansas City Monarchs when he was seventeen years old as a player, as a pitcher. Satchel himself took him there, and I remember my dad telling us, growing up on the job and everything—my dad's a landscaper, that's the family business—and you had a lot of time to reminisce because we all worked together side by side. In the summer months, when the work was done, then it was time to play baseball. But I remember him telling me about when Satchel came to town with what was known as the Hattisburgh Black Sox, way before we got a chance to join professional baseball or the white man's game, or whatever, and my momma told me they would line up the people in town just like it was a parade.

"Satchel's been home, he's been to my house. I met him finally in 1980, when they were making the movie of his life, and my pitching coach, Sippio Spinks, played a bartender in the movie. From a long shot, Sippio was doing the pitching, and I got a chance to meet Satchel. But that was my primary reason for going to Hattisburgh and that was the same season that I was drafted by the Red Sox. And he knew of me, he knew of my dad and my younger brothers and everything.

"Satchel pitched in Meridien in the early '40s, late '30s, around the time that Ted Williams was prosperin' in the big leagues, and he would come through with a team, traveling like Bingo Long and the Traveling All-Stars and Motor Kings. My dad told me that they came to Meridien with only six men on the ball team. Satchel was pitching and they had a catcher, a shortstop, a first baseman, and two outfielders. That was it. My dad said the first baseman put on a show. It was a showman type of baseball, with trick plays and hidden ball tricks and things like that.

"I played for the Homestead Grays in 1978 and 1979, semi-pro ball. I played with a lot of older men from age thirteen to age nineteen, I'd be playing with guys that were forty-five-year-old men who taught me the game of baseball. And my baseball makeup comes from that era of baseball that I grew up with, with old men saying, 'Throw it to me in the dirt, I do not want it thrown to me in the air.' I had a first baseman when I was fourteen years old playing semi-pro ball who'd get mad at me and swear me out for throwing him a good throw. He wanted to pick it out of the dirt!

"They had all this type of lingo goin' on that's not basically heard throughout the game right now, a Negro type of ritual that went on, and the fans in the stands were really into it, and it was just so lively, and the ballplayers back then, the way I understand it, literally played *for* the fans. They acknowledged the fans in the stands, and when they yelled, 'Hit Me a Home Run,' they would turn and bow and call their shot. It wasn't anything to see a guy turn a double play behind his back.

"Cool Papa Bell, my dad knew him personally, from growing up in Birmingham, Alabama, which is only an hour from where I grew up at. They played in Tuscaloosa, Atlanta, Columbus, Mobile, Pensacola, just about the whole southeast, Shreveport,

Baton Rouge. And at the end of the baseball season they would come together and play teams from Indiana and Kansas City against the Monarchs. What they would put together was Satchel, Cool Papa Bell, Josh Gibson, all these cats, man, has played in my home town, all these dudes has travelled down through there.

"Satchel had to pitch five innings every day. He warmed up over a matchbox. I know those kind of things were true because I come up with the same kind of makeup as a ballplayer, knowing that the things that they said may seem kind of farfetched, but they were true. I warmed up as a Little Leaguer, I used to be able to throw a curveball and drop it into a bucket on home plate. That's how I learned to make my curveball go down. I had a perfect curveball. We used to swing a tire hanging from a rope on a tree, and throw the ball through it. My other brother would catch it. My brothers and I used to line up in the backyard, from as far back as I can remember, and get beer bottles and beer cans and line 'em up on the fence post, and throw rocks, and hit 'em from a hundred feet away, like it was nothin'. And people wonder today why my control is so good, where it comes from. If I'm not the best control pitcher in the game, I'm the second best, and that's where it comes from, I've been doing it all my life, and I can count the times that I've made a bad throw.

"I grew up in a neighborhood where every little kid tried everything no matter how daring it was. I grew up practicing to catch a foul tip off the bat. Johnny Bench used to be able to do that, catch the foul tip on the ricochet off the bat, when it was movin', and I learned to do that when I was little. And we worked on trying to do that, and got everything from cracked teeth to teeth knocked out to broken noses. No mask, and it was like if we didn't have a game face mask we'd use a softball face mask, and many times the ball would come right through my face.

"I have seven brothers, two girls. The girls are the oldest. My sisters love the game, and I remember watchin' my older sister playing softball growing up. She was a left-handed hitter, and once upon a time, Blanche, to see a girl hit a ball over the fence was something to see, and she's a big girl, I'm talkin' about five-ten, one sixty, one seventy. I'm the smallest, they're all pretty stout, pretty buck and everything, and I'm by far the least talented out of all my brothers. I am the tallest. Right now I've got a brother a year and a half older than me and there's nothing that he can't do that you can think of in the game of baseball. I had two brothers who were good prospects. They all at one time looked to be at a professional level. But my oldest brother right now is only thirty-three years old, so we're all right there together, like twenty-eight, twenty-nine, thirty, thirty-one, thirty-two, thirty-three—Skeeter be thirty-four in September.

"That was the thing I've enjoyed most in all my experiences playing baseball, was when the seven of us played on the same field together. Playing semi-pro baseball, that's how it was every summer, the whole lineup was Boyd Boyd Boyd Boyd Boyd. And my dad's baby brother was doing the catching, so the whole lineup was eight Boyds. And then you had a first cousin. So the whole team was relatives. And they didn't know which one they could get out or who they should pitch to.

"It's a tough road, being the only one to make it this far, because besides my brothers playing, I had two uncles that were dynamite, and they just played at the wrong time. It was a very racial type thing, the league hadn't turned over yet. And my dad's younger brothers, if they got a chance to play ball, they would have come up in the late '50s, early '60s, and it was tough, especially for a black pitcher, and especially being from the South. They look for football players down there, and they were just overlooked.

"One scout told me, when I asked why they didn't come down to the South and do a lot of recruiting, he said that the type of baseball is not played down there like in New England and Florida, the caliber of baseball is nowhere, all you're going to get is a guy who can run fast and throw hard, but he don't know the game. They figure he's illiterate to the game or whatever, and that type of thing stays with you. And if you're not a Lee Smith . . . they figure that I'm exceptional, a kid 150 pounds who knows how to pitch, but I feel you're not gonna get a Dennis Boyd every day, whether you're black, brown, green, or blue.

"Believe it or not, being a pitcher came to me so natural that I never thought that this is what I wanted to do, because I played every position. I came to baseball, I wasn't just a pitcher, I felt like I was just an athlete when it came to playing the game of baseball. I could field ground balls, I could run as fast as anybody I knew. What probably pushed me more towards pitching is that when I was recruited out of high school to play college baseball, they put down positions played, I put down shortstop and pitching, and the coach had seen me pitch in a semi-pro game, so that's what he wanted me to do.

"The first thing Ted Williams ever said to me, he saw me throw in minor-league camp, the first time he had ever seen me, he was standing behind the backstop, and I'll never forget the day, he called time and said, 'Holy Cow, if it ain't Satchel in reincarnation.' And from that point on, he has been so good to me, he used to say he wanted to represent me, he talked me into the big leagues. He pulled for me every day, with other coaches, he said 'I don't care who you're lookin' at down here, that's the man you should have your eye on.' He was always telling people who were in charge of things to keep their eye on me, and sayin' 'I want to represent him, I want to be his agent!'

"From the day I been here, I been accepted, management has been behind me, they went through some ups and downs with me, but I learned, I know what's goin' on, I know what to expect from myself, and that's to do a good job regardless of the circumstances. You're in a different world now. You're gettin' *paid to play*, and right away, regardless of whether you want to change or not, it's gonna change you, if not right now, then later. The media, when I first got up here, everybody kind of flocked to me right away, because of the colorful nickname, and I seem to be a character. So I've always been focused on very highly with attention, even when I was in the minor leagues."

Pitching for all the marbles in the World Series is a long way from Boyd's beginnings. He looked forward to the challenge, but admitted it wasn't quite what he bargained for. "The World Series was just different," he said. "I got to go back so I can understand what's goin' on. You play for it every year, and it seems to be the greatest thing that could ever come around, you know, you go out there so many times that you think you'll never get nervous, you'll never have butterflies. As soon as the playoffs or World Series comes along, it's like you've never been out there. I'd like to see what it's like again, because I can't even flashback on what I really enjoyed."

Boyd has said he wants to go out of the game "gray-headed," and that he's saving some of his pitches for his old age. Right now, they don't include spitters or other illegal pitches. The only thing he's been accused of is wearing gold chains around his neck to distract hitters. "I've never cheated, I never really thought about it. Some guys go out and they scuff the balls and that type thing. Maybe when I'm an older man, I don't know what I might do, but right now I'm using my youth and my strength and power and I go from there, I'm still a winning pitcher any way you look at it.

"I don't mess with my motion at all, my mechanics are pretty sound. What I work on is the mental part of my game, which varies by the hitter. I try to sharpen it up. I've been blessed in being able to throw the baseball, but I've also been blessed to know how well I can throw it. I can throw the ball over the plate without worrying about when and how and if I can. The Lord has not just given me a great arm, but a great arm and how to use it. That's probably the best thing that could ever happen. So I feel good about it, and basically I can go out there with a game plan, and believe it or not, I really feel like I'm in control all the time.

"I fight with myself and I really don't have to, and that's what I want to get out of myself, that you don't have to try hard and do it, just go out there and do it. It's not gonna do what you want to do, you're not gonna put it in that good spot, if you overthrow. So many things can work against you.

"For me, going in, everything works for me. I never went into a game, even if that slider ain't pinpoint, I can make an adjustment and get it over. I never went out there and said 'I didn't have my stuff that day.' Every day, no matter what, I have all my pitches. I'm just a pitcher. When I go out there, things click. I don't have to worry about what's workin' that day. When I go to the bullpen, it's for just what it is, a fifteen-minute warmup, just to get loose. I already got my game plan, I don't have to try and throw that slider for a strike, I just throw it, I don't have to pinpoint that fastball inside, I just throw it when I see that mitt inside.

"I vary the pattern. I never pitch in a pattern. Let's say I face a guy the first time up, I might throw him this sequence of pitches. The second time he comes up, he might not see any of the pitches he saw the first time, he might see 'em in different locations. And that's what I go out there for, and you have to have serious concentration in order not to get into a pattern, you have to be two pitches ahead, and I'm always thinking two pitches ahead. I've already got the out pitch waiting. The first pitch is not the purpose pitch, the first pitch is to get ahead. The second pitch is the purpose pitch. The third pitch is the out pitch. You've got to set the purpose pitch up right, which is basically, bust the guy way inside. So you do it in that sequence, and I try and throw as few pitches as I can.

"Mentally I try to pick up little things, day by day, that I steal from other guys, not a new pitch, but how to pitch. I talk to Bruce Hurst and I talk to guys about 'Do you pitch off of the plate, why do you pitch off of the plate?' It's very difficult to see the ball, when it's thrown so hard, if it's just off of the plate. It's hard, so if you keep puttin' it there, he'll start calling it, and it's not a strike. It's not thrown over the plate, but you keep putting it there, he'll call it.

"You try to get a guy out front. Their eyes tell me what they're trying to do. It's like a boxer. Where they direct their eyes, eye shifts, head shifts, you watch it all. Sometimes a guy will deke you with that front foot. You can't go for that front foot, because a guy could come up to you with an open stance, you're gettin' him out, then he comes up the next time with a closed stance, you think he's doin' it 'cause you're getting him out, he wants you to think he's gonna dive out there now, so you should bust him inside. But keep pitchin' him out there. I learned, don't second-guess yourself. Keep makin' your pitch until he can hit it with some authority. Not when he hits it, but with some authority.

"In the off season mostly I do a lot of running, and with me, eating is important. I have to have good eating habits to maintain myself. I'm a naturally strong little guy to carry a frame like this. I just try and keep myself thinkin', thinkin' baseball, thinkin' positive all the time. I don't have to face a hitter for five months, but I'm in a game situation when I'm in my car drivin'. That's how I feel about it, I'm always reminiscing about how to make things better. I try to change something every year as to what I'm thinking."

"The biggest adjustment was adjusting to the hitters, learning the hitters. The guys who are tough are the guys who put the ball in play, the big power guys never really hurt me. I mean, I give up home runs because I'm around the plate all the time, but I don't give up three-run shots, I give up solo shots, so I look at it like that. Probably the biggest adjustment was adjusting to the hitters in the major leagues as opposed to the minors. They're more patient, but when they swung, they hit the ball. In the minor leagues they're aggressive, they'll hack at everything, and then they even miss good pitches. In the big leagues, they'll take your best pitch, and hit your worst pitch.

"You get out bad hitters with good stuff, and you get out good hitters with bad stuff. You make a good pitch to a good hitter, *they like that*. That's what makes Wade a good hitter, you pitch him inside and he can line that ball to left field. Instead of trying to turn on the ball, he can do somethin' different. So the guy who's always in front on the fastball gives you room to get him out other places. So I just try and be a thinker out there, try to be a hundred percent thinker out there, and go out with a game plan and an idea. I don't pitch a whole team the same way, I pitch individual players. I don't so much go by the charts, where he hits the ball, 'cause I figure he'll hit the ball where I throw it if he's a good hitter.

"I never think about coming out of a game. I just go out there to win. Mac gives me the baseball and he tells me, 'It's your game.' He knows, I've shown him so many times, more than I haven't, that when I get in a jam, I can get out of it, so he lets me stay out there. He says that's what he likes the most about me. He says 'Right now, you're rated one of the top five pitchers in the game because of what you can do under pressure.'

"He said, 'I've seen you bust the side out with the bases loaded. I've seen you start off the inning by giving up a triple, and strand the man at third,' more so than I've even given up the run. If you can beat the odds of the game when that man is on third and no out . . . For some reason I know how to get out of that. I pound that right-hander inside, I'm gonna try and get him to pop it up. You throw the ball in a certain area and they'll get under it and pop it up. I need that fly or that bloop to left. And you get it by busting that ball out over the plate, and any aggressive hitter with a man on third, he's gonna hack and you know it, you beat 'em at what they want, just make it a little higher than he likes it and they'll pop that baby up. They say, 'Darn' and 'Shit, I just missed it,' but I got one out. I know that I beat you and you didn't 'just missed it,' I need that, and I know how to make that hitter pull it, no matter what. And that second guy, that's the guy you try and punch out. Not the first guy, the second guy, to cut off a rally. You've got to punch him out because it boosts me. I already got the first guy, I want to punch the second motherfucker out, 'cause if you try and punch the first guy out, it works against you. For some reason I've had it happen to me, you try and get too pumped up, you think I've got to get this bastard now, that's the first thing that comes in your mind, instead of stepping off and thinking 'Okay, I've got to try and get a fly ball from this first guy.' Now if you get the first guy, then you're more relaxed for the second guy, now you can make some bastard pitches because you want to get out of the inning now. You're not sure if you're gonna get out of it without a run, but if you walk him, you still can get out of it with a double play. Now if I get the second guy, the last guy I'll get out any kind of way I can, and I'll make some bastard pitches to this guy, too, but not so much with the idea that I'm going to strike him out. This guy, I want to get out with the first pitch. Preferably he's a left-hand hitter so right away I can throw that out pitch.

"Mac has seen me do it so much, he sees that's what I'm doing, I'm making guys beat themselves, and that's the way I take the game out there. It's good to know that even if I could throw the ball only seventy-five miles an hour, they'd still send me out there because I can do the job as a pitcher. They don't need me to throw a hundred miles an hour out there every day, they just need me to be out there every day.

"Pitching the clincher [when the Red Sox won the American League East pennant] was probably the most meaningful ball game to me as a player, but for the club more than anything that was the most prosperous thing that could happen. As an individual game, I've had many good games but the one that stands out is the time I went seven innings of no-hit ball against Baltimore. Mike Young broke it up. He hit a little flare right off of the wall. If that ball had been caught, I'd go to the eighth inning with the weakest part of the lineup coming up and I would have made it to the ninth. But I'd walk me a man to throw a no-hitter. I'd walk their best hitter, if I had to walk three hitters to face the three rookies in the lineup I'd do it.

"But that was the game that was effortless. I wasn't even trying. You just let it keep flowin'. It's a funny feeling, it's a great feeling, but you feel insecure out there, because you feel like you want to do it by yourself. Somethin' else is takin' over. You're wondering if your shit is just that good tonight, and guys are hitting the first ball you throw up there right at somebody and it very seldom happens, and that's the great game of baseball."

The vicissitudes of the great game of baseball were none too kind to Boyd in the 1988 campaign. He began the year getting lit up like the proverbial Christmas tree, and then came the bad news in the second half of the season when a blood clot was discovered in his right shoulder. Medication dissolved the clot and he came back to pitch six shutout innings before another blood clot was found, and Oil Can went home for the year.

A Day at the Batting Cage with Ted and John Henry Williams

*E*very spring, Ted Williams comes over from his home in Cross Keys, Florida, to appraise, encourage, and advise the young hitters in the Red Sox organization. At the age of seventy, in full uniform, wearing dark sunglasses in the brilliant sun, he leaned on the batting cage at the Red Sox' Yawkey Field in Winter Haven. There are undoubtedly more imposing things than initiating a conversation with Ted Williams, but I'm not sure what they are.

I walked up to the cage and waited until he noticed me standing there. "Ted," I said, "there's something I have to tell you. As you know, your autobiography *My Turn at Bat* was out of print for some time. I had never read it, but I found the paperback in a used bookstore six years ago in San Francisco, and since it was only a week to my thirtieth birthday, I decided to read it on that day, so I went up to a hill overlooking the Bay . . ."

"Hey, everybody, quiet!" he yelled, cutting me off. "Listen to this!" I don't think it was to embarrass me, just that he probably thought, "Oh, this is gonna be good." He turned back to me calmly, and now everyone around the cage froze and was watching and listening because Ted Williams so instructed them. How many times, I wondered, have people gone up to Ted Williams to tell him something . . . but I've never been afraid to say something silly if I thought it was absolutely true.

"Well," I continued, "I read the book that day, cover to cover, and it was the closest thing I had ever experienced to the sound of baseball talking." He stopped to digest this, and then nodded. I knew that he was very proud of the book. "Thank you," he said sincerely. "No, Ted," I replied, "I meant to thank *you*, because your book was all I really had. I only had one chance to see you play. It was in 1960 in Briggs Stadium in Detroit. I saw you hit two doubles in the first major-league baseball game I ever saw."

This little exchange didn't make us fast friends by any means, but it was enough for Ted Williams to tolerate me standing by his side at the batting cage, for which I was grateful. Williams gets tugged at a lot. Autograph hunters wait in the morning for his van to show up. "Did you see Williams?" they ask each other expectantly. When he does drive up, he's instantly swarmed upon by people thrusting balls, bats, and pictures for him to sign. He usually stops to sign as many autographs as he can for a few minutes, then gruffly moves on. But it's a losing proposition; there are always people left waiting.

Once he's in uniform by the batting cage, fans cannot approach him, but a CBS crew tentatively moved into his supposed sanctuary with a camera and sound boom. They didn't want an interview, they just wanted to film him and capture the voice that sounds more like his hero, John Wayne, than any impressionist. He looks like Wayne, too, but he didn't afford CBS anything more than the still-classic profile. He barely acknowledged them, and after a few minutes they moved on. The business and pleasure of these days for him is watching and working with these young hitters.

A young player stepped into the cage choking up five inches on the bat, but pulling the ball hard. "He reminds me of Chet Laabs," said Williams. "Remember Chet Laabs? He could hit it as hard as anybody." Another young Latin American hitter reminded him of one of his favorites, Tony Oliva. As a ball was resoundingly smacked into the alley, I asked him if he could tell a good hitter by the sound. "Yeah," he said, "I think a good hitter cracks it a little different."

Overhead floated a large blimp with "Fuji" printed on it. Ted looked up and shook his head ruefully. "They're gonna own everything," he said. I asked him if he heard what Bill Gullickson said when he started pitching in Japan—that the only American words he recognized over there were "Sony" and "Mitsubishi." Ted liked that, but he doesn't laugh very easily.

We talked a bit about the long dinner and many drinks he had with Mattingly and Boggs last spring for *Sports Illustrated*, during which he brought up the oddity of fouling off a good fastball and smelling smoke rising from the bat. "Yep," he said excitedly, "that's the first time I ever told anybody about it. Mattingly thought I was doing coke or something. But I asked Kiner and he knew. Musial said he didn't know about such things—'I never fouled 'em off,' he said. 'How should I know?' "

The smoking bat story amazed a lot of people—it was almost as incredible as the stories about Williams's eyesight. A Navy doctor who checked Williams's eyes in 1942 said he had 20/10 vision, and Williams felt thereafter that his eyes were given more credit than they deserved for his hitting. Williams doesn't think the ball looked any bigger to him than it did to any other player.

"I was a pretty good guesser, and I knew I could hit a fastball, and I knew a lot of guys were afraid to throw me a fastball, so I started looking for the other stuff." But Ted Williams knew when he hit the ball if he was connecting with the seams or not. When I asked him about this, he sloughed it off. "Anybody can see the seams, the coaches can tell if they're hitting with the seams or not." They can? Oh, really?

Where Williams's eyesight really helped was in his knowledge of the strike zone. It was one of his commandments never to swing at a ball that wasn't a strike, for which he was criticized throughout his career. But he would take a walk, because he felt that a good hitter swinging at a good pitch was better than a great hitter swinging at a bad one. His idea of a great hitter was someone who walked three times as much as he struck out.

Both leagues had just made an adjustment in the strike zone for the '88 season, so I asked Williams what he thought about it. "Where's my belly-button?" he growled. I pointed at his midsection, and he said, "Where is it? Show me where it is!" I pointed my finger at his waistband. "No, that's not it!" He pulled down the waistband of his baseball pants, grabbed my finger, and stuck it in his belly-button. So there I was, with my finger in the navel of the greatest hitter who ever lived. "Here it is," he said. "Now this ball at the belly-button has got to be a strike. They only been givin' 'em the low strike, and so everybody's pitching there."

Williams watched the pitchers closely as well as the hitters, as he always did. He saw one he liked, the Red Sox number-one draft pick, Reggie Harris. "Boy, good delivery, good everything. I'd stay with him for forty years. Damn right, damn right," he muttered. "Twenty-four, Jesus Christ." A pitch came in close to the hitter. "He don't like hitters, he don't like you. *He does not like hitters!*"

I asked him what he thought of young pitchers today, compared to those of his generation. "I think they're getting better coaching. You've got to have maturity. The guys who make it look the most natural are the ones who have done it the most, the guys from Florida and California."

He likes to talk about pitching. He gripped a baseball and held it up. "This is the best way to throw a curve," he announced to nobody in particular. "You know why?" The coaches around the cage played dumb. I knew why. "You've got both fingers on a seam to get maximum friction on your release point," I said. "That's right," Williams drawled, then turned and saw it was me who said it and not one of the coaches, and did a slow double take. "Son of a gun," he said, "that's right."

Another young hitter, just a number to Williams, turned on some balls with authority. "How much did you hit, .321? You look good, keep going, that's all. How old are you? Twenty-two? Is that your real age or your baseball age?" He turned to me, muttering. "You gotta watch for these goddamn South American kids, they tell you they're seventeen, they're really twenty-two. They oughta be pretty good." I asked him if he thought Valenzuela was twenty-one when he came to the National League. "What a great pitcher," he said. "I don't know, I don't know, it's very possible that he wasn't twenty-one. It's hard to be as fucking good as he was, the curveballs, everything, a hell of a pitcher."

Occasionally Ted would play with a hitter's style, get him to widen his stance. "I'd like to see you spread out just a fraction, now be quick." The hitter lined one to left. "It's a little solider, but that's for you to decide, something for you to play with. Eliminate a lot of loose stuff. Just try it, that's all. I think it's a little solider. When I started playing I was like this . . . and I ended up like this, and I think you will, too. But you know, through experimenting and practice, I got to there, but you gotta decide, too, cuz you hit the ball just as hard, make a few less mistakes. Even now you feel good there, don't you?. . . Now just for fun, spread out a little bit more, just cock your wrists and rip, that's all right. That ain't changin' a thing, is it? Not a thing, not a damn thing. If you feel it's too much, come back a little bit."

Some of these hitters genuinely excited Ted. He said the crop of young hitters in Florida this year was 25 percent better than the crop that produced Burks, Greenwell, Horn, Marzano, and Benzinger a few years ago. "Jeez," Ted repeated over and over, "ya look good," as the hitters sprayed line drives all over the field. "Atta boy! I'll put my name on him. I want to be his agent. He can't miss . . . that is, unless he's dumb. Ya look good, ya can't look any better than that. Ya look good, buddy." Then *crack*, another shot through the box. "He's got line-drive-itis!"

The last hitter of the day stepped in and lit up the batting-practice pitcher, brightening up Williams as well. When the moon-faced young man left the cage, Ted called him over.

"What's your name, son?"

"Lou Munoz." He said so breathlessly that the coaches thought his name was Loomis or Luminos.

"You're great. You Irish all look the same. How many years you played in school?"

"Three."

"You an outfielder?"

"Third baseman. I'm reading your book."

"Good. You find something in there you don't agree with, we ought to talk about it. I'm glad you're interested in finding some material to read about hitting. And listen, what I say, no matter who talks to you—listen. Then it's up to you to say, 'I like that, it works for me,' or else you say, 'I don't like that.' "

Lou Munoz stumbled away backwards, glowing from the encounter. He had gone to the University of Florida and hit .388 in Division One in Tampa, and expected to report to A ball where his manager would be Doug Camili. Ted said he looked good, and somebody said, yeah, he's got a nice swing, and Ted said, "I'm talking about his looks." I asked if he always considered how someone looked when sizing up a prospect. "Who the hell doesn't look at guys' faces?"

I wondered how many of these young hitters were reading about hitting. "Not enough," said Williams. "There's only one book that they can get a hold of, and that's *The Science of Hitting* that I wrote." And there it was, the vaunted, legendary Williams arrogance, brushing aside Lau and Hriniak, who have also written books on hitting. Williams may have mellowed, but there is still that part of him that is the same guy with such abounding belief in himself that he used to hang around batting cages when he was a player pumping himself up by saying, "I'm Ted fucking Williams and I'm the best hitter that ever lived."

He has a different idea than Hriniak, for instance, about what Wade Boggs's goals should be. Williams has always wanted Boggs to hit home runs as well as hit for average. "I talked to Boggs in the minor leagues, and I always told him, don't let anybody change you. But in batting practice he'll put on a show hitting homers so you know he can do it."

Williams thinks that when you get the pitcher in the hole, 2–0, 3–1, 3–0, that's the time to guess and try and pull the ball. He still holds that with two strikes you have to concede something to the pitcher so you can make contact, which a lot of hitters have refused to do. Mantle, thought Williams, had a great chance to hit .400 because of his great speed, but he conceded nothing with two strikes, he never tried to hit a single.

The day's practice session ended. On another practice field, working out with the minor leaguers, was his only son, John Henry Williams, age eighteen. (Williams also has two daughters.) "John Henry wants me to come up and look at him hit. I haven't seen him the last two or three days. He got so much exercise one day, he couldn't swing the bat. Goddamn, I'll tell you what he had for breakfast, he had a cheese-and-ham omelet, French toast, and he had toast, too. I had a piece of his toast."

Ted abruptly jumped into a cart, riding to the adjacent practice field to watch his son take batting practice. Before the batting-practice pitcher got ready, Ted spied a photographer smoking a cigarette on the bench. "I'd like to see Peter Ueberroth ban smoking around the ball field," he said. I recalled how I used to see Hank Aaron hiding cigarettes in the dugout. "That's right," he said, "a lot of 'em smoked all kinds of 'em, Grove, DiMaggio." I'd heard about DiMaggio chain-smoking Camels in the clubhouse. "Yeah, but he went on to Lucky Strikes . . . DiMaggio was the best player of my era, but I got sick of looking at him, he was so damn good, we were having a harder time beating the Yankees because of him."

John Henry stepped into the cage. He is dark, good-looking, bearing a strong resemblance to Ted when he was that age, right down to the long arms and legs. Another hitting guru, Harry "The Hat" Walker, came by, and Ted had John Henry take a few easy practice swings for Harry, who watched closely. "Just relax and swing through," Ted said. "It's a good swing, isn't it?" he asked Walker, and The Hat smiled appreciatively.

As a hitter, John Henry didn't look too bad, but he was obviously inexperienced, although he's going to get a lot stronger when he fills out. His best hits were looping line drives into the gaps. John Henry shook his head, complaining that his bat was slow that day. "Just ping it now," Ted advised, "just swing at it, wherever it is." After batting practice, John Henry went out to shag some flies, and then Ted got on him good-naturedly.

John Henry was an enthusiastic butcher in the field, and each fly ball was an adventure. "*Charge it!*" Ted yelled as the ball went up. John Henry got a late jump and it fell in. "*Shoulda had it.*" On the next ball, John Henry got a good jump and streaked to his left, glove outstretched. "Yeah," Ted said, "he'll get that." The ball tipped off his glove. "Oh Christ Almighty, he fucked it up. The one-armed bandit . . ." On the next one, Ted remained silent, until John Henry redeemed himself with a good running catch. "That's a boy! *Oh-hoo boy!*"

When the session ended, only a few stragglers were left at the practice field, as the spring-training game between the Red Sox and Royals reached the ninth inning at the main stadium. It is only then that Williams, in relative privacy, picked up a bat for the first time. "I can't hit anymore," he said. "I played in old-timers' games and the last few years I haven't hit so much as a loud foul." But when he picked up the bat, cocked it, and then moved it in slow motion into an imaginary pitch, the hips moving, the timing still apparently perfect, right to the point of imaginary impact, that's all it really took for the years to roll away for a moment, and he was again The Kid, The Splendid Splinter himself.

"He just wants to play," Ted said of John Henry. "He's never gonna be a big leaguer, but he wants to have that extra thing in college for him, because he loves to participate, he loves baseball. It's a motivator. The first school he went to, he couldn't get with it, and I know he's not a dumb kid. Now he likes that school in Maine because it's got a good baseball program."

John Henry didn't spend a lot of time around the Red Sox clubhouse when he was growing up, but the last two years he's been around. They call him "Little Teddy." He's quite popular around camp, personable and very accommodating to autograph seekers and people who want pictures. "Yeah," Ted admitted, "he's a good kid, at least I think so."

I sat with John Henry on the hood of a car in the small parking lot next to the non-roster players' clubhouse, and we began talking about his father's influence on the young hitters down here. "I can see some of these guys just *melt* when he says, 'What's that guy's name up there?' They'll be hitting, and they'll hear Ted say something, and they can't hit anymore."

When John Henry Williams was growing up in Vermont, he played soccer and basketball, ran cross-country, and wrestled a bit. He didn't grow up a fan of the Red Sox or any team, really. Then he suddenly got serious about playing the game of baseball. "I just started the game a year ago. Every year in school I played, but it's only been a thirteen-game schedule in the spring, then the whole thing's over with. Ask anyone here, they've played every year of their life almost. I plan on playing this summer for the first time, then if I do well, in Maine."

The Red Sox got John Winkin the job as head coach at Maine, and John Henry knew him, but didn't believe that would make things any easier for him. "That can work against you, too. He's going to try and be fair with me, and show everyone else that he's fair. He'll have a vested interest in me, but he has to be a coach, not a friend, so he's going to have to worry about what other people might think, that I'm getting a better shot because I'm Ted Williams's son. He may not be trying to make it tougher, but he might make it tougher, I don't know. I've gotten sick of worrying about it. I have no control over it."

Being Ted Williams's son, he is watched closely. "I can remember in school, even, we'd be horsing around, and when I'd get up to the plate, all I could hear was *ssshoop*, just the ball, everybody would have stopped everything that they're doing, just watching. You could hear a pin drop." It was the same way when John Henry first came down to spring training. People asked for his autograph right away, and they still do. "Maybe they think they see something future-wise, but I know it's because of who my dad is. I'm fighting it when I really shouldn't be, I don't want to worry about someone saying 'Ted Williams's son,' I want to be known as John Henry Williams, so it's something that, if I just be normal and forget about it, everything will be fine."

But there are constant reminders that he is Ted's son. He met Joe DiMaggio and the man he respectfully refers to as "Mr. Yastrzemski," through his father. Someone else introduced him to Jim Rice. "He said 'How ya doin' ?', you know, big deal, and then Ted said 'Have you met my son?' and it was totally different. It wasn't me, it was who I was connected to, but I understand that."

John Henry's mother was Delores Wettech, who was Miss Vermont and a model for *Vogue*. "My mom and dad got divorced early, I was never around my dad for a long time, and I rarely see him, and it would be kind of fun if I could become a friend instead of a son, because there has to be a time when it changes so that your dad can stop being a dad and share things and become a friend. Friends can really grow close, and you always have the father and son. I wish I could understand him better, that's why I really wish I could become a friend instead of just his son. It's hard to become a friend. I had a grandfather, and I could tell him anything I wanted, and he was my best friend, my mom's dad, Carl Wettech. He died two and a half years ago. It's weird to lose a person there. If I think about it, I think of what it would be like if Dad wasn't there, and he's in good health, but he could be hit by a truck, and thinking if he's gone, what would I do . . ."

His father was one of the most misunderstood players who ever played, and John Henry's take on the frequent booing that his father endured is that "fans are hypocritical." Even now, he sees the strain on his father of being Ted Williams. "I'm sure Dad wishes sometimes he was not even known, go out to dinner and not be noticed, not even worry about it. Maybe that's why he loves fishing so much."

When Ted says that is son is never going to be a major leaguer, he may be trying to relieve some of the pressure of following in his footsteps—John Henry is more ambitious than that. "I'm not doing it because my dad did it. I want to do it because I want to do it. I just happen to like the game and I feel I can excel in this. It's better to try it and fail than to think that I could have done it and hate myself for not having tried it.

"I feel terrible swinging right now, I don't feel quick, I don't feel comfortable, I don't feel strong, I don't feel secure, I feel awkward right now. If I keep on working on it, I'll click. I can't feel comfortable being a mediocre hitter. I want to be a good hitter and I know I can be a good hitter. It's just, I have to get coordinated up there to just make it natural, see that ball and not even think about it hardly. That's what Dad made it, a natural thing.

"I can pick his brain about hitting. If there's one thing Dad knows how to do, it's hit. We talk about a lot of little things. I pretty much have the idea. I just have to get it toned down. Did you ever see Dad's statue in the Hall of Fame? I remember when they were making it, the sculptor had taken this block of wood, and he took a chainsaw and carved out this general outline, his arms were this big, it was totally raw. That's the way I am now, and I have to chisel it away to make it perfect."

My Mother, the Batting Champ

*B*aseball, wrote the poet and essayist Donald Hall, is fathers
playing catch with sons. In pitcher Mike Flanagan's case,
he played catch with his father, uncle, and grandfather, com-
prising a four-man "King and his Court" that challenged all com-
ers. When Flanagan was eight years old, his grandfather, who
was an ambidextrous pitcher, called him into the basement to
give him a black tube of slippery elm. "Someday," he said, "you're
going to need this." Flanagan didn't even know that he was being handed a rare and favored lubricant used in the art of ball-
doctoring. "I wish I'd kept it," he said.

This cyclical passing of the wand from one generation to the
next is traditionally an exchange between men and boys. Few
ever say that baseball is mothers playing catch with sons. But
that's the way it was for Casey Candaele. Then again, not a lot
of guys have mothers who played professional baseball. Not softball, hardball. Casey's mother, Helen St. Aubin, was a member
of the AAGPBL (All-American Girls Professional Baseball League)
for eight years, and this was a hardball league.

The AAGPBL was started in 1943. It was tied in with World
War II insofar as there was serious talk that the '43 major-league

baseball season would be called off by President Roosevelt because of the war effort. It was Phil Wrigley, the owner of the Chicago Cubs, who had the idea of putting together a women's league to continue bringing out baseball fans even if there was no major-league baseball.

Wrigley's plan was to install franchises in small midwestern industrial cities, and promote the teams as morale-boosting entertainment for war-weary factory workers. With the support of Dodgers president Branch Rickey, he went ahead and held tryouts at Wrigley Field. Two hundred of the country's top women players showed up and four teams of equal ability were put together representing Rockford, Illinois; South Bend, Indiana; and Kenosha and Racine in Wisconsin.

Helen Callaghan had never played hardball before she turned pro. Always athletically inclined, she had grown up in Canada playing softball in the summer, as well as lacrosse and basketball. She easily met the skill requirements for playing in the league, but that's not all there was to it.

Phil Wrigley insisted that the women who played in the league be trained at Helena Rubenstein's Charm School. It was one thing if a woman could hit, run, and throw, but they also had to be able to balance books on their heads and walk the walk. The women were also schooled on how to put on makeup so that their lipstick wouldn't smear in a game situation.

Wrigley wanted the league marketed by having the women project ultra-feminine characteristics along with their ability to play ball, like Pete Roses in the bodies of Nancy Reagans. They even had to wear skirts during the games, so they had to slide on their bare legs, raising rainbow welts and strawberries. But it was just part of the league, and something that they all accepted. The women also had chaperones who prohibited smoking or drinking, at least in public, and enforced a 12:30 A.M. curfew.

Initially, fans came out to see the women play out of curiosity, but after witnessing a well-executed squeeze play or a lightning pickoff, they soon realized that these women could really play ball. Originally the rules were a hybrid of baseball and fast-pitch softball. Nine players took the field, bases were sixty-five feet apart, and the ball was softball-size. The pitchers used windmill, underhand motions. But over the years, the base length went to eighty-five feet, the ball shrank to almost the size of a regulation hardball, sidearm pitching was allowed, and then finally overhand pitching. The league grew to eight teams in 1946 and attendance peaked in 1948, when 910,000 saw the women play.

In 1945 Helen Callaghan hit .299, which led the league. She had her first child in 1947, and although she continued to play, it proved too difficult to be away from home. "It was over," she said, "and time to get on with raising a family." Attendance for the women's league dwindled in the '50s as all manner of new recreational pursuits like television rose to prominence, and the league played its last game in 1954. Once the league disbanded, it was as if the teams and the women players fell into a black hole, never to be heard of again. Indeed, it seems that everyone had forgotten about the league. Even in the heyday of the women's movement in the '70s, when the fact that these women playing baseball could have been made into a cause célèbre, it was never brought up because nobody knew about it.

Casey Candaele grew up without even knowing of his mother's career as a pro ballplayer until he was a sophomore in high school. "What I saw was a newsletter sittin' there, All-American Girls Professional Baseball League. I said, 'Mom, what's that?' She said, 'It's the women's baseball league I used to play in.' Then she opened up and talked a little bit about it. She's a very humble and yet complex woman. I think she's got a lot of memories that are her own that she probably thinks about and doesn't ever offer to anybody unless they dig deep and ask about 'em."

But still I had to wonder, not knowing Casey Candaele's mother, why she didn't talk about such a major part of her life. "I think maybe it was because she didn't want to push us into sports," Candaele said. "She was always a mother who wanted her kids to make their own decisions as to what they want to do in life, and that was probably part of the reason. She offered advice if we asked for advice, and she would do anything you wanted to do. If you wanted to go out there and hit balls or play catch, she would go out there and do it."

The world finally caught up with the AAGPBL when Helen's son Kelly made a documentary with filmmaker Kim Wilson called *A League of Their Own*, which was aired on public television. (An assistant professor at Northwestern University has completed a half-hour documentary about the league, *When Diamonds Were a Girl's Best Friend.*) Now the Hall of Fame plans an exhibit on the women's league. "I was astounded that Kelly wanted to make the documentary about this period in my life," Helen said. "Without his making it, my life would have passed without anyone knowing about women playing professional baseball."

A League of Their Own shows the women at a reunion, having not seen each other for more than thirty years, since their playing days when they sang together on bus rides. At a picnic, the women played catch, and even though most of them were in their fifties and sixties, all you had to see was the way they threw the ball to know that they could really play the game. Hitting was a different story. As Helen said, "You get rusty after forty years."

After the reunions, Helen went to Chicago with a few former teammates to watch her son play in Wrigley Field, where she had once played. Casey remembered calling his mother when he got the news that he was joining the Expos. "You're going back to the big leagues," he told her.

It was quite an accomplishment for Candaele, considering that he had never been a regular at the start of any season he had ever played, including high school or the minor leagues. Wherever he was, he always had to make the team.

He played in the minor leagues three and a half years before he got the call, coming up halfway through the '86 season when Andre Dawson got injured. Candaele had not been with the Expos in spring training, so he thought there was no way manager Buck Rodgers would ask for him when he hadn't really seen him play.

Candaele didn't play much, and then went back to the minors when Dawson returned and he caught fire. "I don't know if it was because I got a taste of the big leagues and wanted to get back so bad or what, but it really turned me around and I had a great offensive year."

However, by the time he was called back to the majors for the end of that season, he had been in a tough pennant race in the International League with Indianapolis, and he was "beat and tired and emotionally drained." He hit .231 in 100 at-bats. He went to spring training in 1987, made the team again, and played a key role in the National League East pennant drive, as the Expos stayed in the race until a doubleheader loss to the Cardinals in September. "It just goes to show how one day in baseball can turn around a whole season." All in all, it was a tremendous experience for someone whose goal was to just play one single day in the major leagues.

Actually, Candaele's first love was football. "I was a quarter-back and free safety, but I thought about college ball and thought I might get crushed up and broken in half. I would have liked to continue to play football but I knew I had to concentrate on one sport, and at the time baseball started to take over from football as the sport that I love more."

He played baseball all through Little League, high school, and college. His father, Robert Candaele, was his coach. "He was a semi-pro hockey player from Canada. His nickname was 'Red-light' Bobby Candaele. We used to watch the Habs all the time. I've got four older brothers and he wanted to make us all into catchers, I think because that was the closest thing to a goalie in baseball. So we all started out as catchers, and then progressed from there."

His mother, of course, was a prime influence as well. "She was a great athlete and taught me the fundamentals of the game. She could run and she was real tough, and taught me to be tough. I'd go outside and play against my brothers, I was the youngest, and I'd play against two of 'em, and one would hit me high and one would hit me low, and I'd come runnin' in crying, and she would just say, 'If you can't handle playin' with the big guys, don't play, but if you want to, then get back out there.' She's a real tough lady, she's been through a lot in her life and overcome a lot of crises. She's probably the toughest person I know. I hope some of it has rubbed off on me."

"When I was young, whenever a game came on I'd want to be outside playin' instead of watchin' it. I'd go outside and make up my own game, throwing the ball against the wall and just doing things like that because I always wanted to be active, doing it and not just watching it. I'll watch the World Series, but I'd rather be playin' it than watchin' it. Now I watch games because they're much more interesting now that I know all the little intricacies of the game."

Despite Casey's size, five feet nine and 165 pounds, his parents or stepfather never tried to discourage him. "They never said 'What are you doing? Get on with your life.' I know a lot of people get told that, and it's very discouraging, it just breaks all their dreams. I've always been the kind of person, if there's something that I want to do, I'm gonna try at it, and at least I'm gonna give it a shot."

"Baseball is a great game. There's a lot of opportunities in it for people who might not have been blessed with the most physical talent like a Strawberry has. But if you know how to use certain things and know the rules of the game and know the fundamentals of the game and learn how to play the game properly, the way it's supposed to be played, and do a lot of little things. . . . You can't become a great hitter, most of the guys who are great hitters are just great hitters. But as far as becoming a great fielder, you can do it, and I wanted to just be the best player I could, and that's how I learned all the positions and how to play 'em. Don't get me wrong, I'd rather play one position and play it every day. But if you can play all the positions, that's a lot of ways that you can help the team."

When he first came up to the big leagues, Candaele was so gung-ho just to be there that he was busting his butt in batting practice, diving for balls and overexerting himself. He learned from the veterans to just get his work done in batting practice and save something for the long haul. "As intense as I am, it's important for me to be relaxed."

For a while his mother wouldn't come to the games, because every game she came to, Casey would never get a hit. "She didn't want to ruin me, so she wouldn't come to games, she would say, 'Oh no, I don't think so . . .'" When I asked Helen about it, she said, "I thought I was jinxing him." "It's funny," Casey says, "because she doesn't want to bother me, but I know deep down she would like to be here every day and be able to encourage me and build my confidence up because that's how she's always been to me, and she's just a wonderful woman in that respect." Candaele finally got some hits in a game in Los Angeles with his family visiting from Lompoc, three hours away, so they're not afraid to come see him play anymore. "It's a lot of fun to have 'em come to the game and talk to 'em in the stands, and just somehow let 'em share in the fun that I'm having and how happy I am to be where I am, and how proud I am that they stayed behind me in the choices I made in my life."

Casey was a popular player on the Expos. When I saw him in spring training, he was fake-boxing with Tim Raines in the outfield, and scored a second-round knockout with a slow motion uppercut. He enjoyed the ambience of the clubhouse, arriving five or six hours before a game so he could put on his uniform and just soak it all up. He took part as well in the awarding of "The 'Zilla," a little rubber Godzilla, to whoever made the stupidest play during the game.

Candaele shared an interest in high-powered rock with Dave Engle, and frequently talked about the game with veterans like Bob McClure, Tim Foley, and Tim Wallach. "It's such a pleasure to play on a team where you can call anybody up and say, 'Do you want to go watch a movie or get something to eat?' I'm sure there's teams where you can be uncomfortable calling up a teammate and asking him to do something."

He signed a one-year contract, and seemed more than satisfied with it. "I want to get as much money as I can, just like any other player, but I don't really care much about it. When it's over and done with, that's it, I don't cry about it. That stuff's important and I understand that, and it's all about providing for your family, and I want to do that myself, but I'm here for the game, and I want to play it every day and I want to be in the lineup every day. I don't want to sit down, I don't like sittin' out. Even if I am sittin' out, I'll be there and I'll be ready, no matter what. But I like playing every day, and if they needed me to play 162 I'd be ready to play 162. If I had settled for five dollars for the whole year, I'd still be playing, because that's what I settled on. Because I'm here to play the game and that's what I want to do."

During the '88 season, Candaele hit miserably for some stretches and got sent down to the minor leagues. The Expos used eight different players at second base and hadn't settled on anybody they felt could do the job. Most of us succeed and fail in private; not so for ballplayers. Helen St. Aubin did not find it to be an easy time.

"Do you want to know what it's like to have a son in the major leagues?" she said. "It's terrible. It's awful. I thought it was so great but I had forgotten what it was like to have the whole world know how you're doing from day to day. It was harder for me with my son than it ever was for me. Finally I just couldn't read the papers anymore. I didn't want to see them."

Casey Candaele went back to Indianapolis and continued hustling, waiting for another shot. He was traded to the Houston Astros in mid-season.

The Rose of Spring

*L*ess than a month after the start of the '88 season, Pete Rose was suspended for thirty days and fined $10,000 by National League President Bart Giamatti for twice bumping umpire Dave Pallone. The umpire had poked Rose in the face with his finger while the two argued a call, and Rose explained later, "I'm glad I didn't react the way I was taught to react, or it would have been longer than thirty days. I might have been out of baseball for life. My dad taught me that when I was hit in the face to hit back in the face."

Rose was unhappy that Giamatti had chosen to make a point by suspending him when his record with umpires was a very good one. What put salt in the wound was that, as he sat on the sidelines, his highly touted ball club continued to lead the league in errors, prove unable to win at home, and suffer crippling injuries. When he finally came back to manage, he got a parking ticket on the downtown street that was named for him—Pete Rose Way.

A few months earlier, as he leaned up against a chain-link fence down the right field line in Plant City, Florida, watching a morning spring-training game between the Reds and the Tigers, Pete Rose would probably not have believed anything like this could ever happen. He exuded his customary confidence and enthusiasm. Despite the early starting time, Pete Rose was already warmed up, delivering the spoken equivalent of successive line drives.

"When I first signed," he said, "I went two months and made $400 a month. The next year I played, in 1960, I made $400 a month. In 1961 I played for Tampa Southern and hit .331. The next year I went to Macon in Class A and I made $500 a month. I remember I came back from New York my first year, I worked at Railway Express. I think that had to develop me. They would give me a whole boxcar to unload. I made $2.83 an hour, a whole boxcar of whatever from twelve at night to eight in the morning. Right down behind Crosley Field. I could work at night and look at the ballpark in 1960, right out the window. I could dream while I was workin'. I wanted to play there."

Rose recalled all his monetary stats with the same pride and ease as his batting averages and hit totals. "Getting 4,000 hits? I couldn't see that for a long time. My first year in the big leagues I made $7,000 a year, made Rookie of the Year, and made $12,500. But I caught up," he laughed. (When Rose became a free agent as a player, the contract he signed with Philadelphia made him the best-paid player in the game.) "I gave 'em all a head start but I come on strong. Like Seattle Slew, when the stretch opens up, if Shoemaker asks him, you take off.

"Fifteen to twenty years ago, we had to get off-season jobs. You know how most players spend their money today? They hire their own coach, they join a health spa. I was telling a guy yesterday that most all the players today approach the game the way I did twenty years ago. I stayed in shape all year."

Rose is now a legend in Cincinnati, but he wasn't very popular with his teammates when he first joined the Reds. He was so intent on playing the game that he didn't notice his being ostracized until years later. "When I came to the Reds, it was a very cliquish team. You gotta remember in 1961 the Reds won the

World Series. In 1962 they had a second baseman, Don Blasingame, who had the greatest year of his career, hit .281. So in 1963 when I came up, they were all set, and they wanted Blasingame to play second. The only guy who wanted me to play second was Fred Hutchinson, but he was the only guy who counted, and he let me win the job. He put me right in the lineup opening day, hometown. I didn't realize it, I was a kid on Cloud Nine, but the guys on the team didn't even associate with me. I didn't worry about that because I was just worried about playing baseball. Except Frank and Vada, they could see where I was coming from.

"The first night of my life I ever had room service was in Chicago," Rose recalls. "I got home ten after twelve and my roommate locked the door. He had a chain on the door. I was out with Vada, so he said 'Come on and stay with me, because Frank is in Cincinnati having his arm checked.' And when we got up the next morning, we ordered room service. It cost $10.75, and that's the first time I had room service.

"Gordy Coleman treated me good, he liked me. I never confronted any of the others, but they all know it. None of 'em ever called me for jobs, either. It was something I didn't realize for many years. Then one day, someone pointed this out, and I said, 'Yeah, those guys didn't like me that much.' They didn't call me names or anything—I'd kick the shit out 'em, or I'd try. I didn't cause any problems, I just wanted to play ball.

"They thought I was just a raw kid. Some people resented the way I played. But there's no reason for resentment if it's legitimate. Running to first on a walk, that's not something I started to do in the big leagues, that's something I've done from the first time I played when I was nine years old. They originally thought I did it just to get my picture in the papers."

I spoke with his Reds teammate Vada Pinson in Lakeland on St. Patrick's Day at twilight around the batting cage. Pinson was wearing a uniform especially made for the occasion, with green socks, green cap, green trim, and green numerals. "Pete hung out with Frank and myself," he said, "and we were his only friends at the time. He didn't notice it. He just wanted to play baseball, he was happy-go-lucky and excited. We were around him more than anyone else, so we noticed it. We befriended him because it was the natural thing to do. He was a young ballplayer, and I was young once, so we talked to him. It was like in the older days, when a rookie would come up, the older guys would shun him because they didn't want him to take their job. When I came up, I had guys like Gus Bell and Johnny Temple, and they didn't do me that way, so I didn't intend to do anybody that way, either.

"When he'd run down to first base, man, they were lookin' for him, calling him 'hot dog.' I think it was Mantle who called him 'Charley Hustle,' " Pinson recalled. "Of course, I wasn't that old, but I could remember Slaughter running down to first so it didn't bother me. Someone asked me, 'Well, why don't you do it?' But that's not my way of doing things. But that's his way, and that's who he is."

Pinson wasn't all that surprised that Rose had managed to endure and establish the all-time hit record. "He batted first, stayed healthy. Age is just a doggone number. I'll be fifty this August. I don't feel it. It's just a number. I'm sure Pete looked at it this way—until he can't *move*. You wake up in the morning, you feel good, you go out and play. Hey, it's your business and if you've got this ideal goal set up of what you want to do, if you're still capable, do it. But there are few people who can do these things at the age of forty something."

At the end of Rose's career, he played the same game, he just choked up a little more to keep his bat speed up to snuff. As Nolan Ryan said in the early '80s, "Pete's one of the best to ever play the game. The only difference since I first faced him fourteen years ago is that his hair is longer and he's gotten a little uglier."

Rose had finished second-managing the Reds the last two years. When a writer asks about the club's chances for the up-coming season, Rose jokes, "We can't win this year, we're worried about '89 . . . We're gonna be competitive. I'll tell you, this is the last year of my contract, we better be contenders. I'm gonna be around, you're not gonna lose me. We're gonna be a good ball club. We've got good power, great team speed, the best bullpen in the league, bar none. We set a record last year for appearances by a bullpen and we had the lowest ERA for a bullpen, so that indicates you've got a pretty good damn bullpen. If you've got something like that, you use it.

"In our division, us and the Giants have the least amount of question marks. You can't name me anybody who had an off year for the Giants. Every team has four or five phases in a game, and our weakest phase is our starters, but that's shrinking. We've got some good young arms in camp. We're getting where we want to be. We're putting more of an emphasis on pitching now. We always put an emphasis on hitting, The Big Red Machine. Back in the late '60s and early '70s, you go to the Cincinnati camp and what did you have, more than anything? Batting cages! In the Met camp, what did you have? Pitching mounds! We're trying to even that out now.

"I'm still going to try to be an offensive manager, but if I could be strong in one area, it would be pitching. Like teams that go to the Super Bowl, it's defense, like teams that go to the Series. I was telling my Triple A manager, you're gonna have a good pitching staff, and there's a reason for that. We come in second, we drew 2.2 million, 1.8 the year before that, and you can put some money into the minor leagues.

"When I came back to this team it was the fucking *Titanic*. They were last place in '82 and last in '83, and they were in last place when I came in in 1984. I can remember, if I'm not mistaken, I forget which year Bench retired, '82 or '83, the point is that they had a Johnny Bench Night in Cincinnati, and they had 56,000 people at the game. And that night only enabled the Reds to outdraw Louisville. Right now we're at an all-time high in ticket sales, and we're sold out now the earliest time in the history of the Reds, so we're doing something right. Some people want to say we're not doing something right because we finished second, but we're making progress.

"I'm a Cincinnati Reds fan, that's why I want the Reds to win.

Do you know anyone whose name comes up more with the Reds than mine? What people don't understand is that when we lose a game, I hurt the most. When we win, I'm the happiest guy. It means I care. Some people don't think I care if I put the wrong pitcher in. I care about the fuckin' Reds. You hear about how much Tommy Lasorda loves the Dodgers. He doesn't love the Dodgers more than I love the Reds. Because when I was a little boy, I was watching the Reds on TV." Pete didn't have any one baseball idol: "My idol was my father."

I asked him who was the smartest player he ever saw, and he didn't have to think long. "Joe Morgan was real smart. He'd make a good coach or manager. His talent is what made him a terrific player. Joe knew what he could do and what he couldn't do, and his preparation was great. He stayed within himself. And they put him in a good situation in Cincinnati. Joe Morgan was the same Joe Morgan in Houston. We just surrounded him with better players. You could book me for 200 hits, you could book Bench for 35 homers, you could book Perez for 90 RBI. We had career years our whole careers, that's why we won."

The conversation drifted around to Eric Davis, as it often does. I asked Rose what Davis would have to do, playing all phases of the game so intensely, to play 150 games in a season. "He has to learn how to rest. Morgan was the perfect example of that. Joe Morgan was a better ballplayer when he got days off. I might add, I was just the opposite of him. I was a better ballplayer if I got 162 games. But I've never seen a guy who knew how to rest like Joe Morgan. Joe Morgan would come to the ballpark, and he'd always take a day off—it wasn't because this pitcher was pitching or that—it was to take a Sunday off when you have a Monday off, then it's like almost three days off if you have a Tuesday night game. He'd come to the park, put his shorts on, he'd go through his mail, he wouldn't go out to take ground balls.

"Boy, if I had a day off, I'd take ground balls for an hour and hit for a half hour. I only missed like ten games in twelve years. The coaches hated me. They wanted me to play. When I didn't play the coaches couldn't wipe their ass the next day. But Morgan would totally rest, and come back the next day like a six million dollar man. That's what Eric has to do, just totally rest when he takes a day off."

Was Joe Morgan the most underrated player you played with? Who was the greatest? "Joe didn't get as much respect as he liked because he didn't play in Houston the way he did in Cincinnati. You can't have any better two years than he had in '75 and '76. All I can say is he's the most intelligent player I ever played with. I played with some pretty good ones. Perez. Frank Robinson. Morgan, Bench, Raines, Dawson, Carter, Schmidt. The best player I ever played with is Mike Schmidt. He could play for me anyday. I'd let him play the whole left side of the infield. Just play in the hole. We'd lose but he could still play it."

There are few keener observers in the game than Rose. He's dedicated his life to the game, and it shows, often. He amazed the Elias Bureau statisticians when they found out which batter had the highest ratio of fly-ball outs to ground-ball outs and asked Rose who he thought it was. He asked, "Is it a regular?" They said yes, and he guessed Gary Redus, which was correct.

While Rose is a mine of inside-baseball trivia, his employer, Reds owner Marge Schott, is something else again. When Marge was asked who she expected to be the Reds' main competition in the division this year, she said, "The Royals." No, within your own division, she was asked, and so she then said, "Pittsburgh." Rose and Schott are an odd couple, indeed, but Pete shrugs off any difficulties between them. "Ask Marge," he smiles.

In twenty-some-odd seasons as a player, Rose has gone head to head with some of baseball's classic characters. Dock Ellis announced in spring training one year that he would hit every Cincinnati batter the first time he faced the Reds. "That was kind of funny, because I led off the game and he plunked me right in the fucking ribs." (When Rose was hit that day, he picked up the ball, tossed it softly underhand to Ellis, and then ran full speed down to first.) "He hit the first three guys, and we only got one run out of it. I only found out that he had announced it about a month later. The next time I saw Dock was years later, he picked me up in a 1930 Chevy at the hotel in L.A. and drove me to the ballpark because he was speaking to the team that day about drugs."

Early in Rose's career, he didn't get the attention that he deserved. Now, surrounded by an ever-growing retinue of scribes, he appeared to relish it. Rose raises his arms and waves across the field to Sparky Anderson with a big smile. "There's Sparky eating his fucking heart out. He knows I'm down here holding court."

When I ask him about the biggest change he's seen in the game since he came in, he instantly pointed at all the writers. "You guys," he said. "I could go out with Cincinnati sportswriters and I could talk about anything I wanted to talk about. Players are scared to go out with you guys now. The old-timers we used to go out with, and everything was off the record. I'm sure players still have a couple brews after the game when it's a hot day, but they keep it under wraps now. You know, there's more TV now, there's more radio, there's more coverage. You don't need all those headaches.

"Players still drink today like they did twenty years ago, players still carouse. But all of a sudden, a guy has a couple drinks and then he's a great drinker. I've been around this game twenty-four years and I've never seen a ballplayer come to the park with liquor on his breath, and I played with some of the so-called big drinkers.

"Some guys like you guys. Other guys think you're a bunch of assholes. I just happen to like you, except you," he said, jabbing me in the chest, "you're an asshole." But he's laughing and grabbing me at the same time, literally pulling my leg. The eerie thing was looking up and seeing Roger Angell taking notes on our exchange.

"Some people don't know how to have fun with the press, but I've had a lot of practice at it, I've been in a lot of World

Series, I've been in a lot of playoffs, the hitting streaks. I won batting titles in '68 and '69, one on the last day and one on the last at-bat.

"You wanna get you some press, go through a forty-four-game hitting streak. I had good material. My writer was a professor from UC, I had good writers. But the best way to make your job comfortable and my job, is to cooperate. I could say I don't want to talk. The only thing I ever worried about during the hitting streak or 4,192, was I didn't want to inconvenience any of my teammates. Concepcion was thirteen, I was fourteen, and Foster was fifteen, and if I got a hit to extend my streak to forty games, they couldn't get dressed. We had a room off to the side, where if they wanted to talk to me before, they could. I got my practice in. It made it easier for them, and easier for me.

"I loved it because we were playing in New York when I set the National League record. If you want to make money, the place to do something is New York, if you're going to break a record. Buddy Harrelson knew what he was doing when he called me a cocksucker in the 1973 playoffs. He knew what he was doing. He didn't know me that well.

"We relived that situation when we were teammates in Philadelphia, did you know that? We were out on the field and little Buddy and little Pete were playin' pickle out on the field in between the games, and they got in a fight during one of our games, playing it out."

On the day in question, it was not a little boys' pretend tussle. "I slid in, I was mad anyway, we were getting beat 8–3, and I heard him say, 'You cocksucker.' And I said, 'Buddy, you don't know me that well.' And the next thing I knew Wayne Garrett came at me from behind and then I got mad. And then Borbon went crazy. Then the fans went crazy. You do that a hundred times a year, like the collision with Fosse. Anything you do, if you do it on national TV, the whole thing is timing.

"I remember the very next year I was on third base, somebody popped one to the pitcher, I was going on contact, and they threw me out at home. It was Opening Day, and Duke Sims was the catcher. The only difference with Fosse was that Sims had the ball waitin' for me. I was dizzy for two innings. He put me back in the middle of the fuckin' third deck, and nobody said anything about it. And you do it in the playoffs, you replay it and replay it and replay it."

Even while speaking at length, with his back to the diamond, he seldom missed what was happening on the field. Right fielder Paul O'Neill turned a single into a double with his nonchalance, and Rose was all over him before the throw got to second base. "Practice right, that's the way you play right. Don't glide! Don't take things for granted in this game.

"Sparky said he doesn't care about winning in spring training, and I said, 'Okay, I want to play you every day. That's the kind of habit I'd like to get into.' " The thought of Sparky continually telling the Tigers during the '87 pennant drive, "Just have fun," brings a guffaw from Pete. "The only way to have fun is to win," he said. "So he was really saying, 'Just win.' "

A lot of people didn't respect Sparky as a manager during his years with the Reds because of the great players he had, but Pete wasn't one of them. "There's been a lot of managers that had a lot of great players who didn't win as many games as Sparky's won. Cuz all you do as a manager is get your players to play good every day. All the time I hear Sparky was lucky, but he still had the respect of all of us, and the way he handled himself is how he got that respect. He's the best manager I ever played for and I played for a lot of 'em. I think I'm the smartest manager I ever played for, but Sparky's the best. The only way you rate good or bad is success, and he won more than anybody else."

"I owe the most to Fred Hutchinson, because he gave me the opportunity to play. I have a different philosophy than most of the players, because I don't think you play for a manager. It just said 'Rose' across my uniform, it didn't say Anderson, Bristol, Virdon, Ozark, Green, Hefner, Hutchinson, it says Cincinnati. I play for the team, the manager is just the one who has to make the decisions.

"I get a kick out of some of these players who say 'I can't play for that guy,' but that's usually a guy who's having a bad year. He probably wants to be traded. The easiest way to be traded is to say you can't play for that manager. It's pretty good psychology. A lot of players have off years, and the first thing they do is start bitching about that team or that organization, because they know if they're gonna negotiate a new contract hitting .220, they're not gonna get shit. But if you get a new player because you think he's got potential, are you going to start your relationship off with that player by cutting his salary? Hell, no! If anything, you're gonna give him a raise. He hits .220 and he gets a raise.

"You don't play for a manager. I never heard Clemente or Aaron or Mays or Musial say they couldn't play for a manager. Good players don't ever complain, they just play, because you don't play for a manager, you play for a team.

"The only problem I ever had with a manager is something I didn't understand. In Game Four of the World Series in '83, they should have told me I wasn't playing. Perez came in the ballpark, he says, 'You're playin' the outfield.' I said, 'No, you're playin'.' There's two guys with twenty years of experience. If I'm not gonna play he should have called me and said, 'Tony's gonna play tomorrow night.' And Flanagan was pitching. That's one guy I had experience against. I wound up getting as many hits as anybody in that Series. We lost, though.

"See, I try to communicate with my players, I try to be fair with my players, I try never to show anybody up, because nobody ever showed me up as a player. No manager ever showed me up, and I just try to treat people like they treated me. Mike Ditka is very successful, but I couldn't do the things he does. First of all, I'm not big enough. And you don't see many baseball managers react like football coaches. Bobby Knight couldn't do that if he was in the pros. He's giving kids a free education so they should listen to him. It makes a big difference, playing every day. Because you get burned for a touchdown, you gotta look at those films, Monday, Wednesday, and Friday—you make an error and lose a game, you gotta play the next day."

I ask what the most amazing thing was he'd ever seen in his career. "We went from Houston to Cincinnati when I was goin' for 4,000 with Montreal and I hit a beebee the first time up, and they walked me the next four times up. I could have gotten my 4,000th hit in Cincinnati. Perez is playin' first, I had a Montreal uniform on and he had a Cincinnati uniform on, and when I got my 3,000th hit, he was playing first and he had a Montreal uniform on and I had a Cincinnati uniform on."

Then Rose recalls a night in Philadelphia. "If I hadn't seen it, I wouldn't have believed it. We were playing Montreal one day, on the Phillies, and Mike Schmidt struck out four times on twelve pitches, and those fans were lettin' him know, they were booing his ass, unmerciful. Now the most unusual thing is he only saw twelve pitches, because he's got the best eye around. Now he leads off the ninth inning against Jeff Reardon, they're booing him for the four strikeouts, he hits the first pitch into the bullpen for a 2–1 win. So he strikes out four times, every one of the 50,000 was booing him, and he was the star of the post-game show.

"It's just like when I hit the home run off of Harry Parker in the '73 playoff against the Mets. I was playing the whole town, I was playing the whole city, people just booed and clapped all at once. I never worried about getting booed, but I never wanted to get booed in a white uniform. And I think it's a compliment to get booed on the road, and I proved that to myself. Because I used to get booed louder than anybody when I went to Philly as a Red, but I hit .245 my first year in Philadelphia and they didn't boo me in a white uniform. It's just like the song says, root, root, root for the home team.

"You can't let it bother you. I remember when I used to go to New York and get booed. I never told people this, but it excited me, it made me want to do better. If you're a Met fan, the best thing to do when I came up was to drink your beer and eat your peanuts so you couldn't do a fucking thing. Then I had a good chance of going 0 for 4. A guy had this sign, 'You Bum,' I'm readin' that thing, I'm gonna try and shut him up. Let sleeping dogs lie. You have certain guys that you just don't throw inside to, because you don't want to wake him up. If their team's losing, let 'em sleep."

Eric Davis reached first base, and Rose looked over at him as he took his lead. "He's got more potential than any of them. More than any player I've ever seen. You can add Aaron and Mays and Clemente and Musial, that's the kind of potential he has. It's up to him. He can be as good as he wants to be. The talent's there. I think he's going to do a pretty good job of it. Yeah, he wants to be a good player. He's got that type of personality, he thinks he should be good, and works to that goal."

Rose looked around, appraising the crowd. "We gotta big crowd, maybe Eric's gonna steal this bag here," he said, as Davis broke with the pitch.

Joe Morgan and the Man Upstairs

J oe Morgan, third-base coach for the Red Sox, arrived in the clubhouse at 3:30 P.M., the day after the All-Star Break, and twenty minutes later, general manager Lou Gorman came up to him and said, "We gotta make a change."

Morgan knew what he was referring to. Manager John McNamara, who had led the Red Sox to within one strike of a world championship in 1986, had been heavily criticized by many for having lost control of a struggling team, and the media and fans were singing "Knife the Mac." For his part, Morgan knew that the Red Sox, who were picked as contenders in the pre-season, were not playing up to their capability.

The firing of McNamara was hardly unanimous. Haywood Sullivan, one of the Sox' co-owners, was a long-time friend of McNamara's and voted against the dismissal. But Mrs. Jean Yawkey is the principal owner and she held the two votes that fired McNamara.

"I didn't expect it," said Morgan, "because if they were going to make a change, they had three days during the All-Star Break to do it. Gorman told me I would be the interim manager for a week or so, and I told him, 'Forget that. I'm your man.' "

The first night of Morgan's reign as manager was the toughest. He got through with facing the hordes of media, but the worst was yet to come. Rain delayed the start of his first game for three hours. "It was torture," Morgan recalled. "At ten they called the game off, and I was glad, I'd had enough. The next day we won a doubleheader."

The Red Sox swept that series, then continued to sweep. They won twelve straight before losing, and then won another seven games in a row, nineteen out of twenty, including the longest home win streak in Fenway Park history. The turnaround was dubbed "Morgan's Miracle," as the team won twice during the streak with dramatic home runs in its last at-bat. The longest winning streak Morgan had ever had as a manager, after managing over 1,100 games in sixteen years, had been nine games.

He soon had his chance to prove his leadership when an incident occurred involving Jim Rice, whom Morgan had managed down in Pawtucket. Late in a ball game, Morgan told Rice that if it was a bunting situation, he would be called back for a pinch-hitter, Spike Owen, and Rice said, "Okay." But after Morgan made the move, Rice returned to the dugout, and having thought this over a bit, pulled Morgan into the runway. Other players had to restrain Rice, and he was suspended for three days, costing him $30,000. "Everyone in the clubhouse," said Morgan, "is on an equal plane, and that's a very important message I had to get across. The only difference between anyone in that room is when the man upstairs hands out the paycheck."

As the streak lengthened more improbably with every game, Morgan fielded interviews around the clock, appearing on the "Today" show and "Good Morning, America" (Morgan thought he was going on "Good Morning, Miss America"), the works, even the foreign media, to the point where they began calling the great Cincinnati second baseman "the other Joe Morgan."

Of course, it had always been the other way around. Morgan used to have kids mail him baseball cards for autographs, thinking he was the black Joe Morgan who won two MVP awards. "I've

signed a ton of his cards. I've got his signature down pretty good.
I got his bats a couple of times.

"I received one of his checks one time from the pension fund,
but I sent it back. One time during the World Series he had my
hotel room in New York, and it took Haywood Sullivan over an
hour to get a room for me. But when he played for the Phillies
and hit a home run in the World Series, I got back to my room
and there was a great big bottle of champagne in it. He never
drank a drop of it. I remember the cork hit the ceiling."

Apparently, even the Red Sox people weren't too sure who he
was, even though he's been a minor-league manager and third
base coach for the team for years. In the Red Sox press guide,
they mixed up coach Rac Slider's picture with Morgan's. Another
case of mistaken identity, which up until mid-season 1988 was
the story of Joe Morgan's life, one of the true Rodney Dangerfields
of the game of baseball.

When I was going to speak with Morgan in Winter Haven after
spending most of the day at the batting cage with Ted Williams,
Morgan said, in his typically self-effacing way, "You don't want
to talk to me, you've got plenty of stuff." He wasn't brushing me
off, he just couldn't believe that someone would really be interested.

He attended Boston College on a hockey scholarship, and although he is modest about his exploits on the ice, teammates
from his hockey team compared Morgan to a Bobby Orr in that
Morgan was a brilliant stick-handler who could, when killing
penalties, keep the puck for as long as he wanted. Morgan's
college hockey team was the only one from BC to ever defeat a
U.S. Olympic team. But by the time Morgan was a junior, several
major-league teams were interested in him as an infielder. He
could have signed with the Boston Red Sox but figured he would
have a better chance of making it with the Boston Braves, which
was not a very good team. "That didn't work out so well. When
they moved to Milwaukee the next year they picked up Andy
Pafko, Joe Adcock, Johnny Logan, and then Eddie Mathews and
Hank Aaron blossomed, and they were doing pretty good."

He didn't make the major leagues until 1959, and never did play very much, eighty-eight games total in four seasons, until 1964. "I never did shit," he says, summing up his fifteen-year playing career. He hit two homers in 1960, his career major-league total. What he still remembers is a game against the Yankees with Yogi Berra playing left field. As a fledgling outfielder, Berra was something of a butcher out there, with extremely limited range. In 1961, in a year when Morgan only had two hits in the four games he played, Berra robbed him twice in one game. These are the highlights of his career.

What sticks out from his playing days are the fluffs and disappointments, the near-misses and the big misses. He was on the Phillies in 1960 playing third base behind Robin Roberts in a game against the Giants in Candlestick Park when, early in the game, he misplayed a bouncer off the bat of Felipe Alou, who was given a base hit. Roberts, who never got a no-hitter in his whole career, retired the rest of the Giants without a hit, and Morgan understandably felt terrible about it.

Morgan left the Phillies shortly thereafter to join the Indians in the American League and didn't see Roberts until a few years later in spring training when Roberts was with Baltimore. Morgan said hello to Roberts and "Robby walked right by me like I wasn't even there. I figured it was because I screwed up his no-hitter." But it was simply another case of misplaced identity in the career of Joe Morgan—Roberts just didn't recognize him.

He came close to getting into the 1964 World Series, but again, no cigar. When Julian Javier of the Cardinals got hurt, he came up to replace him on September 10th. At that time a player had to be on the roster by September 1st to be eligible for the Series. The Cardinals asked the Yankees if Morgan could take Javier's place on the roster, and the Yankees vetoed it.

The '86 World Series against the Mets was still very much on Morgan's mind, Game Six especially. He asked me if I thought Gedman should have caught that pitch from Bob Stanley that got away. His indelible memory from that fateful game was being out in the Sox bullpen in Shea, with two outs in the ninth inning, one Calvin Schiraldi pitch from a World Championship. "Bob Stanley turned to me, and he said, 'What do you think you're worth when we get the final strike, Joe?' "

Joe Morgan began his managerial career with the Pirates at the age of thirty-six. He was only offered $7,500 for his first job, which would have been impossible to accept with a family to raise, but they upped the offer a bit by making Morgan the player-manager, telling Morgan that he wouldn't have to play very much. And Morgan, at the end of his playing career, had no interest in playing. He took the job and then a couple of players on the team got hurt and the farm director came to Morgan two weeks after the season started and told him, "If there's one think I don't like, it's a non-playing player manager." Morgan wound up logging 104 games.

Morgan joined the Red Sox organization as a minor-league manager in 1974 and managed their Triple A farm team at Pawtucket for nine years. He's fond of joking about the year he had Lynn and Rice in the outfield and finished thirty-three games out. "Now that's bad managing," he said. But in truth he put up good numbers just about wherever he went. When he won the championship in 1977, it was his fourth title. He had a .519 winning percentage in the minors, and then there were all the games he managed in the winter leagues. Joe Morgan just kept coming back for more.

"If I didn't want to be in those bus leagues, I should have gotten out. It's just like the winter leagues, you go down there, and it's so hard you say, 'I'll never go back again.' Then you go back, because you know what you're getting into. I always tell guys, 'Don't come back, you know what it's like, but if you do come back, I don't want to listen to any of your bitchin' and moanin' because you know what it's like to play down there.' "

Morgan said he's always had fun managing, and a tight major-league pennant race was no different. "We're in the damn thing now," he said in the middle of August 1988. "Managing is easy. The only pressure I've ever known is trying to hit in the big leagues." After ball games he enjoyed baffling sportswriters by frequently interjecting his favorite nonsensical saying, "Six, two, and even," which he took from the beer-bellied bard, former manager Joe Schultz. The most industrious of Boston's sportswriters have traced the saying to two early Bogart films in which the line is spoken, but it makes no sense in the movies, either.

The Red Sox beat the Yankees in five of their last seven meetings, and held on for the American League East pennant. Morgan's dream season ended when the Red Sox were eliminated in the playoffs by the Oakland A's. The Red Sox signed him for the '89 season, so Morgan won't have to hold down one of his off-season jobs as a carpenter, bricklayer, clerical worker, bill collector, substitute teacher, or snowplow driver on the Massachusetts Turnpike.

Joe Morgan got his opportunity at the age of fifty-seven. Sparky Anderson, by comparison, is only fifty-four. When I spoke with Morgan at the start of the '88 season, I got the sense that he felt his time may have passed for becoming a major-league manager. He had been passed over when the Red Sox replaced Darrel Johnson in 1976, Don Zimmer after 1980, and Ralph Houk after 1984. After getting the Red Sox manager's job, Morgan admitted that this was true. "But once I got to third base, then when they would make a change, I knew that I would have a chance, better than the next guy."

It's hard not to pull for the Joe Morgans of this world. An affable, blue-collar type of guy, he's the evidence against Leo Durocher's claim that nice guys finish last, and the evidence for there being a measure of justice in this world. Pirate general manager Syd Thrift knew Joe Morgan from the time he first started managing in the Pittsburgh organization, and Thrift, acknowledging the power of baseball karma, said, "Joe Morgan is being repaid by the Man Upstairs for all those years he was a good manager and nobody recognized it."

As far as people in baseball are concerned, I think I've always rooted more for those who have known a little adversity in their lives or careers. That player who gets hurt or demoted, who many refuse to believe will fulfill his early promise, who perhaps gets injured or traded and falls into semi-obscurity, and then gets his moment in the sun, his chance to show what he can really do—he's the kind of ballplayer I've always watched the closest. Perhaps I've always identified with those people because I intuitively felt that my own life would obey the same pattern.

One thing that impressed me in my coverage of the Grapefruit League was the tenuous nature of existence in the big leagues. The world of baseball remains filled with countless talented ballplayers who never get a chance to play in the major leagues, and everyone who makes it has a story to tell about how he beat the odds and actually lived out a dream that few ever realize. You see all the young guys suited up trying desperately to impress someone so they could make a big-league roster, and the older players working just as hard, trying to hang on. I asked Rick Dempsey, dressing with the Dodgers' non-roster players, a former World Series MVP trying to make the Dodgers as their second catcher, what he hit with Cleveland last year. "One seventy-seven," he said, with his deadpan expression. "Not too good." Dempsey made the Dodgers late in spring training ahead of catcher Alex Trevino, who latched on with the Astros. Dempsey wound up with another World Series ring, but his old battery mate, Tippy Martinez, was released by the Twins, as were numerous other players I spoke with.

Meeting so many of the people I had been watching and reading about for years was an experience I never thought I would have when Jimmy Piersall first showed me that ballplayers were a breed apart. While it's customary to wax ecstatic over the quaintness of the ballparks, the weather, the relaxed pace, and the close proximity to the game in spring training, it's really the people I met that stick in memory. Tiger broadcaster Ernie Harwell was a one-man welcoming committee to the Tiger camp in Lakeland, helping with introductions, inviting me to lunch, and telling me stories about the morning he interviewed Ty Cobb.

When one depends so much on the kindness of strangers, these are no little things, but we were after all not really strangers, we just had never met.

I must have heard Harwell do a thousand games while I was growing up, enough to know by heart all his signature inflections and phrasings. So when I told him about meeting the Japanese slugger Ochiai, it was more than a small pleasure just to hear him roll the sound (O-chee-I) around in his throat, announcing the name as if the greatest hitter in Japanese baseball history had just homered into the short porch in Tiger Stadium.

I found myself talking about a lot more than baseball down in spring training, enough to nearly lose my voice after less than a week. Most ballplayers love other sports as well. I remember conversations with Mark Eichorn, Jays reliever, about the greatest heavyweight fights of all time, and going over the matchups for a projected NBA final, still three months in the offing, between the Pistons and the Lakers with Terry Pendleton, whose all-time hero is Magic Johnson. And sometimes I was farther afield than other sports, talking jazz and rhythm and blues with Mudcat Grant, who is still a working singer. He said that Lee Maye, the former Indians outfielder, had the sweetest singing voice of any ballplayer.

Some acknowledged the world outside of baseball, as when Grant elaborated on the difficulties many ballplayers have after their baseball careers are over. "I think a lot of times people assume that ballplayers will go into the corporate world and be the president or something. But it doesn't always work that way. I used to work in the post office, and people would ask me, 'What are you doing working in there?' and I'd say, 'What do you think I'm doing working in there? I'm trying to make a living.' An honest job is an honest job. A lot of guys don't say what they do because it may be a job that is demeaning, since this guy is an ex-major leaguer. I don't hold with that, because if you've got a job that feeds your family, you've got hospitalization, you've got dental, there's nothing wrong with it. I was a broadcaster for a while, I worked in the post office, I was a singer. A job is a job, that's the way I see it.

"There's still a lot of guys playing today that are going to have to do the same thing that we had to do. A lot of guys are only making $90,000 or $100,000. The guys making a million dollars, they're not going to have to worry too much about it. But the guys making $100,000 . . . There's no preparation for a ballplayer when he gets through."

For one season I had become a sometime member of the working press, what the ballplayers refer to as "a green fly at the show." Ballplayers are sufficiently tugged at to naturally guard their turf somewhat, and as I buzzed around the camps, I naturally met with all kinds of responses. In the process I had the opportunity to employ everything I had ever learned about adult or child psychology. Some were suspicious of a writer they didn't know, some were hoarding their best anecdotes for their own best-selling celebrity books, and some people are just cantankerous by nature.

Whitey Herzog was one of those who like to challenge writers a bit, to see where you're coming from, if you know anything or have any guts. At the batting cage at the Busch Complex in St. Petersburg, he indicated at first that I would need an axe and a lot of elbow grease to break the ice. "You guys go around and talk to Tommy Lasorda and me and Sparky," he said gruffly, "and you collect all these stories and put 'em in a book and you get all the money." Even though he said later he was just pulling my leg, no one likes to think of themselves as a leech or user or worse, and he did have a point.

Then a low fastball bounced, came up through the batting cage and hit me in the leg, inches from Whitey. He never flinched, like those commanders in Vietnam who walked amid live gunfire and mortar rounds without a care in the world. "They never hit me," he said. "Can't catch The Rat." When I told Herzog that Moe Drabowsky and Stan Musial had gone to Poland to run a Polish baseball clinic, he got going. "Just what they need," he said. "They'll have 'em runnin' from third to first." The conversation drifted around to baseball behind the Iron Curtain, and the Russians' chances of building a good team. Whitey said they had a helluva pitcher, though—"Igor Bittertitoff."

Most of the people I met were actually quite accommodating if I treated them with respect and didn't just stick a tape recorder in their face. If you can briefly demonstrate that you care about the game of baseball and the people in it, you're in the inner circle. But then, even as an unknown, I felt I had a certain advantage over the newspaper reporters because I was not asking players about whether the team could contend this year or how their arm felt, or if they were going to have a good season, or any of the stock pre-season questions that generally elicit eyes-glazed, rote responses. I was looking for much more than that, for reflections on the people that made an impression on them, for the good times they had, for what they really thought about their lives in baseball.

There is a lot of time to shoot the breeze around the ballparks of spring. Baseball is a waiting game, and many have filled the hours of waiting by spinning tales. I felt that I encountered some most experienced practitioners in the art of storytelling—Rose with his push-button baseball memory, Hrabosky's balance of on-the-edge intensity and total command, Dempsey's dry wit, Tiant's kaleidoscopic personality and Robin Williams–like pace, not to mention the unexpected poignance from a Southern rap-master like Dennis Boyd.

Hanging out with these people makes one feel closer to the game of baseball, more attuned to that which can never be filtered through a box score. While baseball is a game where nearly everything that happens is recorded statistically, it is nonetheless loaded with intangible influences. At times I even considered the possibility that, while wandering amid palm trees and practice fields and spring-training clubhouses, I may have had some small effect on the '88 pennant races.

I was in the Tiger clubhouse talking with Bill Freehan about the time Denny McLain dumped the bucket of ice water on seventy-year-old sportswriter Watson Spoelstra, two feet from Willie Hernandez's locker where he was dressing. The next day Hernandez, in a most uncharacteristic outburst, dumped a bucket of ice water on Detroit sportswriter Mitch Albom. He then promptly changed his name from "Willie" back to "Guillermo," in an attempt to cast off two years filled with blown saves and vociferous booing in Tiger Stadium. It worked for at least half a season, as he got his screwball back and led the league in earned-run average for a time as the Tigers made a valiant effort at a second consecutive division title.

Did Hernandez just happen to dump a bucket of ice water on that writer, or did the story about McLain give him the idea? A similar incident at Vero Beach also gave me pause, after I had spoken with Jesse Orosco, newly of the Dodgers, about some of the pranks he pulled with Roger McDowell on the Mets. Orosco had smiled, remembering some of the better ones, and the next day he put shoe polish on the inside of new Dodger Kirk Gibson's hat. When Gibson found his forehead smeared with black grease in left field, he stormed off, making it clear that he "didn't want to be part of anyone's comedy act." Orosco came forward and confessed, and some observers have traced the Dodgers' division-leading play this year, culminating in a world championship, to this symbolic incident. The Dodgers of 1988 finally shucked their much-criticized laid-back attitude and style of play, while led by the fiery Gibson, who at this writing is one of the favorites for the National League MVP award.

Did Orosco decide to initiate Gibson with the shoe polish prank because I happened to come by his locker? Everyone would like to think that his mere presence on the scene has been a part of two major-league pennant races, but then again, grandiose self-delusions are part of most fans' psychological makeup. It's not only the grade-school fans who believe that if they don't change their chairs, the last out will be mercifully recorded, as if the slightest shift, eating the peanuts from the left hand instead of the right, could unalterably affect the baseball cosmos forever. Finally, this kind of magical thinking, which the most statistics-oriented analyst will occasionally resort to in a crunch, may be our way of acknowledging that baseball is more than diversion, that it has become in some way a part of us.

There is no way, however, of completely separating what appeals to us about baseball from the problems of the players' union, agents and contracts, drug-testing clauses, and all the things that serve as reminders that we are dealing with a highly competitive big-business institution, a near-circus-like TV spectacle. Living in New York affords one a glimpse of baseball at its farthest remove from the joys of playing it.

The Mets grew very weary of having to apologize profusely for not running away with their division by the All-Star break, and by September numerous players wanted out of the Yankee organization. Jack Clark, never known as a wimp, talked about being "drained" and "broken down" because every game from Opening Day on had been as tense as the World Series. Don Mattingly, despite being paid $2 million a season on his current contract, joined the ranks of the disgruntled, demanding to be treated with a little respect, revealing that he "had to fight himself every day in order to play."

The question is whether players who are so highly paid to perform should complain that they aren't having enough fun, but being a ballplayer is a special kind of job. The first words the umpire says before a game, after all, are "Play ball!" So many '60s players that I spoke with—Harmon Killebrew, Boog Powell, Frank Thomas, Luis Tiant—feel very fortunate indeed to have played when they did, because of the people they got to know and the experiences they were able to have in baseball. Society has changed radically in the last twenty-five years and there was never any reason to expect that baseball would not change along with it. The '60s have become baseball's new "good old days."

You look around a major-league clubhouse today and the increasing homogenization of the players is noticeable with many of the teams. The ambience of some locker rooms is like *Top Gun*, populated by young, strong, talented guys making a lot of money. There seems to be less and less room for the cutup, the prankster, the off-the-wall clubhouse philosopher, the guy who's survived by his wits. The great baseball characters are without question a vanishing breed, no less endangered than the bald eagle.

If the present-day structure of baseball discourages wacky individuals whose lives are monuments to free expression, the fans and the media still hunger for these kinds of players. Whenever a ballplayer makes a witty comment, he finds himself quoted all over the country. Fans across the country are awaiting the next great Coming of the Oddball, the next Hrabosky, the next Fidrych, but like no one we have ever seen before. He will have a name that makes you smile when you pronounce it, he will have great difficulty combing his hair, one of his webbed feet will be larger than the other, and when doing interviews he will sound alternately comatose and brilliant. He will probably be a pitcher who not only talks to the ball, but gets the ball to talk back to him. He'll be loose-limbed, with more soul than Ray Charles, and blow hitters away with his eyes closed. And he will be a true keeper of the flame, insofar as he will remind us once again that it is, after all, a game.